W9-DIR-674

Cocaine

Cocaine

Seduction and Solution

Nannette Stone, Marlene Fromme, and Daniel Kagan

Clarkson N. Potter, Inc./Publishers
DISTRIBUTED BY CROWN PUBLISHERS, NEW YORK

The people described in this book are composite portraits of
real people whom we have either treated or interviewed
in the course of our research. All of the facts in these
stories are true, but the details and identities of the individuals
have been altered to protect their privacy.

Published by Clarkson N. Potter, Inc., One Park Avenue,
New York, New York 10016, and simultaneously in
Canada by General Publishing Company Limited

Manufactured in the United States of America

Library of Congress Cataloging in Publication Data
Stone, Nanette.
  Cocaine.
  Bibliography: p.
  Includes index.
  1. Cocaine habit—United States.   2. Cocaine.
I. Fromme, Marlene.   II. Kagen, Daniel.   III. Title.
HV5810.S86   1984   362.2'93   83-23116
ISBN 0-517-55175-6
10 9 8 7 6 5 4 3 2 1
First Edition

Contents

Acknowledgments

To everyone who has taught us, helped us, encouraged us, and inspired us, we thank you for making this book possible.

In particular we want to acknowledge Alan Stein, Arnold Washton, and Bert Fromberg for information, guidance, and support; Mark Gold and Jeffrey Shore for providing valuable information; Gwen Gordon and Rhona Lawrence for their dependability and patience; Carol Southern, Michael Fragnito, Valerie Monroe, and Ann Coleman for their talents and interest in this project; Mark and Linda Reiner, Susan Jacobi, Jon and Robin Kellner, Ben Moss, Mildred Washton, Nadine and Edward Smart, Alex and Martha Stone, Mr. and Mrs. J. G. Blumenthal for their encouragement; and Jon Goodman and Julie and Anita for making us feel beautiful.

Our sincerest thanks and gratitude go to the many people we interviewed, our patients, and to our Creative Solutions staff.

We especially appreciate the efforts of those patients who had the courage and conviction to step forth and participate with us in media interviews (Valerie, Mike, Marilyn, Andrea, Kim, Elaine, and Bruce).

N.S. and M.F.

I'd like to thank the following people, whose friendship, honesty, and support made writing this book possible:

Ian Summers, for sound advice; Josiah Greenberg, for good counsel; and Ed Svasta, for helping to keep things in perspective with patience and good humor.

The most special kind of thanks is for Valerie Fortune, who always calls them as she sees them.

D.K.

Introduction

We are Nannette Stone and Marlene Fromme, directors of Creative Solutions, an organization providing consultations, counseling, and referrals for the treatment of excessive behaviors. For ten years we have worked together as researchers, psychotherapists, lecturers, and, more recently, self-help consultants for local radio and television shows. (We've been nicknamed Stone and Fromme—The Habit Breakers.)

We first began working together at New York Medical College, coordinating early studies about who uses cocaine and what treatments might work to break the habits of chronic cocaine users. Since that time we have seen cocaine become the drug of choice, not just in ghettos, subcultures, and among jet-setters, but for the middle class. People who had been taking cocaine for recreational use, or to gain a feeling of control in their lives, began telling us that they were suddenly feeling that cocaine had gained control of them. It had become a dangerous, destructive, and all-consuming habit.

We soon realized that the traditional clinic settings for treating "hard-core addicts" frightened away many of those people who were eager to understand their problem and get their cocaine use under control. This new breed of drug abuser objected to the clinic environment for reasons that made sense to us. Middle-class abusers told us that they were put off or frightened by the locations of many clinics and of standing in line with rowdy people who were sometimes even armed. They said it was difficult to relate to some of the ex-addict counselors whose language and values were so often different from their own.

The alternative route, private psychotherapy, had proved unsuccessful for many of them. Therapists frequently refused to see a drug-abusing patient. This was due in part to stigmas about drug abuse, but it was also because traditional psychoanalytic methods are unsuited to the treatment of addictions. Many therapists are inexperienced, untrained, and uncomfortable with the drug-abusing patient.

We realized that some drug abusers were having great difficulty finding therapists willing and able to treat them. So we put our heads together and came up with the concept of "Creative Solutions." We established a new kind of organization with a "living room" atmosphere: comfortable, private, and anonymous. Our hours are arranged to accommodate people who cannot disrupt their work schedules. There are no lines at Creative Solutions, nor back-to-back appointments. Everything is discreet; there is no sign on the door, only help behind it.

Word about our organization spread and we received many calls. A lot of the people referred to us did not require long-term therapy but were able to make successful use of direct advice, encouragement, support, and information. Sometimes a telephone conversation alone was enough to clear up some misinformation or provide the motivation for someone to help himself. We set up a telephone helpline offering information, advice, and referrals. It was the first in our area and we were amazed that *within one hour* after our first public-service announcement aired on a local New York radio station we received 128 calls from cocaine users and their families. We heard from all kinds of people, from secretaries to celebrities.

Soon we were appearing on local television and radio talk shows and news programs. By this time our helpline was ringing continually. Many of the calls were from people who did not need or want treatment but who had immediate concerns and questions about the effects of cocaine on their physical and emotional health. About half of the calls were from family or friends of cocaine users who wanted advice on how to approach someone they love about a problem with drug use.

Many people benefited just from knowing that they could help themselves and from talking over suggestions about how to take control of their lives again. In hundreds of letters and phone calls, people told us that seeing us on television discussing experiences so similar to their own made them feel as though there were people in their corner—people who understood.

We know that feeling alone with a problem makes it harder to bear and more difficult to overcome. This book is our way of "being there" with you. If you are a cocaine user, we will help you to understand the power of cocaine, why you respond to it the way you do, and how to get help. You will probably find someone like yourself described in Part II of our book, among the true real-life stories of people we have treated or interviewed.

If someone you love uses cocaine or if you live with or depend upon someone who you think is abusing cocaine, this book will give you information about how to help that person and how to save yourself.

And if you have never used cocaine, we will help you understand why and how people use it and why its use has spread dramatically in the last few years.

Drug abuse is a forever kind of problem. A person who has become dependent upon a drug will always have to be on guard against relapse. We wrote this book to help all those people who are trying to break their habits, or who have stopped using cocaine, stay on the side of control and recovery. We have learned most of what we know from the many courageous people who have sought us for treatment or just shared their experiences with us. They have helped us to help others. We hope this book will help you.

Nannette Stone and Marlene Fromme

New York
September 1983

Part I

Behind the Cocaine Mystique

The widespread use of cocaine today grew out of the experimentation in marijuana and hallucinogens that emerged during the 1960s as an expression of the social upheaval of the times. The sixties represented a collective breaking away from the constricting social, political, and psychological atmosphere of the forties and the conformist fifties. We were a society in the process of freeing itself, changing definitions, altering the shape of our reality, stretching the limits of what was acceptable. And marijuana and hallucinogens offered to those who used them a drug-induced feeling of understanding and change.

If the emotional and social message of the sixties was "turn on, tune in, drop out" and "free yourself," then the message of the eighties is "gain power, consolidate, take control"—invest, excel, own, succeed; make yourself invincible.

Cocaine delivers these feelings of power and control better than any other drug. Users say it makes them feel optimistic, competent, completely in control of themselves and whatever they do, masterful, joyous, possessed of tremendous physical stamina or remarkable intelligence, supremely confident, sexually turned on, intently aware, superalert and creative, vigilant, content, invincible, fulfilled. If ever there was a drug that suited the mood of an era, cocaine is it.

The economy is uncertain, the shadow of nuclear war looms over us, and it seems that people either hope to succeed in a very big way or not at all. No wonder cocaine, which delivers feelings of triumph and fulfillment, is the drug for our age. It yields up all the feelings we crave and gives us a sense of security.

From 1980 through 1982, the number of Americans who have used cocaine at least once rose from 10 million to 20 million. The number increases every twenty-four hours: 5,000 people a day try cocaine for the first time. Government figures indicate that at least 4 million to 5 million, and possibly as many as 8 million, Americans use cocaine regularly, at least once a month. It is estimated that between 5 percent and 20 percent of those are seriously dependent on cocaine, so this means anywhere from 200,000 to 1,600,000 Amer-

3

icans can be classified as addicted, or nearly addicted, to the drug.

The fastest-growing group of cocaine users is made up of Americans in their late twenties through early forties, including both men and women. Most people who have tried cocaine are over 26 and include blue-collar through upper-class Americans: average, upwardly mobile, educated people who by all outward appearances are successful. According to a *Time* magazine poll conducted by Yankelovich, Skelly and White, 11 percent of the adults in the United States have tried cocaine at least once, and 25 percent acknowledge that someone close to them has.

A 1981 survey done throughout New York State by the New York State Division of Substance Abuse Services (NYSDSAS) revealed even more startling data.

■ A survey of households showed that cocaine use had increased three times from 1976 through 1981. When asked, "Have you used cocaine in the past six months?" 135,000 people said yes in 1976; 437,000 said yes in 1981.

■ Cocaine-related hospital emergency room episodes in the New York City area increased 158 percent from 1979 through 1980. In 1979 there were 771 cases; in 1980, 1,991.

■ Also in the New York City area, cocaine-related deaths increased 197 percent in just one year, from 1979 through 1980. Nationally, cocaine-involved deaths increased 183 percent during the same period.

■ In the New York City area, cocaine use doubled between 1978 and 1980.

■ In New York State, hospital treatment admissions by drug-abuse clinics, with cocaine as the primary drug of abuse, increased 28 percent from 1978 through 1980. Nationally, admissions to federally funded treatment clinics for cocaine-abuse problems tripled between 1977 and 1980.

■ From 1970 through 1982 there was a *500 percent* increase in people seeking treatment for cocaine abuse in the United States. This figure increases steadily. In May 1983, a New Jersey hospital specializing in the treatment of cocaine abuse launched a national telephone-referral helpline for cocaine abusers. From the moment it began, 1-800-COCAINE has re-

4

ceived more than 100 calls per hour, more than 1,000 calls per day.

Experts in the law-enforcement and drug-abuse fields believe that the trend of cocaine use has not even begun to approach its apex. Many estimates gloomily anticipate that the incidence of cocaine use and serious cocaine abuse will at least double before it begins to level off or recede.

History
of Cocaine

The stimulant properties of cocaine were familiar to South American Indians who chewed coca leaves as long as thirteen hundred years ago. The two coca plants that contain the drug, *erythroxylon coca* and *erythroxylon novogranatense*, were used by the pre-Inca Indian cultures living on the slopes of the Andes in what is now Peru, Colombia, and Bolivia. Archaeological data indicate that coca-leaf chewing was relatively widespread and uncontrolled among the social organizations of the Indians of that period.

With the establishment of the Inca empire, the chewing of coca leaf became regulated and its use was limited to the nobility and the priesthood. Religious connotations were attached to the plant; it was seen as a divine gift specially bestowed upon the Incas by the sun god. Coca-leaf chewing by the public was permitted only under special circumstances and only by certain people—soldiers, workers on imperial projects, and those who were being rewarded for special services to the empire. This political and religious control progressively eroded as the Inca empire developed and then declined from the year A.D. 1000 through the mid-1500s. By

6

the time the Spanish conquistadores arrived in Peru in the 1530s, coca-chewing had again become widespread throughout Inca society. Spanish chroniclers of the time frequently recorded how the Indians routinely chewed quids of coca leaves to stave off hunger, help them endure cold, and enable them to work longer and harder with little food or rest.

It has been estimated that as many as half the rural Indian population of Peru still use the drug and also use the same method to obtain the drug's effects. Several coca leaves are stuffed into the side of the mouth against the cheek and chewed until a moist quid forms. Then a black alkaline substance the size of a pebble, called a "tocra," is tucked inside the cheek while the coca leaves are chewed. This facilitates the release of the cocaine from the organic material of the leaf and aids the body in digesting it. Chewed coca gives subtle and long-lasting effects: mood elevation, mild stimulation, reduced appetite, and increased physical stamina, very different from the intense mental and emotional excitement that processed cocaine produces.

Although coca leaves were brought back to Europe by explorers as early as the 1600s, the plant and its effects aroused nothing more than passing botanical and scientific interest until the mid-1800s, when physicians became intrigued by its reported medicinal potential. The credit for finally isolating the active substance from the leaves is usually given to the Viennese physician Albert Nieman, who also gave the substance its name. The material he produced in his laboratory was the same white, crystalline, odorless powder, cocaine hydrochloride, as that in use today. Doctors in the United States and Europe began experimenting with the new drug, usually in the form of an infusion—cocaine dissolved in water and taken by the teaspoonful—or taken on the tip of the tongue in its powdered form. There was no Food and Drug Administration in those days, and as long as a drug appeared to be safe, physicians freely prescribed it to patients, using it as a means to wean those addicted to morphine and other opiates away from their addictions and also as a tonic for fatigue.

In early 1884, Sigmund Freud began his now-famous experiments, using himself and several close physician associates as subjects. He published a paper lauding the drug's exhilarating and euphoric effect, and recommended it for medicinal use to alleviate depression, fatigue, and nausea, to treat opiate and alcohol addiction and asthma, and as an aphrodisiac. He also suggested that it might be useful as a local anesthetic because it numbed the tissues to which it was applied. The definitive work in that area, however, was done by another Viennese physician, Carl Koller, who developed cocaine as a local anesthetic for eye surgery, a practice still followed today by some doctors. Cocaine also began to be used in dentistry and in other kinds of surgery. It was used as both a topical anesthetic and, like Novocain, as an injection into the tissue to deaden sensitivity.

With this progressively wider medicinal use of cocaine came further experimentation and the first recorded instances of serious cocaine dependency and abuse. Physicians who prescribed the drug to patients for fatigue and depression noticed that they often rapidly developed a dependency on it. And several physicians, notably Freud's friend Dr. Ernst von Fleiscl-Marxow (who used cocaine to try to cure himself of a long-standing morphine habit) and the well-known American surgeon William Halstead, developed severe cocaine habits.

By the end of the 1880s Freud and others who had initially proselytized for cocaine as an all-purpose wonder drug withdrew their support of it in light of increasing reports of dependency and abuse. Interestingly enough, neither Freud nor the others saw cocaine as addicting because it failed to fulfill the criteria that opiate addiction did: there was no observable tolerance to the drug requiring increased doses to achieve its effects, and there were no clear-cut physiological withdrawal symptoms when the drug was discontinued. Fleiscl's and Halstead's compulsive cocaine abuse apparently did not qualify as addiction.

By 1890, unregulated cocaine had been discovered by the patent-medicine industry, which was entering its golden age of popularity. Opiates, including morphine, codeine, and heroin, were added to over-the-counter nostrums, and

8

legal narcotic addiction was common. Patent-medicine man-
ufacturers began adding cocaine to their potions and often
touted the cocaine-laced products as helpful in curing addictions to other patent medicines that contained narcotics.
Medicines containing cocaine were claimed to be helpful for
everything from headaches and the common cold to vene-
real disease, nausea, alcoholism, and asthma. These tonics
and powders often contained substantial amounts of cocaine. It was no wonder that they initially made people feel
better.

In Europe, a Corsican named Angelo Mariani began
marketing a cocaine-spiked wine called "Vin Mariani" that
was enthusiastically endorsed by well-known people in the
United States and Europe, including John Philip Sousa, Pope
Leo XIII, Sarah Bernhardt, Thomas Edison, and Ulysses
Grant. Mariani produced a whole line of addictive products
including lozenges, tea, and candies, all of which were consumed with great enthusiasm.

In 1886 an alcohol-free soft drink syrup containing coca
leaf and kola-nut extract appeared on the market to compete
with Vin Mariani. It was to be mixed with soda water and
was sold first as a medicinal drink and then solely as a re-
freshment. It was called Coca-Cola. This new product was so
popular that eventually sixty-nine other cocaine tonics were
created to compete with its growing market. But around the
turn of the century, with negative medical and public reactions on the rise, the Coca-Cola Company voluntarily removed the cocaine from the cola and replaced it with another
stimulant, caffeine.

In 1901, the American Pharmaceutical Association
formed a special committee to examine cocaine and opiate
consumption patterns in the United States. The committee's
report revealed, among other things, that between 1898 and
1902 the American population had increased by 10 percent,
while the importation of cocaine had increased by 40 percent. At the same time, a mythology grew up surrounding
the southern black population's affinity for cocaine medications with stories appearing in the popular press. There is no
evidence to support these stories, and southern blacks prob-

ably used no more or less cocaine than any other racial group. Nevertheless, these myths cemented a public association between cocaine, minorities threatening the established order, and crime. The growing body of medical evidence pointing to the danger and addictiveness of cocaine in patent medicines set the stage for legislation to control its sale and use.

In 1900, eight states had laws prohibiting the dispensing of cocaine without a prescription; by 1914, forty-six of the forty-eight states had such laws. In 1906 the federal Pure Food and Drug Act was passed. It was the first federal law to regulate the distribution of narcotics and cocaine. It required that all patent medicines explicitly state on their labels whether alcohol, cocaine, opiates, or any derivatives of these were present in the product. In 1908 an amendment was added to the act forbidding any interstate shipment of patent preparations containing cocaine, opiates, or alcohol. This evolved into the Harrison Narcotics Act of 1914, which declared that anyone who imported, manufactured, sold, or gave away opiate or coca-leaf derivatives, including cocaine, had to register with the Internal Revenue Service and pay a special tax on the transaction.

In 1922, an amendment was passed to the Narcotic Drugs Import and Export Act, a companion bill to the Harrison Act, banning the import of cocaine and limiting the importation of coca leaves to the amount needed for medical or other purposes. By 1930, although narcotics were regarded as addictive and dangerous, they were also accepted as having great medicinal usefulness as pain-killers. Cocaine, however, had lost its public appeal. It remained underground, intermittently in favor in the ghetto and in the Bohemian, music, and arts subcultures until its rediscovery during the drug renaissance in the late sixties and its subsequent climb to popularity beginning in the early seventies.

In 1970, Congress enacted the Comprehensive Drug Abuse Prevention and Control Act to replace the jumble of drug laws that had developed since 1914. Part of the new law is called the Controlled Substances Act, and it divides all drugs into five schedules according to their potential for abuse and their medical value. Cocaine is classified under

Schedule II, as a drug with a legitimate medical use, but also with a high potential for abuse and a strong tendency to lead to physical or psychological dependence.

Legal penalties for cocaine possession and sale can be harsh, involving stiff fines and long prison terms in some cases, but the laws are selectively administered. Enforcement has followed the general trend of drug law since the 1960s: most enforcement agencies tend to ignore or only lightly punish people who merely consume cocaine, or buy and keep small amounts for their own use, while they pursue and punish smugglers and dealers. This follows the informal "decriminalization" of drugs that has achieved some degree of social acceptance. Cocaine's illegality does not deter the millions of otherwise law-abiding citizens who use it.

Most of the cocaine sold and consumed in the United States today is cocaine hydrochloride. The finished cocaine product comes in three forms. True "flake" is pure white and technically refers only to the legally manufactured drug intended for medical purposes. It is 90 percent pure and can be acquired only from a medical source. More common is a 70-percent cocaine, refined from illegal coca crops in South America and smuggled into the country, or 30-percent pure cocaine, known as "rock," that comes in the same way. Almost all of the cocaine sold in the United States is grown in Peru, Bolivia, and Colombia, where it is refined and sent on its way to the United States.

The cocaine bought and sold outside medical channels is rarely close to pure. Profit margins and accepted practice dictate that all cocaine is progressively adulterated ("stepped on") as it moves from hand to hand in the chain of distribution. A kilo (2.2 pounds) of raw cocaine paste may sell to a Colombian processor for $350, and after it is refined and smuggled into the United States, the same kilo may fetch $10,000. At that point a dealer may split this single kilo into two kilos, stretch them with additives and sell each 50-percent kilo for $30,000. The kilo may then change hands again or be broken up into pounds or ounces and sold, again being adulterated at each step of the way. A gram of cocaine currently sells on the street for $100 to $150; thus a kilo of well-cut cocaine is worth at least $100,000. The most common substances used to stretch cocaine are lactose (milk sugar), mannitol or bonita (baby laxative), amphetamine (which adds staying power to the high), caffeine, or procaine (Novocain) or lidocaine (Xylocaine), two local anesthetics that mimic cocaine's local numbing qualities at a fraction of the price, but without the euphoric high.

Cocaine
and American
Society

It has frequently been observed that the psychological problems of an individual will reflect the values, trends, ideas, issues, and habits of the society in which he lives. When society changes, so do the most common psychological problems. Freud saw many cases of hysteria, for instance, because that particular neurotic disorder reflected the repressed Victorian era in which he lived. As society became less repressed, that disorder became less common.

Cocaine use and abuse are similarly products of our time. The cocaine high offers a short, sweet taste of how we think it must feel to succeed at the American dream in which so many of us believe. It lets us in on the triumph, the ecstasy, the flush of success. It also feeds the common perception that one need not tolerate unhappiness, disappointment, or bad feelings, because there is an instant cure that will make all those feelings disappear. We tend to think in terms of the quick fix, the technological marvel that will suddenly make a bad situation good. The cocaine high gives us the illusion of instant happiness.

The majority of Americans who use cocaine are between 30 and 40. They are members of the baby-boom generation, which is at the center of most of the trends that have rocked this society since the sixties. This is the generation that broke a fifty-year social taboo against casual and open drug-taking. They challenged the taboos and myths about marijuana and experimented with hallucinogens. They adopted drugs as a casual means of relaxation or escape. As a result, recreational drug use became acceptable throughout much of American society. And many people made the assumption that since marijuana didn't turn people into junkies, as the old myths said, then even drugs like cocaine and heroin must not be as risky as once believed. Consequently, there has been a rising rate of cocaine and heroin experimentation and addiction among the middle class.

This same generation, the original "youth culture" of the sixties, is now, along with the rest of society, constantly bombarded with messages about staying young. Cocaine helps ease our confrontation with this and some of our other distorted social values. The fears of growing old, of not having time left, of not having made it fast enough, or of losing what we've made are intensified by our vision of the American ideals of youth, success, and instant celebrity. The cocaine high can give us the illusion that we've achieved those ideals.

Ironically, cocaine connects with the solid middle-class traits of energy, confidence, control, drive, and willpower. Since cocaine's effect is not antithetical to middle-class values, it appeals to people who otherwise would not consider using drugs. They are pleasantly surprised to find a drug that instantly makes them feel the way they are striving to feel anyway, not incapacitated or out of control.

Unfortunately, the problems of cocaine abuse and dependency are predictably increasing in the middle class. Recent statistics from a questionnaire submitted to people seeking help from a cocaine hotline at a New York drug-abuse clinic revealed that the median age of these admitted cocaine abusers was 32½ years, 60 percent of them made between $15,000 and $50,000 per year, 78 percent were either blue collar, white collar, or self-employed. Only 12 percent were unemployed. This profile does not fit the typical population of drug users, but it does fit a broad segment of the

U.S. population. Our own survey made through Creative Solutions indicated that the average income for cocaine users and abusers is around $40,000 a year.

When marijuana was achieving wider social acceptance during the sixties, it became the "great differentiator" in many social milieus. To smoke pot at a party in the mid-sixties, or be the one who offered it, conveyed an instant image of the user as progressive, youth-oriented, open-minded, and adventurous. In a more general sense, smoking pot was what symbolically separated idealistic, uninhibited young people, or older hipsters who empathized with them, from "up-tight," square parents and authority figures. Anyone who did not use pot was looked on by smokers as suspect, untrustworthy, uncool, socially inept, or chicken; anyone who smoked was probably basically okay.

Smoking marijuana was a way of saying you were tuned in to the spirit of the times, on the cutting edge of what marijuana symbolized—rebellion, change, new directions, freer sex, love, brotherhood, peace, and antimaterialism.

Cocaine has replaced the role of pot as a great differentiator and serves the same social purpose. Coke use carries with it the glamour of high living, money, success, sex, power, the ideals of our time—the implication that one is bold enough to use it and well off enough to afford it. Using it implies one is special; because one uses the drug of the stars of finance, the jet set, and Hollywood, one must be a species of star himself. Being the one to offer cocaine at a party is a gesture of power and style. The world is divided into coke users and nonusers as it used to be split into "heads" and "straights," and where nonpotsmokers would be looked at with suspicion, noncocaine users in such a situation are viewed with a bemused tolerance and indulgence for their hopeless pedestrianism, their lack of taste for things expensive, rare, forbidden, and wild, their failure to understand the value of a chic and electric experience.

There are specific areas with which cocaine is most often associated in our culture: money, work, sex, and relationships. And there are two other areas that also seem to reveal special trends: cocaine and women, and cocaine and love.

15

Cocaine and Money

Every aspect of cocaine use or abuse revolves around its extraordinarily inflated expense. At approximately $2,000 per ounce and $100 or more per gram, cocaine is worth roughly five times the price of gold. This means that its cost is a limiting factor in its use or abuse. People often stop or curtail their use because they simply cannot afford more. Many a Cokeaholic's life has been saved by bankruptcy, and more than one professional who treats people with cocaine problems has expressed thankfulness that the drug is expensive. Money, then, directly controls one of the key factors that determines the extent of one's cocaine use or abuse: access. More generally, money is only one resource that provides access. Trades can be made to gain access to the drug—sex, or goods and services, for instance—and this pattern of bartering for cocaine is common.

Cocaine's expense is at the root of its many symbolic social roles. Its high price makes it chic. Cocaine is a mark of status. Having it, using it, and displaying it bolster self-esteem.

In August 1983, our survey of 113 problem cocaine users revealed that 56 users had consumed from 1 to 5 grams per week, 31 from 6 to 10 grams, and 26 from 11 to 35 grams per week. Costs per person ran from $0 per week to $900 per week. The average cost was nearly $500 per week. That's more than $26,000 per year just on cocaine. Not too many people earn salaries that allow them to spend so much on drugs. It isn't surprising that 102 of them said cocaine use had caused them negative financial consequences. A survey made by New York Medical College, May 1983, revealed the average cost for a problem user was over $800 a week.

Obviously, these figures refer only to people with serious cocaine problems, but anyone who uses even a gram a week needs to find an extra $100 or more every seven days. To do this, many people are engaging in acts that are unethical or illegal. There is a steady rise in nonviolent and white-collar crime associated with the growth of cocaine use in the middle class. Borrowing money from banks, businesses, friends, and families and not repaying it is frequent.

Shoplifting, credit card scams, prostitution, passing bad checks, and embezzlement have been reported, as has theft of goods from jobs for resale.

Another level of crime involves intimate, personal acts that are more actions of betrayal than criminal acts—stealing money or jewelry from friends or family. There is also a growing population of cocaine abusers who do not actually commit crimes, but who exchange their skills and services with large-scale cocaine dealers in return for the drug. An article in the December 13, 1982, issue of the *New York Times* details how middle-class cocaine abusers bartered their skills to cocaine dealers in New York's Lower East Side tenement-based drug-supermarket neighborhood, for payment in cocaine. The dealers' warrens in the decrepit buildings have been outfitted with elaborate intercom and surveillance systems, baffles of steel-jacketed doors, and trick getaway routes with complex piping systems to catapult drugs from one building to another in case of a police raid. All of the work was done by plumbers, carpenters, and other tradesmen who were dependent on cocaine and took their pay in drugs. There are some lawyers and doctors who take their pay in cocaine.

The most common illegal means of raising money for cocaine, however, is to sell it. People begin to deal because they need constant access to cocaine for their abuse or dependency. Most people who sell a few grams to support cocaine abuse do not consider this a crime but rather view it as a favor to their friends. A 1981 study of low-, medium-, and high-level cocaine users showed that among low-level users, almost a quarter (23 percent) sold cocaine more than ten times to get some for themselves. Forty-three percent of medium-level users and 52 percent of heavy users sold cocaine. We've all seen reports on the results of the more dramatic forays by noncriminals into cocaine dealing—the arrest of John DeLorean is one, as was the arrest in December 1982 of Bermuda's contestant in the Miss World Contest, who tried to smuggle $300,000 worth of cocaine into Britain. In fact, the *New York Times* reported in October 1982 that the DEA and FBI were concerned about the rapidly rising number of middle-class people being lured into the cocaine trade to raise cash and to maintain their own habits.

Cocaine and Work

For regular or dependent users, work is a resource for cocaine; services are exchanged for the drug. But there is another link between cocaine and work; cocaine use damages the frequent user's ability to perform his job. With up to 8 million regular users, this has broad negative consequences throughout our society and economy.

Absenteeism tends to increase among frequent users, who, energized by the drug, will stay up all night or all weekend and then cannot make it in to work the next day. The more frequently one uses cocaine or the more one abuses it, the higher this rate of absenteeism becomes.

Regular cocaine use tends to foster irregular sleep patterns and insomnia, leaving people tired and ineffective. The drug also diminishes appetite. Frequent use can cause weight loss and fatigue with related loss in job effectiveness.

People who use cocaine frequently have a tendency to feel depressed and irritable in between cocaine highs. A regular user who feels this way at work may have diminished productivity and may cause difficulty with co-workers.

These side effects also reduce the quality of a person's judgment on the job and impair skills. This can have disastrous results if a cocaine user is, for instance, a doctor, nurse, truck driver, airplane pilot, mechanic, or air traffic controller.

Many people use cocaine at work for energy. The "coke break" instead of the coffee break is becoming increasingly popular. There is a special temptation for people who work second jobs, or late or long hours: firemen, emergency room staff, and transatlantic flight crews, for example. At first, these people use it to improve their performance; it allows them to work longer hours without feeling tired. This is particularly strong motivation in these difficult economic times. The extra work, though, makes the person too tired for leisure time after work, so he often has some cocaine then as well, to have enough energy to be able to enjoy himself.

This cycle is a seductive trap. When cocaine becomes

integrated into one's life this way, the potential for abuse skyrockets. The user may come to believe he needs cocaine just to keep functioning.

Cocaine-related reduction in productivity is so widespread that many major companies have instituted employee drug counseling programs focusing on cocaine abuse. These include several Hollywood studios, Lockheed Industries, and all the major airlines. There are more than 5,000 such programs nationwide, operating in 60 percent of the Fortune 500 companies. A 1981 study of low-, moderate-, and high-level cocaine users revealed that 69 percent of the high-level users felt it harmed the quality of their work; 86 percent had missed work because of it; and 37 percent said it caused them to get fired. The figures were not encouraging for the low-level users, 25 percent of whom reported a drop in quality of their work and absenteeism as a result of cocaine. Forty-two percent of the medium-level users said cocaine hurt their work's quality; 56 percent missed work because of it; and 20 percent got fired due to cocaine. An August 1983 survey of cocaine abusers calling Creative Solutions helpline in New York revealed that 68 percent reported problems related to work.

Most people who use cocaine with regularity are using it to give themselves a feeling of competence, relieve performance anxiety, alleviate stress, and avoid coming to terms with uncomfortable feelings not only at work but in all kinds of life circumstances. Many of them have problems with self-esteem and confidence, and fear taking risks such as initiating changes, meeting new people, asking for a raise, asking for more responsibility. Many people feel threatened when confronted with an untried challenge. Cocaine often gives them a short-term feeling of confidence. But, as indicated by the studies, the good effects bring a host of problems with them.

Cocaine and Sex

Cocaine has a reputation for being a spectacular aphrodisiac; its mythology is rich with sexual superlatives; it is called "the sex drug." It is believed to create sexual desire, to heighten it, to cure impotence or frigidity, to increase sexual endurance, and prolong erection in men. These beliefs are partly true, partly untrue; with excessive use, however, the negative long-term effect of cocaine far outweighs any short-term pleasures.

As to why cocaine heightens or encourages sexual arousal, the answer is subtle and complex. So far as we know, there is no "sex center" in the brain, no nucleus of cells that when influenced by a chemical gives rise to erotic impulses. Sexual arousal results from associations: memories, sights, smells, sounds, and touches, a web of delicate interactions between emotions, physical reactions, and cues in the environment. Cocaine works on these components to create its aphrodisiac effect. Cocaine can also make you feel good about yourself, and that is one of the most important factors in enjoying sex.

In addition, its chemical effect closely resembles the effects of sexual arousal: exhilaration, elation, increased heart rate, sense of anticipation, a rise in body temperature, heart palpitation, breathlessness, and sense of excitement.

Cocaine's reputation as an aphrodisiac predisposes users to have a sexual response to it. Because of its reputation, people often choose to use cocaine expressly for sex, and this adds to the suggestive factor in creating a sexual response.

Because it makes people feel good about themselves cocaine also makes them feel less inhibited. Under the influence of cocaine, many people will enact sexual fantasies that they are afraid to ask for or initiate without it. Many couples have told us that the ritual offering and acceptance of cocaine by another couple can mean a willingness to engage in group sex or mate-swapping. Similarly, cocaine occasionally acts as a catalyst for people who have wanted to explore homosexuality or bisexuality, lowering their inhibitions enough for them to try it.

Cocaine's renowned ability to prolong sexual performance stems from two factors: its tendency to delay orgasm, as alcohol does, and its numbing local anesthetic effect. Its delaying effect is hard to control and can result in the inability to reach climax. Its local numbing effect results when it's applied to the penis or vagina, and although this may give some very short extension of arousal before climax, it is also dangerous. Cocaine absorption through the vagina can easily lead to overdose, and the thin skin of the penis is especially sensitive to the accumulative damage of cocaine's local vascular constricting effect.

Too much cocaine at one time will not only inhibit orgasm, but can also cause temporary impotence. Frequent users report a diminished interest in sex and a marked loss of sex drive. This is often the symptom that forces a cocaine-abusing man or his wife or lover to recognize and acknowledge their problem.

Women and Cocaine

Cocaine use has been increasing among women. A 1975–76 survey of cocaine users showed that 39 percent of the people who reported recent cocaine use were women. In the same survey done in 1981 that statistic increased to 51 percent.

Expanded business and social opportunities for women, along with economic conditions necessitating many more women to join the work force, have increased their exposure to cocaine. And women's new responsibilities have brought with them added stress. The responsibilities of a woman who works outside the home and is also raising children and running a household can be grueling. Some of these women are using cocaine for extra energy and as a release from tension. Women are now expected to enjoy sex, and a woman may be drawn to the drug to free her from inhibitions. Men sometimes give women cocaine as a gift, as they would flowers or candy, and it has become incorporated to some extent in courtship rituals. There are also the housewives, often mothers of young children, who may feel unstimulated and isolated, stuck in a routine they regard as repetitive, boring, unsatisfying, and fatiguing, who are turning to cocaine.

Cocaine's appetite-suppressant effects account for another increasing use of it by women: for weight control. It kills hunger and its euphoria makes a woman feel good about herself and her body. Many women say they make it a habit to snort cocaine before a party to ensure that they don't eat.

Cocaine and Relationships

Cocaine use will exert an influence on the user's relationships in direct proportion to the extent of its use, abuse, dependency, or addiction. Statistics tell a cruel story: 93 percent of the admitted abusers who called a drug-abuse helpline in New York in May 1983 reported significant interpersonal problems due to cocaine use. And in another study, 95 percent of frequent users, 69 percent of moderate users, and 41 percent of low users reported cocaine had harmed their marriage or love relationship; 77 percent of the high users, 56 percent of the medium users, and 23 percent of the low users said their cocaine use had caused their divorce or separation.

Cocaine's effects often result in a marked sense of connectedness to the people one is with, and this false sense of intimacy inhibits the real thing. In the singles scene the drug functions as a "social leveler"—snorting breaks the ice in a group and gives everyone the same high, the same good mood. But sharing *only* cocaine gives imitation intimacy and can't substitute for real friendship.

"Cocaine romances" are the affairs that begin with cocaine as a central element right from the start and courtships or marriages where one of the most important things the couple does together is use cocaine. Cocaine becomes a substitute for common interests, love, and passion. It often becomes the only thing these couples are able to really give each other, since they have trouble feeling or sharing strong emotions. A new relationship usually begins in a burst of passion, infatuation, sexual obsession. If a new relationship needs cocaine in order to induce this intensity, then something is wrong.

After the first flashes of new romance wear off, lovers have to start dealing with other feelings and demands. This can be a difficult transition, but it is twice as hard if cocaine use has induced much of the excitement, togetherness, and security and has displaced real attachment. Generally, in these early stages of a cocaine romance, the basic emotional groundwork for the future of the relationship is never laid. The couple builds on the false emotions of the drug, as the cocaine-induced sensations distort and displace the real connectedness, excitement, newness, and passion necessary to bind two people together.

Most cocaine romances cannot survive if one partner stops using the drug; he or she will sometimes discover that cocaine was more of an attraction than the other partner. Often one partner will encourage the other to continue dangerous and destructive cocaine use in order to maintain a familiar balance that binds the relationship. He may fear his lover will get better and abandon him. One partner generally controls the cocaine and thus controls the relationship. If the other partner stops using it, the controller is frightened because he loses his source of dominance. If the controller stops, then the cocaine receiver becomes frightened because the source of the drug is gone and he or she must take responsibility for his or her own actions.

When cocaine becomes a major factor in an established relationship, it usually indicates that something went wrong before the drug appeared—emotional distance, a waning sex life, problems with trust. Couples often drift into joint cocaine abuse from the pressures of their life. Both may work, then try to pursue leisure while tired and stressed, and attention to the quality of their life together becomes a low priority. Cocaine is initially a way of feeling good together and it can thus be seductive. Unfortunately, if a couple uses coke to feel good instead of talking and confronting problems, things will only get worse. The drug can become a convenient way for them to procrastinate, avoiding the less romantic, less pleasant issues that make a lasting relationship—agreements, limits, understandings with each other, shared responsibilities. Cocaine can feed into the desire many established couples seem to have for perpetual good times.

All the apparent benefits can erode very quickly. With sustained cocaine use, sex will inevitably deteriorate and be displaced by anger and other unresolved destructive feelings. The last word on cocaine and intimate relationships is this: cocaine as a solution to problems will inevitably backfire.

Cocaine and Self

Cocaine may become a substitute for love for those people who have not learned to accept, love, and care for themselves. When a person feels loved he feels adequate and accepted. A person who feels accepted for his good and not-so-good self feels safe and secure; he feels lovable. He's then able not only to give to others but to give to himself when he needs it—when he's under stress, when he's lonely. If a person is unable to do this, he may respond strongly to something that helps to obscure unwanted feelings, and a drug like cocaine, which replaces them with quick elation, can be extremely magnetic.

Using cocaine can feel as if the user is giving himself something—a good feeling. It can be disguised as a self-affirming act, the gift of a bit of euphoria. Actually, it is a tease.

If taking cocaine is the only way a person has of loving himself, he'll never learn to tolerate unpleasant feelings, feel gratification, feel pleasure, use his imagination to make himself feel good. He will always yearn for these feelings.

If a cocaine high touches this deep well of need and delivers what feels like real fulfillment or gratification, it can make the user feel as if he has just discovered the heart of the universe. He may feel "real" for the first time, truly alive, or more deeply calm and secure than he ever imagined.

That is how cocaine becomes a substitute for love. Some people seek their salvation in the drug, in the same way that others go through life believing that if they can just find the right person to love them, everything will be wonderful.

As long as a person depends on something or someone outside of himself to feel good, he is bound to be disappointed. For many of the people whose stories are told in Part II of this book, cocaine seemed at first the panacea that made their lives worth living. But it is only after cocaine made their lives unbearable that they were motivated to begin learning how to live.

How Does Cocaine Work?

Besides being a local anesthetic, cocaine produces a pattern of easily identifiable physical stimulant effects. Its action on the brain results in a marked increase in heart rate, measurable elevation in blood pressure, and constriction of blood vessels. It also increases the rate of breathing and raises the inner body temperature as its vasoconstrictor effect limits blood flow to the arms and legs. This is why the Andean Indians find that the cocaine from coca leaves helps them endure the cold. The deep body temperature rises, while heat loss from extremities is limited by diminished blood flow.

But it is not for these physiological reactions that people in our culture use processed cocaine. Although cocaine is legally classified as a narcotic like heroin and morphine, it is actually unrelated to narcotics in its action. Narcotics are "downs"—their effects are sleepiness, laziness, numbed warmth, blissful lack of care and tension. Cocaine's stimulant properties deliver the opposite effects—increased energy, alertness, a sense of physical and intellectual power, energetic elation.

These effects are the result of the cocaine's chemical action within the brain. The drug interrupts the normal action of chemicals called neurotransmitters—"brain messengers," substances released by nerve cells to carry signals to other nerve cells. These signals control the chemical basis of our moods and emotional states; if the chemicals are altered or disturbed, the result is a perceptible change in our emotional state. The actions of the brain transmitters dopamine, norepinephrine, and epinephrine are known to be central in controlling powerful mood states, particularly depression, elation, and sensations of pleasure. So cocaine delivers its high by disturbing the most potentially consequential chemical cycles in the brain—those that control our basic state of being, the foundations of how we feel: good or bad, sad or happy, motivated or dejected, depressed and hopeless or satisfied, energetic, and able to cope.

The purely chemical intoxication of the cocaine high is variable, depending on the general psychological and emotional condition of the person using the drug. The emotional texture, the richness or lack of it, the sense of fulfillment, gratification, or happiness, the value of the high is determined by the very subjective experience of the user.

Some people do not like the feelings they get from cocaine. For them, effects such as racing heart, rapid breathing, tingling fingers, and dry mouth are associated with fear and illness rather than stimulation and excitement. A 45-year-old dentist who had previously had a heart attack told us he was terrified when he experienced heart palpitations from his first and only experiment with intranasal cocaine. Lisa, a publicist, graciously thanked her boss for a generous cocaine bonus and then flushed it down the toilet. She hates the tingling sensation she has gotten each of the three times she tried it. "I just feel like my hands and feet are falling asleep." Joan thought she was a "freak" until we told her she wasn't alone in her tendency to get "weepy and jittery" after taking a sniff of cocaine. It happens. Some people get headaches and some find that cocaine acts as a powerful laxative. Each person's physiology and psychology are different.

Cocaine's potential for either casual or damaging use depends on its chemical effects and the way those effects and induced emotional states interact with an individual's existing emotional strengths, weaknesses, needs, wants, fears, and pleasures. This is why cocaine can be used recreationally by some people, while others become trapped into using it more than they'd like to and often more than they can tolerate. Cocaine's effects essentially heighten and distort normal feeling states: the cocaine high is an artificially induced and often twisted, amplified, and overstated version of familiar emotions. For some people this means cocaine may be a very pleasurable but inconsequential source of enjoyment. But for someone who has difficulty feeling pleasure, or who may be taxed with emotional problems or stress, cocaine can become a potent diversion, a form of psychic camouflage, a way to enjoy exaggerated emotions and to avoid unpleasant buried feelings.

These factors become particularly crucial when balanced against the other side of the cocaine high—the "crash" that sets in as the drug begins to wear off. Cocaine's action, unlike that of heroin or alcohol, is extremely short-lived. The enjoyable part of a cocaine high generally lasts from ten minutes to half an hour, depending on the dosage and how the drug is ingested. When it wears off there is a noticeable "comedown," technically referred to as dysphoria, usually comprised of feelings of pessimism, irritability, impatience, and depression. This is the crash known to, if not experienced by, almost all cocaine users.

Generally, the higher the dose and the faster it gets into the bloodstream, the greater the crash. Emotional factors further contribute to the crash; the greater the cocaine high diverges from the person's predrugged emotional state, the more intense the crash will be. Again, the chemical and psychological aspects of cocaine combine to create the drug's total effect. Some people never feel the crash at all.

There are a number of ways people try to alleviate the discomfort of the crash: some drink alcohol (brandy is often preferred) or take a tranquilizer like Valium. Some take a stronger hypnotic like a Quaalude or a barbiturate or take a narcotic like codeine or even heroin. But the most effective tactic to delay the crash is to take more cocaine. This means that cocaine use has within it a built-in self-perpetuating cycle of compulsive reuse to alleviate the crash, as much as to remain high. People who are prone to repetitive, compulsive behavior are especially vulnerable to the cocaine high-crash-reuse cycle. If they have enough money to buy the drug in quantity, or some other means of access to it, they can rapidly find themselves in deep trouble.

There are three ways of getting cocaine into the bloodstream and the brain, and each of them has its own sets of dangers.

Snorting (or Sniffing)

Snorting is the most common technique for injesting cocaine. Users pour the powdered cocaine on a mirror, glass, or any hard surface, and with a razor blade, knife, or credit card arrange it into thin "lines" or "rails" about an inch and a half to two inches long and about an eighth of an inch thick. A crisp, rolled bill or a straw is used to snort two lines, one in each nostril. Sometimes a special miniature coke spoon or a specially grown little fingernail is used. Surveys and analysis have shown that this average two-line dose contains about 10 milligrams of cocaine—about half the weight of the two lines. This is consistent with cutting practices, which leave most street grams of cocaine only about 50 percent pure, if that. The high from snorting comes on in seconds and usually lasts from ten to thirty minutes.

Occasionally people report a longer lasting good mood. Usually these are cases where cocaine has been used to facilitate a transition to a very pleasant or absorbing activity that sustains the feeling of well-being without additional cocaine.

Snorting can lead to irritation of the nasal membranes and sinuses and can reduce resistance to colds and upper respiratory infections. It also can cause sinus-related headaches. Because of its local anesthetic effect and the fact that it limits local circulation, excessive snorting will break down the sensitive mucous membranes in the nose and cause persistent and painful nasal sores, nosebleeds, and chronic sinus congestion. If snorting is continued over any length of time, the breakdown of the nasal membrane can extend to the soft cartilage of the septum that separates the nostrils and result in ulceration and then complete perforation of the septum—a hole through the septum from nostril to nostril.

Snorting is only one form of a general technique of applying a drug to any of the moist and capillary-rich mucous membranes and letting the moisture dissolve them while the surface blood vessels absorb the substance into the bloodstream. The lips, tongue, floor of the mouth, and gums are all mucous membranes, and cocaine has been ingested by rubbing it on them. The insides of the eyelids are also mucous membranes, and a few people take cocaine by putting either the crystal or an infusion of cocaine and water into their eyes. There are also many reports of cocaine and water used as nose drops. The entire digestive tract, from esophagus through anus, is a mucous membrane that will absorb cocaine. This means that it can also be eaten or drunk, although it takes effect more slowly this way. Cocaine users have been known to make a cocaine suppository or an infusion and deliver it into the rectum via an enema. This results in an extremely rapid absorption of the drug and a very fast manifestation of its effects. It is also one of the most dangerous ways to take cocaine, since a fatal dose is dependent not so much on the concentration of cocaine in the blood as in the rate of its increase in the blood over a given time: the faster it is absorbed, the more dangerous it is. Similarly, some female users place cocaine inside their vaginas. This is often done just before or during sex, when the vaginal tissues are engorged with blood and the absorption of cocaine is especially fast. The effects are rapid and intense, but again very dangerous. The rapid rise in the cocaine level in the blood can cause a fatal reaction.

Freebasing

In the past four years or so, freebasing has rapidly gained in popularity. It is complicated and requires time and expertise, ends up being far more expensive than snorting, but has become chic, and causes heightened cocaine effect.

Freebasing involves processing the common white cocaine hydrochloride to rid it of impurities and to release or "free" the more potent cocaine sulfide "base" from its hydrochloride bonding. The drug is cooked in a mixture of sodium hydroxide and ether in the top of a double boiler. This is then dried until it resembles a rough version of the original cocaine powder. The yield is about half a gram of freebase from one gram of cocaine, so freebasing doubles the price of a cocaine high.

The freebase is then smoked in a glass water pipe. It is placed in the pipe's glass bowl, which is heated with a butane lighter or a small blowtorch: the freebase melts and vaporizes and the purified cocaine vapors are sucked into the lungs. Since the lungs are the most blood-enriched organs in the body, the absorption of cocaine is instantaneous and the freebaser is hit with an intense "rush" of cocaine effects—a flood of euphoria, pounding heart, a warm flush. With repeated heavy doses there can be hallucinations and a jolting sensation. The freebase rush is almost always referred to as "orgasmic." The rush is gone within two minutes, and the user feels a residual glow for the next ten or twenty minutes.

The speed and intensity of the freebase rush is almost the same as the warm orgasmic rush from shooting cocaine intravenously, and it circumvents the sometimes bloody and painful process of injecting the drug. Many people who would never use a needle will readily freebase. Unfortunately those with a proclivity to develop compulsive cocaine-use problems will be just as easily snared by freebasing as by injecting. Because there are no limiting factors as with needles, freebasing is potentially more dangerous than shooting because it seems less dangerous, though it is not.

The crash from freebasing is more severe than the crash from snorting. This makes the compulsion to immediately smoke more cocaine that much more irresistible. It's not unusual for freebasers to smoke all the cocaine they have or can lay their hands on in a binge until the drug, or their available money, is gone.

Freebasing has its own set of damaging physical side effects. The heated, purified cocaine vapors irritate the tongue, mouth, throat, and lungs. Excessive use can result in chronic sore throat and mouth and a swollen tongue. Those who smoke cocaine excessively often experience breathing problems and may cough up black phlegm or blood.

Injecting

Shooting cocaine is the most direct way to get cocaine into the bloodstream and also yields the fastest and most intense onset of its effects. It is also the least common method and probably the most dangerous. Before freebasing became popular, it was also the most expensive, since people who inject cocaine will typically inject 10 to 25 milligrams of cocaine every ten minutes. Often they do not even bother to take the needle out of their arm between injections. Blood is drawn out of the vein and reinjected with each cocaine mixture. This is called "booting."

People shoot cocaine for the rush, the nearly heart-stopping, stunning, orgasmic punch. The vibrating sensation races throughout the whole body, leaving a charged, tingling feeling. Some people experience a thrilling and nauseating "turning over" in their stomach, like the sensation of dropping off the first fall of a roller coaster. Auditory hallucinations like roaring or ringing in the ears can occur, along with the involuntary clenching of the fists and jaws.

Along with these physical effects are equally heightened and overwhelming psychological effects: elation becomes euphoria, manic joy; confidence becomes a feeling of omnipotence. One of the descriptions of the rush that we hear again and again is that it makes the user feel like God for a few minutes: all-powerful, all-knowing, immortal, invulnerable.

The height of the sensation lasts from one to three minutes and fades very quickly after that, usually leaving only traces for the remaining ten to thirty minutes. With repeated injections, the intensity of the high is followed by an equally intense crash: plummeting depression, shaking hands, diarrhea, nausea, chills, irritability or anger, a feeling of deep despair and loss.

As with freebasing and to a lesser extent snorting, there is an overwhelming drive to cut the effects of the crash, but again, the best short-term "cure" for the crash is to take more cocaine immediately. Consequently, cocaine injectors will often shoot coke compulsively. People who like needles often report their passion for the rituals involved in shooting cocaine: "tying off" their arm with a tourniquet; mixing their own blood with the drug in the syringe ("booting"); a heightened kick from doing something dangerous.

But the largest segment of the cocaine-using public—mainstream, achievement-oriented people—have strong inhibitions against using needles. Needles call up images of hard-core drug use. There are also mechanical complications: finding a source for needles ("works"); learning how to prepare the cocaine, tie up, hit a vein. There's the fact that injecting hurts and draws a palpable amount of blood—both of which are guaranteed to put off most people. And there are the medical consequences.

Street cocaine is neither pure nor sterile; it can contain bacteria or be cut with contaminated or dangerous chemicals. Contaminated or unsafe cocaine can damage heart, arteries, lungs, or any organ it passes through, including the brain.

There is also danger of infection from contaminated hypodermic needles. Skin abscesses, hepatitis, strep or staph infections, blood poisoning, and endocarditis can result. All of these are painful, serious, life-threatening illnesses.

The Importance of Set and Setting

All drugs with psychological effects work along the same principles as cocaine: the chemical effects are heightened, diminished, or colored by the individual's psychological state at the time he takes the drug. The psychological factors at work during a drug's effect are grouped under the heading of "set and setting."

"Set" refers to all the intellectual and emotional predispositions and expectations the person brings with him to the drug experience. These include short-term notions as well as deep-seated psychological images and associations. If someone tells you cocaine will make you joyously happy and you expect that effect, it is likely that the drug will have that effect on you. In a broader way, if one is disposed to look on drug experiences as "good," they are likely to be good, and vice versa.

"Setting" refers to the influence of the environment on the drug's effects. If, for instance, cocaine is sniffed by a man in a comfortable, low-lit room with soft music playing, and it is given to him by an appealing woman, it may yield a very high degree of pleasurable stimulation and elation and little or no crash. The same dose given by a medical researcher in a white coat and snorted in a cold, brightly lit laboratory with hard chairs and many observers may result in a bad case of the jitters and a thoroughly unpleasant sensation that far outweighs the euphoria, followed by an uncomfortable crash. Setting is a powerful factor in determining a drug's effect. It is also the source of an infinite number of environmental cues that can become deeply associated with cocaine use, often without a user's realizing it. For instance, if he listens to a particular song or kind of music while using cocaine, the music will become a subliminal cue for cocaine use. He may hear the music later and want cocaine, or play the music when he uses it again to enhance the effect. This subconscious link between environmental cues and cocaine's effects becomes significant when we investigate how cocaine-taking can go beyond mere casual use to abuse.

The Cycle of Reinforcement

If one's set and setting promote a positive, euphoric, pleasurable experience of cocaine, then one will often want to use it again. This is called "reinforcement"—the pleasant effect of the drug reinforces or endorses the behavior of getting it or using it. The stronger the reinforcement, the greater its pleasurable effect and sense of reward, the more deeply ingrained the behavior will become.

The pleasant effect of the reinforcer imbues the person with an expectation that the reward will be pleasant, and this anticipation further enhances its pleasure and increases the person's motivation to attain it. The reinforcer tends to work in conjunction with setting. Certain environmental cues— objects, smells, music, people who tend to be in the setting where the reinforcer is given—become associated with the reward.

Users emphasize (and extensive laboratory studies with monkeys confirm) that cocaine is the most powerful reinforcer drug known—even more powerful than heroin.

Experiments with monkeys have shown that if they are mechanically set up to freely inject themselves with opiates, amphetamines, other drugs, and cocaine and are then given a choice between these drugs and food or sex, they will follow a similar pattern with all the drugs except cocaine. They will learn to reinforce themselves with the most pleasant drugs and will then inject them regularly, but will also ignore the drug and select food, sleep, or sex as they need it. But monkeys with access to unlimited cocaine injections will quickly learn to choose cocaine over sleep, sex, and food, even when they are hungry. They will starve themselves to death if not stopped. Experiments that allowed monkeys to learn to increase the frequency and dose of cocaine demonstrated that they will do this as long as the supply lasts, until they overdose, have seizures, and die. Animals will not do this with any other drug. This behavior resembles the bingeing behavior of people who are chronic cocaine abusers.

The Crash

There is another powerful kind of reinforcing pattern that works just as effectively as reinforcement by pleasure or reward. This is called "aversive conditioning" and involves learning through associating negative reinforcement or punishment with certain actions. Negative reinforcement generates behavior to *avoid* displeasure or pain. If a rat learns to walk down only the right side of a chute to avoid getting an electric shock when he walks down the left side, the rat's behavior has been changed through negative reinforcement.

The cocaine crash is a powerful negative reinforcer. And the behavior people learn in order to defer the crash is to take more cocaine. The negative reinforcement of the punishing crash combined with the positive reinforcement of the pleasure of the high makes cocaine doubly magnetic.

Cocaine inherently contains the capacity to draw a user on and on into a binge or into cokeaholism.

Compulsive Behavior

Cocaine problems, whether in the form of addiction, dependency, or general abuse, always involve compulsive behavior.

Someone who displays true addictive behavior with cocaine experiences a drug craving that is truly irresistible: he cannot prevent himself from doing whatever he has to do to get the drug's effect, and once he starts using it he cannot stop. Someone with a less intense dependency may find that he can successfully resist the desire sometimes, but not at others. These users will often deny that they have a cocaine problem. Even if they acknowledge it, their conscious understanding of what is happening often does no good in helping to resist the impulse. A person may understand he has a compulsion, may strongly desire to resist it, may understand that there are harmful consequences if he allows himself to submit to it, and yet may still be unable to resist.

The trickiest aspect of compulsive cocaine-using is that it is easily triggered by reinforcing cues that become associated with the drug's rewarding effects: the song heard when high on cocaine, the person who offered it, the emotion felt just before taking the drug, the place, all become subliminally connected to the drug's effect. Hearing the song, talking to the person, or going to the place can kick off a cocaine craving.

This kind of learned, subliminal drive that expresses itself in uncontrollable, compulsive behavior forms the basis for all addictions—to cocaine, to heroin, alcohol, chocolate, work, gambling, food, sex—any pleasurably rewarding reinforcer that may be uncontrollably used to excess, at inappropriate times.

Use, Abuse, Dependency, and Addiction

We define the use, abuse, dependency, or addiction categories by examining these factors: frequency of use, dose, means of ingestion, reasons the drug is being used, cost, and consequences of cocaine use in other areas of the person's life.

Use

Recreational cocaine use is characterized by low frequency, about six to ten or fewer times per year. It is also characterized by cocaine use that is unpatterned—it tends not to be strongly linked to a particular set of factors, cues, or circumstances, but tends instead to be irregular, largely by chance, and unplanned. A purely recreational user may use the drug more often than ten times per year, but no associations or patterns emerge—cocaine is not always used with the same people, in the same place, or while participating in a particular activity like sex or socializing.

The cocaine dose we define as recreational always remains within moderate to light levels: no more than ten lines per episode, no more than two at a time.

Recreational cocaine is almost always snorted. Freebasing is not common among casual users, and shooting is almost unheard of. A recreational user may try freebasing if it is offered to him, but he will not purchase his own equipment or make freebasing his preferred means of taking the drug.

A recreational user has one aim: fun. He almost never uses it to counteract an unpleasant emotion. He does not use it in order to allow himself to have a good time when he would not have one without cocaine, but rather to improve upon an already enjoyable situation. He does not use it to *help* himself in any way.

The legal risk taken by a recreational user is minimal; he is seldom caught and seldom prosecuted. He suffers no health consequences. Cocaine does not interfere with his work, leisure pursuits, or relationships. Cocaine has no greater value in his life than any other casual pleasure.

Abuse

Cocaine-taking is abuse when it causes any negative effects in a person's life. These do not have to be catastrophic. Many cocaine dependencies and addictions start out with a pattern of small but gradually accelerating negative consequences. For instance, in terms of frequency, this may mean that he is buying it often enough that he has to put money aside especially for it or reduce the money that might have gone to other things in order to pay for it.

The emergence of *any* sort of pattern in cocaine use indicates that the drug is an established part of the person's life. It indicates that the drug now has a special value, that actions will be arranged around getting and using it. If this is so, then the potential is there for cocaine-using to compete with other important things, and when cocaine begins to win out, the foundations are laid for abuse.

Increasing the dose is another indicator of abuse. A cocaine abuser may take so much that his high becomes unpleasant, or causes paranoia, or leads to an unpleasant crash when he stops. An abuser may begin to stay up all night to take cocaine, losing the next day to recover from the effects.

He may also find that he requires another drug to cope with the crash. Any threats to the individual's work and any needs for other drugs to counter cocaine's effects can signal abuse.

An increase in frequency and dose also means an increase in the risk of an overdose or other harmful effects. Cocaine use that involves heightened risk is abuse.

A change in the ways a person takes cocaine can also be an indicator of abuse. Switching from snorting to freebasing can be an indicator or precursor to abuse, since it delivers a more intense high, raises the cost, and exposes the individual to greater risks. A developing interest in shooting cocaine also signals the onset of abuse.

Abusers generally don't use cocaine just for fun. Using cocaine to "feel better" is an indicator of a developing dependency—it means that the drug is being used to deal with uncomfortable feelings and that the use is purposeful, not casual. Continuing to use cocaine after one has unpleasant experiences with the cocaine high may also indicate abuse— compulsive behavior may be driving a person to keep taking the drug. Using cocaine because one believes one will not enjoy a particular occasion (a party, for instance) without cocaine is also a sign of abuse. It means that the individual may be starting to feel that he cannot function without being fortified by cocaine's effects, and this is the cornerstone of dependency.

With abuse, cost goes up noticeably. There's no doubt of abusive behavior if money for life's necessities is diverted to purchase cocaine. Borrowing money to buy cocaine also points to abuse.

With cocaine abuse, we begin to see that cocaine-seeking and cocaine-taking exacts consequences in the individual's life. Work regularly missed as a result of cocaine use the night before indicates abuse. Unpaid bills, recurring physical or emotional discomfort as a result of cocaine, noticeable strain on marriage, love relationships, or friendships as a result of cocaine also indicate abusive behavior. Significant change in social habits in order to increase access to cocaine may also point toward cocaine abuse.

Dependency

Dependency exists when cocaine use ceases to be a choice and becomes a necessity. If and when one feels he "needs" cocaine for any reason, he has crossed over into dependency. A dependent user will often refuse to undertake a task unless he has cocaine first, or he may believe that he cannot succeed without the drug, or he may find that doing the task without the cocaine he "needs" is profoundly unpleasant or painful.

With dependency, frequency is determined by the intensity of the negative emotions associated with doing without the cocaine and by the strength of the craving. A user who is dependent will take cocaine as often as he needs it; his discomfort regulates his schedule.

In cocaine dependency, the dose is regulated by how well it delivers the effect the user needs. It is often not enough for someone dependent on cocaine merely to feel high; he often needs to feel high enough to gain some sense of control, confidence, or energy to accomplish a task, or elated enough to ignore feelings of anxiety, depression, or loneliness. Consequently, cocaine-dependent people will increase their dose of the drug until they achieve the effect they're after. The trend in cocaine dependency is to use more, rather than less.

Since someone dependent on cocaine will usually want to feel the drug's effects as intensely as he can, dependent users are more likely to switch to freebasing or shooting.

Although a dependent user has only partial control over his cocaine use, he still retains some choice about it. This is one of the things that differentiates cocaine dependency from addiction: the cocaine-dependent person will feel that he cannot do without it, but *will* do without it under highly motivating conditions. He is dependent, but not psychologically addicted.

With cocaine dependency, the expense of maintaining drug use may become a problem. Sometimes the user finds a level where he can (often with great sacrifice) maintain his elevated cocaine-dependent use without completely destroying or reordering his life, and he stays there as long as he can, for months or years. His dependency can explode into full-scale addiction if stress, access, or any number of psychological factors tip the scales. Or the user may resist his cocaine craving successfully for weeks or months at a time and then give himself up periodically to expensive, short-term binges. Another alternative is that a user's dependency may become focused on certain activities only—sex, making sales pitches, parties—and he may be able to confine his use to those situations. There are other styles of use as well, but they all converge on one point: in dependency, cocaine must be written into one's budget. Often, this means that money is taken from other areas.

Even if the dependent cocaine user is able to bear the increased expense, cocaine dependency leads to recognizable consequences in other parts of his life. There are often health, work, or relationship problems. There may be fights over his drug use. His sexual performance may suffer as he encounters impotence or difficulty in achieving orgasm.

Perhaps the most dangerous consequence of cocaine dependency is its cyclical self-defeating effect. The more one chooses to use cocaine when under stress rather than make use of one's coping skills and psychological strengths, the more one gets used to depending on the drug. When this happens, coping skills are used less and less, and like unused muscles, they atrophy. As a person becomes less able to exercise his strengths, he becomes more dependent on cocaine. If this cycle continues, the dependent user may find himself living with an addiction.

Addiction

Until recently there has been a debate about whether or not cocaine is addicting, and until the last few years the technical answer to this question has been a qualified no. Lately, however, the definition of addiction has changed, and cocaine is now understood to be extremely addicting.

For years, the definition of addiction was thought to lie solely in the chemical action of the drug rather than in the pattern and quality of the behavior attached to the drug use. So the test for addiction was based on the model of opiate addiction and defined as a chemically predictable increase in tolerance for a drug, requiring larger and larger doses over time in order to achieve the same effect, coupled with physical symptoms of withdrawal when use of the drug was discontinued. It was believed that any drug that did not meet these criteria was not addicting.

It has now become clear that these two factors are no more important than the behavior patterns that evolve around getting, using, and experiencing the drug's effects. It is now recognized that there is a psychological element involved in addiction that is far stronger and longer lasting than the physical component. Truly addictive behavior can appear in conjunction not only with drugs like alcohol and heroin, which are physically addicting, but also with food, sex, other people, sugar, or chocolate—anything that gives a positive reinforcement. On the most significant level, the propensity for addiction lies in the person, not in the drug.

Cocaine addiction is defined by the same behavioral criteria that apply to alcohol and heroin abuse and all other forms of addiction.

Loss of Control. The inability to resist the compulsion to use cocaine. This occurs even when there is a strong desire to stop using the drug and the user is not able to resist.

Continued Use in Spite of Consequences. The inability or refusal to resist the compulsion to take cocaine despite damaged or lost relationships, threats of financial ruin, loss of one's job, threat of legal punishment, sickness, even the threat of death.

High Involvement with the Drug. Cocaine becomes the central and most important focus of the addicted user's existence. It is his first priority, above everything, including his own survival.

Symbolic Use. Using cocaine or giving it to someone else to use can be the expression of an unspoken psychological dynamic operating between two or more people. For example, a daughter symbolically thwarted her controlling mother by using cocaine to the point where she ruined her appearance and health.

A Cycle of Use-Recovery-Relapse. This is the psychological component of addiction that transcends the short-term effects of the drug's reinforcement. Someone addicted to cocaine will typically break away from the drug repeatedly, either by sheer will or because of limiting factors like money or illness. Long after the drug's chemical actions have ceased to affect him, however, he will tend to return again and again to compulsive use.

There may be physical withdrawal symptoms that go with the termination of acute cocaine abuse. People who come off a long bout of addictive cocaine use or an intense binge often experience severe depression. It is known that depression is chemically caused by a depletion of norepinephrine in the brain, and the abrupt cessation of high levels of cocaine can have exactly the same effect. The depression can be interpreted as the withdrawal symptom of stopping cocaine. This is further supported by the fact that a dose of cocaine actually "cures" the depression for a short time, just as a shot of heroin or whiskey will momentarily stop withdrawal from opiates or alcohol.

Someone addicted to cocaine may need to stop but cannot, no matter what. He has no limits at all on frequency or dose.

An addicted cocaine user may snort, shoot, or freebase—or do all of them; he will have the greatest tendency to gravitate toward the more intense highs of freebasing or shooting.

Cocaine expense for an addicted user can be devastating, because an addict will spend every penny he can lay his hands on for cocaine. Other damaging consequences of addictive cocaine use can also be devastating: destruction of marriage and family, loss of jobs, destruction of careers, bankruptcy, descent into crime to raise money for the drug, jail, hospitalization, social isolation, death. The health risks are enormous and can result in any number of debilitating diseases. The psychological consequences include guilt, depression, suicidal remorse. High doses of cocaine can bring on cocaine psychosis—paranoia, hallucinations, delusion, violence leading to murder or suicide. The inevitable consequence of addictive cocaine use is self-destruction.

Who Is at Risk?

Anyone who uses cocaine regularly or who goes out of his way to seek it is testing the boundaries of his control. First, it is often impossible to tell where the limits of one's resistance to compulsive cocaine use lie until one encounters them. Often, cocaine use seems casual, and a user may increase its frequency or move from snorting to freebasing or shooting for a more intense high, and suddenly he finds himself with a cocaine problem. Second, the psychological factors that determine if one will go past casual use into abuse are often obscure. Third, the influence of the other determining factors is constantly shifting, and frequently one can't know until it's too late if one's cocaine use during a particular period might blossom into a serious problem.

The determining factors that influence the degree of one's cocaine use are access, stress, emotional makeup, and chemical sensitivity to the drug's effect.

Access. The ease with which an individual can get cocaine. It sometimes makes the difference between cocaine use and abuse, dependency or addiction.

Stress. The pressures in a person's life that cause discomfort or psychic pain—fear, anxiety, depression, loneliness, change, loss. The more intense the person's experience of stress, the stronger and more unremitting it is, the more appealing cocaine may become as a means of relief.

Emotional Makeup. A person's basic personality structure and psychological problems. High or low self-esteem, the ability to love and feel loved, experience happiness and satisfaction, all determine how well or poorly one is able to control cocaine use.

Chemical Sensitivity. A person's unique biological response to cocaine. Chemical sensitivity varies from person to person and can also vary from day to day for each individual. It is not clear what determines individual sensitivity to drugs, especially central nervous system drugs like cocaine.

Access, stress, emotional makeup, and chemical sensitivity work together to determine one's tendency to develop a cocaine problem. Any one factor can heighten or diminish the effect of any of the others. A person with strong psychological predisposition toward compulsive use, but a low chemical sensitivity to the drug and good resources for handling stress, may not develop a cocaine problem. If his stress level goes up past his capacities to cope, however, he may.

The problem is this: it is impossible to predict who is at risk. Any regular cocaine user is vulnerable.

Part II

Real-Life Profiles

Over the past ten years, talking to thousands of people who use cocaine, we have categorized cocaine users into five different user types: we call them Social Sniffers, Routine Users, Performance Users, Boredom/Stress Relievers, and Cokeaholics.

Although these types of cocaine use are quite different from one another and the reasons for the use differ, there are also differences within each group. For instance, someone who has used cocaine only once but might use it again is categorized as a Social Sniffer; so is the person who predictably uses it ten times a year at parties.

These five user groups do not represent a progression of ever more serious cocaine use. A Cokeaholic, for instance, does not start out as a Social Sniffer, then progress from Routine Use to Performance Use and then to Boredom/Stress Relief until he reaches cokeaholism. He may begin as any one of these and rapidly evolve toward addictive behavior without ever passing through another type of use, or he may be a Cokeaholic from the first time he uses cocaine.

Social Sniffers are not "abusing" the drug and may never do so. Users within the other categories are abusers, to a greater or lesser degree. The Cokeaholic users, many of whom are addicted to the drug, are the most extreme abusers.

In the following real-life stories, you'll read about users in each of the categories.

The
Social
Sniffer

If you use cocaine or know someone who does, the odds are that you or they fall into the group we call Social Sniffers. Like social drinkers, Social Sniffers are by far the most common kind of cocaine user, and their relationship to cocaine can be summed up as, "I can take it or leave it."

Since the Social Sniffer uses cocaine infrequently and in no particular pattern, cocaine does not interfere in any significant way with his work, finances, or personal relationships. The Social Sniffer generally does not want cocaine when it's not in front of him, and the thought of how to arrange to get some almost never crosses his mind. Although he might find cocaine pleasant, it does not fulfill a significant function for him.

The Social Sniffer almost always uses cocaine with friends, almost never alone, and he usually doesn't buy the cocaine he uses. He generally uses it only when it is offered to him by someone else, and even then he may not take advantage of an opportunity to use cocaine.

The Social Sniffer's cocaine use is almost always secondary to a more important social occasion. He may go to a party, be offered cocaine there, and opt to use some on the

50

spur of the moment, but his main motivation will have been the party, not the cocaine. His use of the drug is incidental and largely unplanned. He uses cocaine far less frequently than a social drinker takes a drink, perhaps half a dozen times a year or less; perhaps only once every year or so.

There are also limits to the quantity of cocaine a Social Sniffer will use at any given time: he will usually snort between two and ten lines of cocaine within a period of about six hours, and usually he will not repeat use within twenty-four hours, probably not for several weeks or months. He does not inject the drug or freebase.

A small percentage of Social Sniffers may actively seek out cocaine once or twice a year, usually through a friend they know who has access to it. They don't actually go to a dealer to buy it. They would rather forgo the drug than put themselves at risk.

Social Sniffers report a wide range of feelings from the effects of cocaine, from almost no effect, a mildly pleasant feeling, a sense of being greatly energized or noticeably sexually stimulated, to euphoria. Many feel a flush of camaraderie for the people with whom they're using it. Sniffers usually recall the intimate, all-night conversations, celebrations, parties, dancing, and good times they've had while using cocaine, rather than the drug's effect.

The most significant characteristic of the Social Sniffer is that although he may feel decidedly powerful effects from the drug, it does not transform his basic emotional makeup. He will not feel anything with cocaine that he has longed for but never experienced. Instead, he will recognize feelings he has had before, intensified by cocaine. It does not give him feelings he lacks without it, and this is one of the reasons he is unlikely to develop a dependency on it.

The Social Sniffer does not experience an intense crash when the effects of the drug wear off. He may feel a mild sense of dysphoria—a transient bad mood or feeling of mild depression that passes quickly—or some difficulty falling asleep. This, too, is significant. Since the Social Sniffer is usually in good psychological health, the pleasant feelings of a cocaine high are not a profound departure from his normal emotions. As the drug wears off he does not experience a precipitous drop from a dizzying pinnacle of stoned ecstasy.

The typical Social Sniffer is a stable, functioning member of society. He may have any one of a variety of sources for occasional cocaine—a boss who gives his employees cocaine as a bonus, a physician friend who has access to pharmaceutical cocaine, a musician friend who uses the drug; he may have an active social life, attending parties where cocaine is offered.

Cocaine has become an icebreaker at social gatherings, much as alcohol and marijuana have been. Not only do its effects often loosen people up, but the shared activity of cutting up the cocaine, passing it around, and snorting it can create an atmosphere of excitement and intimacy.

As the following true stories indicate, many different kinds of people are Social Sniffers. Because cocaine has become a symbol for a glamorous life, using it gives some people the feeling they are indulging in a wickedly expensive treat.

———

Jane is quintessentially sensible. She is high-spirited and fun-loving, and though she sometimes seems scatter-brained, she possesses a deep and finely tuned intelligence. She's adventurous and creative, and her judgment is sound. She's quick to try out new experiences, but she knows the difference between adventure and serious risk. Jane knows her limits, her strengths and weaknesses very well.

With her round, angelic face and ripe figure, Jane looks younger than her 35 years. She's the mother of two girls, 13 and 15, and she's been married for 16 years to Tony, who manages his family's diner/restaurant. They've always lived comfortably—the restaurant does well. Tony spends twenty hours a week there supervising, and he and Jane have plenty of time to be with each other and with the children. Each of them has many friends. Theirs is a solid marriage; they get along remarkably well.

Jane has little interest in drugs. She may smoke pot once or twice a year if someone offers it to her, and she'll down a martini or two at a wedding or another social occasion. Drugs have never especially interested her. She took a Quaalude once just to see what it was like, and though she found the warmth and satisfaction the drug gave her very pleasant, "it was no big deal," she says. She cannot understand how people get into trouble with it.

Since both her daughters are in school and involved in outside activities, Jane has plenty of leisure time. She and a group of her friends sometimes spend their afternoons shopping or having lunch—comparing notes on relationships, finances, and children. A few months ago the lunch patter at her friend Maryann's house turned to cocaine. A recent celebrity cocaine-abuse scandal had just been reported in the local paper and the five women discussed how often it seemed that cocaine was in the news.

One of the women asked if any of them had ever tried it. A chorus of no's rose from around the table.

"But I'd try some, once, you know," someone volunteered.

Maryann looked around the group, glancing from face to face, a mischievous look in her eyes. In a shy voice she said:

"I have some. Some coke." She held her breath, not sure what to expect.

There was a long moment of silence. Jane giggled and soon everyone else was laughing at Maryann's timidity. The idea that *she* would have cocaine was probably the biggest joke of all. Maryann needed nothing more than a sniff of a cork from a wine bottle to get a buzz.

"No, really," she said, after they calmed down. "Johnny gave it to me."

The girls knew Johnny, Maryann's brother-in-law. In fact, he was a frequent topic of conversation. At 26, he was managing local bands and music acts. It was generally agreed that Johnny was gorgeous—taciturn, yet quick with the perfectly timed compliment, tall, slim, dark-haired, mysterious. He'd given Maryann the coke when it accidentally fell out of the glove compartment of his car as he dropped her and his sister off at the shopping mall last week. The tiny plastic envelope was half full. A musician friend had given it

to him, but Johnny frowned on using drugs. It made his musicians unreliable, so he set an example by never using any himself.

The five women looked at one another around the table; everyone knew what everyone else was thinking. Jane broke the silence: "Why not try it now?" Their kids were at school. Their husbands would not be home for three or four hours and dinner didn't have to be started until five. Jane, like the others, was excited and a little scared.

Maryann left the group and returned with the plastic bag of powder, gingerly placing it on the table. Now what? None of them had prepared coke for snorting before, but they knew you had to have a tube to sniff it through.

"Anyone have a hundred-dollar bill?" Debbie asked. They laughed.

"Maybe we should call Johnny," another said.

"Well," Laura broke in, rummaging through her purse and producing three paper-wrapped straws, "I took the kids to McDonald's for lunch. I heard someone say once that they used cut soda straws for coke. We could try it."

Someone else had heard that you had to lay the cocaine out on a mirror or a piece of glass and arrange it into lines with a razor blade. After some debate, they poured the coke out on the top of Maryann's glass-and-chrome coffee table and used a cheese slicer to line it up. Someone cut the straws and passed them around, and they found themselves seated on the baby-blue wall-to-wall carpet around the coffee table staring at the white lines in front of them. No one moved.

"Well, hell," said Lorraine, who prided herself on having guts. She grabbed her straw, bent over the cocaine, and, with surprising ease, snorted up two lines, one in each nostril. The rest of the women quickly followed.

They wiped their noses, screwed up their faces in discomfort at the stinging in their sinuses, tasted the bitter drip going down their throats, and waited. Jane noticed she was clenching her teeth; she felt a glow of quiet intensity, an excitement deep in the pit of her stomach, the same feeling she had at her wedding, and when she won on a lottery ticket.

"My heart," said Lorraine. "It's going a mile a minute."

"I feel, I don't know, very awake, like I could go home and clean the whole house," said Debbie.

"Yeah," said Maryann. "You feel like you're ready for anything, right?"

"That's it," Laura added. "Ready for anything. I wish Jim were here." Jim is Laura's husband. "I'm horny."

Jane was also turned on. She felt like a teenager: full of mischief, sexy. The women all felt very close to one another, as though they were members of an exclusive club. They began to talk about what they thought other people did when they used cocaine, then about more personal things. They swapped fantasies about which movie stars they'd like to go to bed with. They talked about old boyfriends. They played some what-if games—What if they hadn't had kids? What if they had married other men? They even asked one another what might have been potentially explosive questions at some other time. Had any of them ever fantasized about making love to any of the others' husbands? They shared sexual fantasies. Jane divulged one she had never told anyone.

She lay in her bed, alone in the dark staring out the moonlit bedroom window. It was the middle of the night. Suddenly, a dark figure filled the window frame and slowly, noiselessly, raised the sash, and slid into the room. He was a burglar dressed in a knit cap, mask, dark turtleneck, thin leather gloves, carrying a satchel for his loot. Jane lay in bed rigid, petrified, but also aroused. The thief stealthily crossed the floor, and when a bright bar of moonlight fell across his face she saw it was her Tony. He came to her and made love to her. The mixture of terror, relief, and ecstasy was perfect. The fantasy was a hit with the rest of the women. No one could top it.

They had enough coke for one more round. When the effects began to wear off, Jane compared the cocaine high with others she'd had. Like all other drugs she'd tried, she could only characterize cocaine as "no big deal." She felt more high, more raw effect, from one martini. She liked the implication of cocaine, though—the glamour, the sexiness, the sense of having done something chic. Even so, she wouldn't cross the street to try it again. It was an experience she wanted to have once, like the time she had insisted Tony take her to ride on a roller coaster. She couldn't wait until Tony got home so she could tell him about her afternoon. He'd get a kick out of it.

There was one unexpected benefit from the experience. The following Saturday night, while both of her daughters were sleeping over at friends' houses, Jane lay in her bed in a negligee, exquisitely terrified and excited. Tony appeared at the window in a burglar's costume, quietly entered the room, and wordlessly began to make love to her. The intensity of her fantasy under cocaine had made her want to tell Tony about it. It was his idea to actually play it out.

Tom is a roofer. At 34, he's vigorous and works long hours to make a good living for himself and his wife, Vicky. The money goes far, since they have no children.

Tom gets cocaine only on very special occasions. He has two requirements for this rare treat: the day is usually a holiday like New Year's Eve or someone's birthday and he has been recently paid in cash. Since Tom contracts out to large construction companies, he usually receives a paycheck. Less frequently he is paid in cash, which feels to Tom like found money—"magic money," he calls it. As long as the rent and the bills are paid, Tom's magic money usually goes for extras—a gift for Vicky, something special for the house, a new piece of fishing gear for himself, a night out. A couple of times a year it goes for cocaine.

Tom is very much aware of the connection between the cash payment and his choosing to use cocaine.

"It's fast," he says. "The money comes in fast, you know. A customer puts it in my hand and there it is. Very informal. I don't have to go to the bank or sign anything. And coke's fast, too. It comes on fast, makes me feel fast sometimes. It's a real, you know, instant high. First the money is, then the coke is. It feels nice to do that once in a while."

Tom notes that the feeling he gets from spending the

money is very similar to the one he gets from using the coke—a thrill from feeling special, living high. Easy come, easy go. He would never dream of spending a nickel from a check on cocaine, though. He says he would feel bad if he did that. For him, paycheck money, regular money, is for handling responsibilities. He's accountable for the paycheck, it has to be endorsed, he keeps records on it. He does not have to account for the cash, nor for the cocaine he occasionally buys with it.

Like almost all Social Sniffers, Tom would never risk going to a dealer to purchase cocaine. Rather, he will chip in with a friend or two when one of them will buy the drug. Cocaine is generally available around the building trades these days, so this is easy to arrange. This kind of communal buying is also part of the enjoyment of cocaine for Tom. He likes to participate in the social action of putting his money into the pot, anticipating a good time, talking about it with his friends, and then splitting up the cocaine with them when it arrives. This is more important to him than the drug.

He and Vicky don't use coke by themselves. Usually, they invite one other couple over for dinner. They buy a bottle of wine, and Vicky makes her special homemade hors d'oeuvres. No one wants to eat much once they start sniffing cocaine. Since sharing the cocaine is as much a part of the pleasure of using it, they bring it out as soon as the other couple arrives, and everyone has some. They drink wine, everyone becomes very talkative, loose, and funny. They tell jokes, flirt, and have some more cocaine. Sometimes they play charades or gin rummy with lots of talk. Often they just talk all night. Everyone feels great, and by the end of the evening the cocaine is gone.

Sometimes, after the other couple leaves, Vicky will curl up in bed with Tom and they will often talk for a long time before they finally make love. They will also talk during sex, what Vicky calls "talking dirty." Vicky and Tom both enjoy this because she is usually inhibited about talking during sex and he loves it when she does. Their sex life is good without cocaine, but under the influence of the drug, it feels better and it's a kick for both of them.

At 34, Juliette is one of the youngest partners in her prestigious law firm. She was married to a highly successful businessman at 26 and now they have a lively 3-year-old daughter. Juliette is a cosmopolitan, accomplished achiever who excels at just about everything she does.

Juliette first tried cocaine nine years ago, and she has used it once or twice a year since then. Her business connections bring her into contact with people who are serious connoisseurs of cocaine and who offer it and use it at elegant parties. Juliette has used cocaine but only at these parties. At the most recent affair, a woman she knew waved Juliette and another friend into the ladies' room for a quick powder-room snort. They giggled over the secrecy and hoped no one would notice that three grown women had locked themselves in the bathroom together. The incident reminded Juliette of how she used to feel sneaking cigarettes in the girls' room in high school. In fact, that surreptitious thrill, the stealth, the sense of doing something forbidden, gave her at least as much pleasure as the effect of the cocaine.

Her first experience with cocaine stands out vividly for her. It took place at a small wedding reception in a suite at the Pierre Hotel in New York. Juliette was still single then, and her date had been invited to the wedding and then to this more intimate soiree. This party was clearly staged for maximum theatrical effect by the hostess, a slim, elegant woman wearing a pair of sheer silk lounging pajamas who greeted each guest at the door of the suite. She flitted from guest to guest, touching an arm, a cheek, batting her eyelashes, complimenting and flirting with everyone. It was a show.

When everyone held a glass of champagne, the hostess disappeared for a moment and returned with a silver tray on which was what appeared to be a neat mound of Sweet 'n Low. Juliette had never seen cocaine before, but it was clear that this was it. For each guest, man or woman, she performed a ritual dance with the cocaine. She would approach her guest, who would often be poised expectantly, smile with pleasure, move her tongue over her glossy lips, dip a finger into the guest's champagne, then into the mound of cocaine, and place the crystals on the tip of the guest's tongue. Then she'd do the same thing for herself, making a point to use the same finger. Juliette was struck by the blatant sexuality of the woman's actions. By the time she'd passed the first four or five guests she'd had that many tastes of cocaine, and even from a few feet away Juliette could tell that she was flying. The hostess performed her minuet with Juliette and her date, and slid away to make her offering to the other guests.

Juliette was surprised at the bitterness in her mouth, followed by the swift numbness on her tongue. She felt no other effect. Looking around the room, she noticed that this crowd was clearly paying far more attention to cocaine than to one another. Some people had clearly brought their own, produced mirrors, and were busily using their credit cards to shuffle small piles of it into slender lines on the glass surfaces. Others fished hundred-dollar bills out of their pockets, rolled them into tight cylinders, and used them to snort the lines of cocaine. The way they all fell on the drug told Juliette that this crowd had been prepared for what was happening. It seemed that everyone had brought crisp, high-denomination bills for the occasion. One fellow created a stir by producing a five-hundred-dollar bill. Some of the others used plastic room-service straws that had been snipped in half.

A tall, elegantly dressed man, the Pajama Lady's partner, now made a round of the suite. He was handing something to all the guests. When he reached Juliette and gave it to her, she looked into her open hand at a tiny brown glass vial filled with white powder, obviously cocaine. "Peruvian flake," the man whispered. Juliette nodded knowingly, thinking at first he was joking about the swarthy bridegroom.

Her date tipped out his vial, scratched it into several lines, and showed Juliette how to snort through a rolled bill. She carefully observed the effects—the accelerated heartbeat, the flush of euphoria, the elation, the sexual arousal. The evening slipped by as she savored the sense of feeling more relaxed, self-confident, and uninhibited.

Although she has a smooth, cool exterior, Juliette is prey

to the same anxieties, agonies, and doubts that afflict most people. She likes the way the cocaine relieves tension and allows her to feel less reserved. Usually Juliette won't cut loose when she dances at a party, yet she can after some cocaine. She's also able to leave her professional perfectionism behind for a few hours. Cocaine releases her of her inhibitions, and when she accepts an offer of a snort she is giving herself permission to ease some of her self-control.

Juliette considers the occasions when she decides to use cocaine—far fewer times than she's offered the drug—as once- or twice-yearly treats. She feels safe from any legal repercussions as a result of using an illegal drug, since she knows quite a few other lawyers who indulge as she does and she is careful to use cocaine in the safest circumstances and with people she knows.

Cocaine holds for Juliette a mixture of pleasant surprise, spontaneous indulgence, and unexpected fun. Her attitude toward the drug is so casual that she completely forgot about the party-favor gram of cocaine she was given at the wedding. She discovered the unopened vial of white powder years later, tucked in a corner of the purse she had carried that day.

———

Sheila will be the first one to tell you that she's not the adventurous type. "I'm not exactly Jane Fonda," she says peering over her horn-rimmed specs with an air of resignation and wit. Sheila has a knack for being funny and self-denigrating at the same time.

She is a 36-year-old elementary schoolteacher who has been looking for "Mr. Right" since her early twenties. She seems to be offered cocaine, she says wryly, about as often as she's able to establish a hopeful relationship with a man. Sheila has used cocaine three times in the last eleven years, and she says she'll likely use it again if offered it under the right circumstances. She vividly remembers her first time, and tells the story in her typical deadpan, comic style.

Sheila first used cocaine in 1972, when she was 25. She had gone away with four friends to "another one of those" singles weekends in the Catskill Mountains. She took it as a sign of her desperation.

She felt stuck. Alone in the Catskill hotel suite, she studied herself in the mirror, ticking off her good and bad points. Sweet smile, nice eyes, thick thighs, wide bottom, mousy hair. She looked away from the mirror and shrugged. Who could argue with genes? She was just as her mother had always told her: not glamorous or exciting but even-tempered.

Sheila sighed. This must be the hundredth disco night in three years. She took out her arsenal of makeup, gave it her best try, and appeared in the lobby promptly at 8:00.

At the "disco," actually a darkened dining room with strobe lights, Sheila danced once with a podiatrist whose toupee was slipping and with a shoe salesman with two left feet.

Then she danced with an easygoing guy named Ira three times in a row. He seemed interested in her. He was likable, "acceptable," her mother would have said. He was a teacher, too. He was funny, almost cute. They talked, drank, and danced. Around 11:30 he invited her to a party in his room. His friends had already gone up there, he said. Could she bring the four other girls he'd seen with her?

In the suite, a radio was tuned to a soft rock station and Ira's friends, dressed in an assortment of blue blazers, madras ties, and Topsiders, sat cross-legged on the floor around the coffee table. There was an open tinfoil package on the table and one of the guys hovered over it, absorbed in measuring out quantities of white powder from the foil onto a piece of hotel stationery.

Sheila noticed that all the guys were "ranking out" and joking about the school where they taught. Sheila noticed that they were happy and silly, but with none of the sloppiness of a beer-drinking crew at a fraternity party. Just as she connected the white powder with their "horsing around," Ira asked her if she'd ever tried cocaine.

So that was it. That was why they were happy and silly. That was what was in the foil. Cocaine. Hard drugs.

"Want to try some?" Ira asked. He was so innocent. All of them were. Sheila said yes.

Her girl friends had distributed themselves around the

coffee table. Everyone was focused on the fellow in the shirt sleeves—the "druggist" was how Sheila thought of him—who was busily working with the cocaine. Ira spoke to him.

"Hey, Mark, set up a tray for the girls, will you?" Mark looked up. His eyes were glittering. He had sniffed two lines of cocaine in the few minutes since Sheila had been in the room. "Sure," he said. "Mark will take care of it." He went right back to his pile of crystals, deftly shaking some from the paper onto a shaving mirror. Concentrating, Mark cut the pile with a razor blade into slender lines about three inches long. Then he quickly took his rolled-up ten-dollar bill and snorted up one of the lines, half in each nostril. He sat up straight, admired the parallel network on the mirror, and turned to pass it carefully to Ira, who was sitting on the floor next to Sheila. Mark was distributing red-and-white plastic straws he had cut into three-inch lengths. Everyone seemed to hold their breath in anticipation. One of the guys switched off the Dylan song in the background and the room filled with silence. Suddenly, Sheila started to feel afraid. Ira passed the mirror to his friend, who took two snorts and passed it to Nancy. The mirror moved around the group, everyone taking a hit. Ira and Sheila would be the last to get it.

Sheila felt silly and scared at the same time. What if cocaine made her crazy? What if she didn't know where she was and what she was doing? What if she died because the cocaine was mixed with rat poison? She imagined Walter Cronkite's broadcast: "A teacher attended a sex orgy last evening and died from poisoned cocaine." But there had to be a sex orgy before that happened. Better to go one step at a time. Besides, just this once she wanted to explore something risky firsthand.

The mirror was only three people away now. Those who had already passed it were rubbing their noses, sniffing like head cold victims, smacking their lips as if trying to taste something. The air turned electric. Everyone was laughing. Cocaine seemed to be a social lubricant. Sheila's friend Stephanie, a.k.a. by the group as "Miss Proper," had taken off her shoes and, with a limpid gaze, listened to one of Ira's friends tell an endless joke.

Sheila watched as Marsha tried to snort her lines. She was having trouble. She didn't want to actually put the straw into her nose. Ira's friend next to her was laughing so hard tears streamed down his cheeks. "Put it *in* the nose, all the way *in*," he kept repeating. Marsha finally got the hang of it.

At last, the mirror came to Sheila. There were four lines on it: two for her and two for Ira. They were a couple. Ira gently took the mirror from her and said, "Watch me."

She watched closely as he put the straw in one nostril, held the other closed with a finger, sniffed once, deeply, and repeated the act with the other one. It looked easy. He handed her the straw and the mirror and smiled.

Quickly, she followed Ira's instructions. There was a sharp burning sensation high in her sinuses under her eyes; she immediately disliked the rough, bitter taste dripping down the back of her throat. She sniffed and winced. She concentrated on the sensations, closed her eyes. She half expected that when she looked up, everyone would applaud because she was the last, and now they had all had coke. But everyone else was involved in feeling good, and no one but Ira paid attention.

"How do you feel?" he asked.

"Nothing yet," Sheila shrugged. But there was something happening—a quickening sensation, a feeling of mischievousness. Sheila found herself grinning at the happy scene in the room. Here were two of Ira's friends rolling over on their backs laughing as Marsha and Nancy giggled along with them; there was Stephanie in a sincere tête-à-tête with the joke-teller. She really liked being part of this group. She felt close to all of them. They were all having a good time together. There was magic here, a fine chemistry. The only one not part of this was Mark, who still was bent intently over his cocaine. He spoke with no one and everyone left him alone.

Sheila found herself telling Ira about her job, her mother, about growing up. They traded teaching stories. Marsha overheard and joined in with one of hers, and then they all entered what quickly became a round robin, each teacher trying to top the other's most outrageous story.

Sheila could not remember ever having felt so energetic

and uninhibited. She looked at Ira and wondered if this might be the start of a relationship, but the idea was not accompanied by the anxiety that usually came with it. Whatever will be will be, she thought.

They stayed up all night. The shaving mirror made the rounds every half hour or so. By the time she and her friends got back to their rooms it was after sunup. They were exhausted and woke long after noon.

When Sheila awoke, she "replayed" last night's adventures. The cocaine, she decided, was very nice, but the good feeling was too short-lived. She had sparkled, outdone herself. But it was over. She was already worrying about Monday: preparing the lesson plan, the kids, the teachers' room politics, the grind.

Sheila's subsequent cocaine experiences have been similar to the first, although she's never had so much at once. It usually goes like this: "I use it with a few girl friends. Men always share it with us." It's always been when she's away from home—on vacations, visiting someone out of town, on a cruise. And each time she experiences the same thing: tensions and inhibitions evaporate. She feels at ease, on equal terms with everyone. And that is why Sheila, who doesn't usually feel so great about herself, enjoys cocaine.

———

At 33, Judy has accomplished what she always said she would: she married a doctor before she was 30. Judy traded up into her current position through two previous marriages. She divorced each of her former husbands because neither could give her what she felt she needed: security, status, and wealth.

She married her first husband, an X-ray technician, for love. She left him for her second, who was the controller of a medium-size corporation and who positioned her securely in the upper middle class, a few notches higher than her own middle-class family. She left her second husband for the physician. They're not millionaires, but to Judy they're rich—they can buy whatever they want and they own a Mercedes-Benz.

Judy has always traded up. She does it with her friends, always seeking more powerful, glamorous people and dropping her old acquaintances as she rises in what she perceives is a pantheon of acceptability and chic.

In the sixties, Judy didn't use drugs; she thought drug-taking was lower class. But in the mid-seventies cocaine became for Judy the exception to the rule. It was different. It was a mark of elegance. It got rave reviews from the "A" list, the rich friends she had cultivated, those who could afford to sniff it.

She used cocaine two or three times a year: at a party in the Hamptons, at a gathering in the loft of a Soho art dealer. "Oh! It's terrific," she'd flutter. "I feel just great."

In truth, Judy felt little effect from cocaine. It might as well have been powdered sugar for all the impact it had on her. She usually had a hard time telling if she felt better before or after she sniffed it. What was important was the aura of glamour and cachet she felt she assumed when she used it.

When, in 1978, Judy married her physician husband, she found herself exactly where she wanted to be. She stopped using cocaine. Judy had decided that women her age who were truly successful did not have to prove their status with chic drugs. For a Social Sniffer like Judy, who only used cocaine given to her by someone else, there was no way the drug showed off increased material wealth. The only way to do that would be to buy it and give it away, and she had no interest in doing that. Judy preferred to wear her success or drive around in it. She moved up from using cocaine, just as she moved up from her second husband to her third.

———

Tommy is a fireman in the Staten Island community where he was raised. At 26, he is athletic, well built, with piercing blue eyes and dark hair. He's appealing, friendly, and maybe a little "macho."

About a year ago when Tommy had a fight with his fiancée, Roseanne, he rounded up a bunch of his buddies and drove into Manhattan to an East Side disco, a well-known singles pickup joint. Tommy often runs with "the guys" when he's upset or angry. His friends give one another a sense of themselves; they support one another's male egos and commiserate about their problems.

Tommy wasn't quite sure exactly why he had come to the disco. He certainly wasn't thinking about splitting up with Roseanne, and he hadn't really planned to pick up another woman to ease the sting of his anger, but as he looked around, he was excited that the place was jammed with gorgeous girls. Tommy and his friends stopped at the bar and ordered drinks while they scanned the talent on the dance floor.

A burst of brilliant color flashing under a strobe light caught his eye. It was the vivid, hand-painted image of a parrot on an oversize silk shirt. He couldn't take his eyes off the woman wearing it. She was tall and blond and she danced like a dream. Tommy maneuvered closer for a better look. Her eyes were green like a cat's and she had a sultry look that turned Tommy on. This girl was as different from Roseanne as his red GTO was from his grandmother's Dodge Dart. Not that Roseanne didn't like sex—she was only technically still a virgin—but this girl was obviously all about sex, and she put it right out there. Roseanne was young, inexperienced—she was a virgin because both she and Tommy wanted it that way, but, well, he always felt a dull ache of frustration. This woman looked like she might have the cure.

It was a half second before Tommy realized that Nancy was staring back at him. He asked her to dance and they moved out onto the floor.

Tommy was hit by "the thunderbolt," as the Italians call it. There was immediately an unspoken contract between him and Nancy: they would go to bed. The only question was when. They moved to the music, touching each other. Finally, Nancy said:

"Come with me. I've got something special at home."

Nancy lived only a few blocks from the club. As soon as they left the bar, she took his hand. At the first corner, waiting for a red light, she said, "Give me a kiss." Before Tommy could respond, she put her mouth to his. Roseanne did not kiss like this girl.

Later, at her apartment, he looked up to see Nancy standing in the doorway, looking at him provocatively. In her hand she was cradling a tiny turquoise-colored egg and a miniature silver spoon. She sat down next to him.

Tommy had never seen cocaine. But when she snapped the top half of the egg and Tommy saw the white, crystalline powder inside, he knew what it was.

He was reeling with excitement and fear. He was used to being the aggressor with a woman, not vice versa. And he was afraid of what the drug might do to him. But he had heard that coke was some kind of superaphrodisiac and here was this sexy blond going to give him some. Nancy smiled and twice dipped the tiny spoon into the egg, sniffing the white powder first into one nostril, then the other.

"When she offered me a hit I was scared shitless," Tommy says, "but I wasn't going to let that chick get wind of it. So when she put that little spoon to my nose," he says, "I took one snort and then another. I was floating, man, and more turned on than I've ever been." As he began to feel a tingling sensation in the back of his throat, Tommy realized he had an erection like nothing he'd ever experienced before. It was as though his penis had a life of its own. Nancy caressed him through his jeans.

He was simultaneously more turned on and more in control than he had ever been before. "I was just touching her arm, man, and I got completely lost for twenty minutes just feeling the smoothness of her skin," Tommy says. He and Nancy began to undress each other, one piece of clothing at a time, kissing and touching each other all the while. Tommy had never been able to sustain lovemaking like this before, but now it was as if the cocaine had given him endless patience, energy, and staying power. Every time he got near to coming Nancy would slow him down, and he never lost it, never went over like he often did with Roseanne. He had never been able to have an orgasm more than twice a night, but tonight he came and recovered four or five times.

Every half hour for the rest of the night Nancy gave Tommy a couple of snorts (and had some herself). She knew exactly what she was doing. For Tommy, it was a night of revelations. There had always been anxiety, unsureness, and guilt with sex for Tommy, but tonight he soared above it with Nancy and her little cocaine spoon.

They kept it up until noon the next day with only a short break for a brandy to toast the sunrise. Then the cocaine ran out. A mantle of exhaustion heavier than anything he'd ever felt settled over Tommy, and he succumbed to the black weight of it. When they woke up it was dark outside.

By the time Tommy got back home, he was starting to feel guilty and anxious about his night of sex. When he saw Roseanne he quickly forgot how frustrated and enraged he'd been at her. He felt terrible about deceiving her, but didn't tell her where he'd been.

Tommy swore to himself that he wouldn't see Nancy or use cocaine again. But he did see Nancy.

"I'm not sure what'll happen," Tommy says. "I mean, there's no way I'm going to leave Roseanne, but I do like to see Nancy every couple of months and we go to bed. No cocaine since the first time, though. It was okay, but I don't want to make a habit of it. And besides, I think Nancy uses too many drugs—she's always smoking pot or taking a Quaalude or something. I don't like that. Drugs are not my thing."

Tommy will probably not seek out an experience similar to his first night with Nancy, and the odds are he won't be using cocaine again. For him, Nancy and that coked-out sexy night will be enough: a vivid, erotic memory.

––––––

Cindy is a 40-year-old free-lance graphic designer. She's moderately successful, but she can't seem to rise to the top in her field. She does excel to her complete satisfaction in her hobby, though: distance running. She runs at least five miles a day and has finished in several marathons. She takes vitamins and eats health foods. She calls her body "the machine." She's in great shape—at least physically.

Cindy is lonely. She lived with a man for twelve years, and when they split up a few years ago, he almost immediately married another woman. But between her relentless pursuit of her work and her intense devotion to running, she kept from brooding about it.

Cindy doesn't use any other drugs but cocaine. Drinking makes her feel hung over, and smoking pot makes her feel tired. "I really have to keep my energy up," she explains.

Cindy never uses cocaine by herself, but the circumstances in which she has used it seem to have arisen more frequently over the past year or two. Every six weeks or so, Cindy or one of her women friends in her apartment building will invite a group of regulars over for a Sunday of socializing and watching football or baseball on TV. There's the usual beer, wine, and food, but lately there's also been cocaine. Cindy and her friends never buy it. They'll invite a couple of the women's husbands or boyfriends along, and one of the men will supply the cocaine. Cindy has learned how to use cocaine cautiously.

"The one time I really binged I got this blinding headache and couldn't eat or sleep right for a couple of days," she said. "It was really depressing."

Although she doesn't binge, she consumes a respectable amount when she does use it. She and her friends will consume a gram or two of cocaine in an afternoon.

Since Cindy's become single again, she goes out with many different men and sleeps with a substantial number of them. Her dates will often give her cocaine, and she readily admits that more than once cocaine has tipped the balance in favor of finding a man attractive.

Almost all of Cindy's relationships with men that go beyond one- or two-night stands turn out to be dead ends. She sadly finds herself involved with a man she works with who she knows will not leave his wife for her or will not make a commitment to her. She beats her therapist and friends to the punch with the obvious—she always chooses men she cannot have, she says; she only enters relationships guaranteed to end in disappointment.

"I was forty a couple of weeks ago," Cindy says. "I'd been anticipating the trauma for weeks, thinking about it, talking about it. I mean, I'm not married, I've given up my dream of having children. I got together with my friend Emily and my friend Jill and her husband and we did cocaine. I thought, 'Thank God it was a good evening.' I wasn't as depressed or lonely as I was afraid I would be. Actually, the coke wasn't even all that necessary that night, but I think it made us all feel closer. I even felt cheerful calling my mother in Florida. That usually is a real trial.

"I was okay. I thought, 'At least I know I can get through the night.'"

Marilyn gracefully juggles too many responsibilities, too little time, and a tiny budget. She's 34, divorced, and the sole support of her 11-year-old son, Jerry. She lives in the small town in eastern Colorado where she grew up. Though she has a college degree, she works as an administrative assistant in a small company, and her salary isn't nearly enough to make raising a child an easy task.

Marilyn has the kind of wholesome prettiness that can be transformed into an infinite number of looks. Until Jerry was born, she harbored dreams of being a fashion model. But now with her low income and her responsibilities, there's little room for glamour in her life. She treats herself to glamour twice a year. Every winter she buys the best cloth coat she can find, and every summer the most outrageous bathing suit. She takes pleasure in seeing that she can still turn the heads of men fifteen years younger than she when she strides down the lakeside.

Marilyn doesn't complain, but she and Jerry subsist on what she calls a "meatloaf and tuna diet," and since there's not much money, she spends many of her nights reading or watching TV and eating popcorn with Jerry. She exchanges child care with her friend Barbie, who works with her, so that they both can save on baby-sitting costs. She used to worry about Jerry being a latchkey child who let himself in after school and watched TV until she came home at 5:30. She's since gotten him into after-school clubs and a Little League team. Now she doesn't feel as guilty when she goes out on weekends and leaves Jerry at Barbie's house.

For a break, Marilyn sometimes goes to a neighborhood bar where she spends time with a few of her co-workers. She's not much of a drinker, so she goes for the socializing and nurses a beer. She always hangs out with the same crowd, and she dates three of the men regularly. There's a note of resignation in her voice as she describes them.

"Two are married and one is adorable, but definitely not marriage material."

She will drink more if she's out with one of them, and she'll also smoke a joint. She finds that she likes sex much better when she's smoked some pot first.

Once in a great while one of her regular dates gets some cocaine. She grimaces and shakes her head as she explains.

"It's always George who gets the coke. Of the three of them, he's the wimpy one. His hands shake when he rolls a joint and when he very . . . carefully . . . unwraps . . . the foil around the cocaine. He calls the coke his 'goodies.'" She rolls her eyes upward.

But Marilyn likes cocaine. The drug energizes her and infuses an evening with optimism and adventure. Being with George, she explains, is only tolerably better than being alone, but when he has coke, it's not that bad.

"I know cocaine is probably bad for me," Marilyn says, "but two or three times a year it makes me feel like I'm twenty-one again. I forget about all the things that are wrong with my life, and with me for that matter, and for a couple of hours I feel like I'm going to go right out and conquer the world. Is there anything wrong with that?

"I have no interest in using cocaine more than once in a long while. The stuff really leaves me wiped out," she says. "How could I take care of Jerry and do my job if I used it regularly? I'm not the type to go overboard with anything, anyway."

The truth is, Marilyn is remarkably well disciplined about almost everything. She is iron-willed about her diet and never leaves the house in the morning without rinsing out her coffee cup and straightening up. Her bed, she explains, is always made. Cocaine will never be a problem for her.

Max's father started out poor, as a janitor. But he eventually saved enough to start his own building-maintenance company, and by the time Max and his sister were born, he was making a solid middle-class living. Max's parents yearned to have style and sophistication, and they brought their children up to value those characteristics. When Max and his sister went away to college, they were each given a car and a small allowance.

His sister, the student in the family, was accepted at Northwestern University, studied hard, and finally became a lawyer. Max, in contrast, was extremely bright but not scholarly. He was just getting by in college when his father died. The business, Max was told, was in debt, and his tuition and expense money would have to be cut off. Faced with the choice of struggling through college or quitting to go to work, he dropped out of school (with relief, he confides) and went to work to help save the family business. He had a good head for business and began to do well almost immediately.

He knew he was good-looking and very young to be earning such a hefty amount of money, but he felt he was "just a janitor." His parents had emphasized the importance of transcending their own working-class origins, and he always "felt funny" about how he made his living. He tried to compensate by concentrating on his image. He wore only the most stylish clothes he could afford, he drove a foreign sports car, he took up tennis, backgammon, skiing. He tried hang gliding, dirt-bike motorcycle riding, and everything else that would indicate that he was a mobile, socially advantaged young single.

But none of these ever made him feel any better about who he was or what he did. He always felt that the other young men he spent time with had the edge on him. He was ashamed to tell anyone what he did for a living.

When cocaine became a socially acceptable drug, Max discovered that it eased his self-consciousness in social situations. It helped him slip into conversations with women and breeze right by the discomfort of the "What do you do?" question.

Max's first encounters with cocaine were typical: someone would give him some, usually at a party. The drug did not make him feel high so much as it made him feel relieved, at ease, and confident. Soon, Max began to use cocaine regularly, once every two months or so, and he found himself spending money on it, as well.

"I never got into it heavily," he explained. "I used it fairly often for a couple of years. I used it at parties. I used to buy some; I'd go in on some with a friend and split it, you know, usually very small amounts, just enough for an evening or two.

"I found that even if I didn't pick up the woman of my choice, or if the vibes weren't just right, a little coke would make sex really nice anyway."

About a year and a half ago Max married a woman who didn't like him to use cocaine or any other drugs.

"I wouldn't buy it now," says Max. "Nancy really hates it when I use drugs. She even gets up-tight when I snort a little with good friends at a get-together. She doesn't like my old crowd, and I really don't see them much anymore."

Max at 35 now finds himself in a different social milieu. The social and psychological reasons that induced him to enjoy cocaine in the first place no longer exist.

"Nancy and I are trying to have a baby," Max says. "She had a miscarriage recently, so we're trying again. I'm much more involved with that right now. Look, cocaine was great for kicks, but it's not an important thing to me anymore. And I don't like to get Nancy upset."

Max can easily live without using cocaine, but the tone of his voice betrays a mixed message. If it weren't for Nancy, he might still be snorting it every couple of months.

Mitch is 50 and has never been married. He's witty, well read, and makes a respectable living as a systems analyst in the electronics industry. He's also starting to show the effects of years of bachelorhood. He's set in his ways, and everyone in his family, with whom he is actually quite close, would like to find him some nice woman to settle down with. His mother, his aunts, and his cousins have all been trying to fix him up.

Mitch sustained a relationship with one woman for about eight months but ended it recently. He declared that this was the last time he was going to let himself get so caught up in romance. He gave no explanation to anyone beyond this. Those who love him know, but don't like to admit, that Mitch has some serious problems with women. Though he's charming and courtly with them, and women his age find him appealing if not exactly handsome (they've been known to ask him out—he's fun to be with), it's clear that Mitch is uncomfortable with women in anything beyond a casual relationship. He admits that he's afraid to get too close to people or let them get too close to him. He doesn't like to discuss this. Instead, he'll shrug his shoulders in a "What can you do?" gesture and change the subject.

Mitch uses cocaine every two months or so. For years he has gone to a local bar where he knows the bartender well. Sometimes the bartender will offer him a snort or two of cocaine in the back room. Sometimes he will get together with a few of his friends and use cocaine, and sometimes he'll use it with a woman he may meet, in which case he'll get a small amount from the bartender or one of his friends. Mitch sometimes uses cocaine with his cousins. Mitch never pays for the cocaine, nor does he chip in with others to buy. Instead, he does favors for people who give it to him.

Mitch describes the effect of cocaine as a "lift" rather than an intense high or euphoria. Cocaine makes him feel he is in what he calls "a better mood." While on the surface he's an affable, agreeable Mr. Nice Guy, there's another, darker side to him. "Nice," applied to Mitch, can also mean woefully unassertive. There is a sadness about his good-natured resignation.

He's not in serious trouble with cocaine, but Mitch has some of the characteristics that could turn him into an abuser. He gets a special feeling from cocaine that he rarely gets elsewhere—a relief from his constant underlying sadness. This is where the danger lies for him.

Mitch doesn't run into difficulties with cocaine because his strengths outweigh his weaknesses. These act for him, as they do for many of us, as "brakes," self-limiting devices. He does feel pride in his work and happiness from his relationships with his friends and family; he loves the feeling of responsibility that comes with being "Uncle Mitch" to his brothers' and sisters' children; and he has an image of himself as a reasonable, moderate man. He's living proof, he says, patting his ample belly, that one can be moderate in everything but ice cream.

The odds are against Mitch's becoming a cocaine abuser, but it's possible that circumstances such as losing his job or the death of someone in his family could "set him off."

The Routine User

The Routine User does not use cocaine for recreation. He uses it to keep going, to cope with what feels like an unbearable work situation. He takes cocaine at regular and frequent intervals and uses extremely small, controlled amounts throughout the day. He may, for instance, snort two very short lines every three hours over a nine-hour period. He would not use four lines at a time, for example, nor would he be likely to continue to use the drug after work. The Routine User's most remarkable trait is the minuscule amount of cocaine he uses at a time, all day. A gram that may last only an evening for someone on a one-night binge typically lasts a Routine User a month or longer.

The Routine User is unique among all user types in that he does *not* feel high or euphoric from the drug, but feels energized enough to do his work. He'll feel renewed, less fatigued, and alert through long periods of routine work. Cocaine augments his reserves of physical or emotional stamina and allows him to act pleasant when without the drug he would be exhausted and irritable. He will use such small amounts that he won't crash when he stops using it for the day.

It's not surprising that people in certain demanding professions are drawn to routine cocaine use. People who must stand on their feet all day, perform repetitive or stressful work requiring concentration and a high level of dexterity, or who must be consistently pleasant to clients no matter how they feel—haircutters, dentists, bartenders, and factory workers, for example—make up a significant percentage of Routine Users.

In addition to using cocaine to help him work faster, longer, and more comfortably, the Routine User might "self-medicate" with cocaine, using the drug to treat emotional problems, such as the "blues" or "burnout."

Since routine use is almost exclusively associated with work, this person takes cocaine with him to his job, where every few hours he'll snort his carefully titrated dose to maintain his energy and enthusiasm. This user takes a "coke break" the same way most of us take a coffee break, and enjoys a similar ritual.

We call the Routine User's ritual a "modus operandi" (M.O.) and we find it among all the groups of cocaine users except Social Sniffers. The M.O. gives the cocaine user a kind of gratification that is often as significant to him as the effect of the drug. The Routine User's M.O., for example, might entail returning to the same location to snort the drug, buying it from the same person, using a special coke spoon or straw, keeping the cocaine in a special container or a special hiding place.

An M.O., no matter how flexibly it's followed, indicates a strong emotional connection to cocaine. Routine Users often report powerful feelings of anticipation as the set time when they'll use the drug approaches. The experience is worth a great deal to them. Many Routine Users describe the feeling of having cocaine as their "ace in the hole," their security. When there is this much value placed on cocaine, there is also the beginning of a dependency.

Since cocaine is a regular (often necessary) part of the Routine User's life, he has an organized, businesslike means of procuring it. He buys his cocaine regularly from a trusted source with whom he's carefully cultivated a relationship. The source is sometimes a cocaine dealer, but more often a "civilian" who "moves" (sells) a small amount of cocaine in addition to his regular job to provide himself with a steady supply. The Routine User often buys cocaine in quantities larger than a gram because it tends to be cheaper and less "stepped on" (adulterated) and also because he knows exactly what his needs are and can estimate his use over time. Since he tightly curtails his cocaine use, the Routine User does not usually spend an inordinate amount of money on it: the average Routine User might consume a gram about every month to six weeks, at the rate of $100 to $150 per gram.

The Routine User doesn't dwell on the notion that his cocaine use might be dangerous to his physical or mental health. He seldom thinks of it as symptomatic of underlying problems. He generally sees only the benefits he gets from the drug.

The cocaine effects mask so well the unpleasant consequences of his unsuitable work and life-style that he never feels compelled to face his problems and take appropriate action. The danger here is that over time these unacknowledged problems just tend to get worse. He doesn't know it but he is in trouble. His cocaine use can easily escalate.

Eric has done remarkably well as a hairdresser. He never finished high school and comes from a poor family, but now he's at the pinnacle of his career at his own exclusive salon. All his clients use the same word to describe him: "fabulous." This is because Eric has mastered all the specialties of the hairdresser's art. A successful stylist must cultivate regular clients and so must be not only talented with scissors, but also part confidant, part therapist, and part admirer. Eric is all of these things to perfection, and at 34, with his clean-cut good looks and his immaculately tailored wardrobe of designer clothes, he's the picture of success.

The money is good. It's so good, in fact, that Eric is convinced he could never live on less; consequently he feels trapped in a job that literally takes everything out of him. He's been cutting hair for fifteen years, and although he's not seriously entertaining alternative ways of making a living, he'd like to stop. He told us that the only way he's managed to get through the last five years has been with the routine use of cocaine.

He was introduced to the drug by one of his adoring clients, who came in for her 9:00 A.M. cut and offered him a "wake up." The first time he had cocaine, he was amazed by the jolt of energy and connectedness to his work. In less than two minutes he was awake, alert, and even looking forward to his day. He called this client later and asked her to get him some cocaine the following week. At that time, he was not making as much money, and he willingly cut his socializing by about a third for the first few months in order to afford the drug on a regular basis. This same client still hand-delivers Eric's "magic flake" every six weeks when she comes in for her regular trim.

"My clients get on my nerves sometimes," Eric says, screwing up his handsome face. His bright, quick repartee sometimes becomes sharp and hostile. When he feels this tension rising in him, as he does three or four times a day, he excuses himself and hastily slips into the colorist's tiny supply room for a little "one and one," one snort of cocaine in each nostril. Almost immediately he begins to feel better, amused instead of annoyed, even entertained by what only moments before made him feel angry. Fortified with these new feelings, he's able to continue for several more hours.

Through his clients Eric attends an endless stream of parties, gallery openings, and dinners. He's often offered cocaine when he's out, but he never accepts it. He uses it only at work.

"It's what gets me through the day," he explains.

Eric's life is a paradox. He's successful at work. He makes a lot of money. He dates the kind of women who turn every head when they enter a room. Yet he often feels frustrated, drained by the demands, the repetitiveness, the exhaustion, the strain of servicing his clients.

He doesn't like the draining, tedious aspects of his job, but he needs the good times, the money, and the glamour. Cocaine reduces the conflict Eric feels. He says he does not have a problem with cocaine: he uses it only at work, and a little bit lasts him such a long time. But when he's asked if he thinks he might stop sometime, his sharp answer slices the air like the flashing blades of his scissors: "I wouldn't even consider it," he says.

━━━━━━━━

Elizabeth is an overachiever who uses cocaine because she is dissatisfied with her work. Her job is intensely demanding and repetitive, and she frequently feels depressed.

She's a rarity—a 30-year-old female dentist. She was the only woman in her dental-school class, graduating fourth out of two hundred. She always did well—she had a lot to make up for. She is the only child of an internist who died suddenly of a heart attack when she was 19. For him, she had always been a disappointment: first, that she, his only child, was not a son, and, second, that she had not gotten into medical school, but had to settle (in his estimation) for becoming a dentist.

Elizabeth had always been a model daughter—pretty, perfectly behaved, very proper—a straight-A student who never gave anyone any trouble. Not surprisingly, she did so well in dental school that she was invited to join a lucrative group practice immediately upon graduation.

Once she found herself practicing six days a week, Elizabeth made a devastating discovery: she despised dentistry. She was terrified. She'd tried for so long to fulfill her father's wishes that she had no idea what she really wanted. She felt trapped.

She hoped she would adjust, but after a year she hadn't and she was getting depressed about it. She barely ate and got thinner. She was tired all the time and had trouble relaxing and focusing attention on her work. She worried that her colleagues would notice. She had even stopped dating. But one night she was coerced by some old roommates into attending a party.

She regretted going as soon as she entered the room. The crowd was fashionable, self-possessed, and attractive. Elizabeth felt out of place, tired. She was waiting for the bathroom to be free just so she could be there alone when suddenly the door popped open and a fellow dentist friend,

Peter, poked out his head. He looked sly. She could see that behind him the cramped, brightly lit bathroom was full of people.

"How about a treat, Lizzie?" Peter asked. He grabbed her wrist, yanked her inside, and clicked the door shut behind her. Everyone laughed. There were eight people jammed into the room. She could barely turn around. Balanced on the edge of the sink was a small mirror with several lines of cocaine on it. Peter raised his eyebrows at her and offered her the tray. The look on her face told him she didn't know what to do, so he pulled her onto his lap, set the cocaine on hers, and demonstrated with a rolled-up bill how it was done. Elizabeth was ambivalent about using the cocaine. Finally she thought, "Why not," and concentrated on Peter's instructions.

A few minutes later, back in the living room, she felt great. She didn't feel high; she just felt better. She was alert, not tense, and she felt energetic, not exhausted. She felt as if she had suddenly discovered a hidden reserve of good feeling. She felt so good that she asked Peter if she could have a little cocaine to take home with her.

The next day she tried it again. After only two lines she had a feeling of well-being for hours. "Here's a drug that works on my depression, my boredom, my exhaustion," she thought. With a kind of perverse logic, based on her medical training, Elizabeth concluded that the best course of action would be to take this useful medication as many times a day as reasonable and necessary, for the times she felt worst.

Now, after two years, Elizabeth is still practicing dentistry. She prescribes herself cocaine in minute amounts four to six times a day, every day, at intervals of about two to three hours. Not only is this a typical Routine User pattern, but it further reflects Elizabeth's style in everything she does—set, routine, orderly. She takes no chances with street drugs and orders her cocaine through her practice. She uses such small amounts that it hasn't been noticed yet. Her routine cocaine use hasn't helped her begin to enjoy dentistry, but it has significantly diminished the acute unhappiness she felt until she discovered the drug. Elizabeth finds this satisfactory; she has never been a pleasure-oriented person. Her emphasis is on functional, correct behavior. The fact that she can now tolerate dentistry for up to twelve hours a day, and can just about bear the dread her patients have of her and her drills, feels to her like a victory.

Elizabeth is a typical Routine User. Her work has become the most important thing in her life, even though she doesn't enjoy it.

Elizabeth has entertained the notion that she might have a problem, both with her cocaine use and beyond it, but she generally dismisses the idea. Because she is knowledgeable about pharmacology, she asserts that her use of "chemistry" in the form of cocaine is a good solution to her difficulty in dealing with her demanding practice and full schedule. All in all, she says, she uses cocaine because it is the right medication for the problem of too much to do in not enough time.

In four and a half years Elizabeth has never reduced or increased the amount of cocaine she uses. She has not reported any medical consequences. She continues to work a forty-five-hour workweek and has been dating a man for the last two years who is encouraging her to "slow down" and cut back her schedule.

———

Corky, 39, used to drive a taxi on the graveyard shift, from midnight to 8:00 A.M. At the time, his wife, Marie, had a late waitressing job, so there was no conflict of schedules at home.

"We did pretty well between the two of us," he explains.

Corky would use cocaine every night while driving, in typical Routine User fashion—two lines, about three hours apart, for an eight-hour shift. He would never begin his shift by snorting cocaine, since he wasn't tired at the start. He would drive until he began to feel fatigue, usually in the second or third hour, and only then would he take his first snort.

"I know some guys who ran into bad trouble doing that with cocaine," he says, "but for me it was no problem. I only used it for driving at night."

Corky says he never had any real crashing problems when he stopped using cocaine for the night. But sometimes when he returned home he had trouble getting to sleep ". . . probably because I was just hitting the rack when everybody else was starting to hit the boulevard," he explains. Even though he worked a night job, Corky was essentially a day person and he never got used to the hours.

Corky was always aware that cocaine use can get out of hand. "I guess I always knew I had to be careful with the stuff," he says. Corky feels strongly, though, that there was never any danger for him.

"For me it was just a way to stay up, but not *up*, if you know what I mean."

"Up but not *up*" is a perfect way to describe many Routine Users' experience of cocaine.

A year or two ago Corky and Marie's marriage began to fall apart. He went into therapy when the constant tension at home started to take its toll. He and his wife separated. He became depressed and lost a good deal of weight. During this time he experienced no impulse to use cocaine for a lift, and, in fact, he gave it up completely in order to begin taking Nardil, an antidepressant. This was another indication that Corky's cocaine use was probably exactly what he said it was—a means to stay alert and awake.

Corky benefited from the antidepressants and from the therapy. Since he had few ties to New York other than his destructive marriage and what he called "the dead-end job I hate," we encouraged him to take what we call "the geographical cure." After on-again, off-again reunions with his wife, Corky finally moved to Alabama to work in a factory and start a new life. He is happy, unstressed, and hasn't thought about cocaine since he moved, even though he's working another repetitive, intensely demanding job that could easily generate routine use. Corky says he gets more relaxation and enjoyment from women now than he could ever get from drugs.

"You know, up north my Brooklyn accent gets labeled as no-class. But down here, it's unique. The women go crazy for me. They think I sound like Sylvester Stallone."

When Cleveland-area commuters on their way to work in the morning switch on their AM car radios, most of them tune in to Alan's show. He's known by his colleagues as the "Duke of Drive Time"—from 6:00 A.M. to 10:00 A.M.

Before he took this job, Alan had worked in the radio business for sixteen years as everything from a weatherman to the host of a country-and-western show. He's a high-energy person and he's witty and amiable on the air, but there's a lot of pressure on him now to maintain his audience and his high ratings.

He loves his work, but he's acutely aware that he can never afford to be less than 100 percent while he's on the air. He can't be affected by outside pressures or by fatigue. He also can't think too much about the fact that in terms of career advancement and industry standards a DJ his age—he's 38—with his abilities should have been out of Cleveland and broadcasting in New York or Los Angeles a few years ago. Until he came to Cleveland seven years ago, Alan overcame these pressures with sheer discipline and showmanship. Since then he's had something else to help: cocaine. On his first shift here, Steve, whom Alan relieves after the 2:00 A.M. to 6:00 A.M. show, introduced him to a station tradition.

Steve reached up to a high shelf in the broadcaster's booth and took down a rectangular mirror holding six neat lines of cocaine.

"Here's the way it works," Steve explained. "This is fuel for the late boys. Tim, on the late shift (10:00 P.M. to 2:00 A.M.), sets up the coke for himself and you and me. Two lines, every two hours, times three. That's six apiece, so you can get a boost right away when you start. Timmy's real compulsive—he usually scrapes them up into neat little separate grids. He'd put everyone's name on them, too, but he knows we'd never let him live it down. I don't know if you've ever done this before. If you haven't, try it. It really helps you keep your edge."

Alan immediately discovered that Steve was right and fell into the routine. The cocaine is now as much a part of his broadcasting job as keeping his program log up-to-date. Just as he expects his headphones to be there, hung over the mike boom, when he comes in, he expects the coke mirror to be set up on the panel right next to the morning paper and the clips from the news ticker.

Every week Alan gladly contributes ten dollars to the "coke kitty" with Tim and Steve. The price is low because they use so little among them and because their coke comes out of the larger quantities regularly purchased by one of the executives from the network.

Alan thinks of the cocaine as a special perk. At the station it's taken for granted and used openly. He feels free to pass up all or part of his share on mornings when he doesn't feel it will give him anything, and he does this about once a week. No one bothers him about it, and his engineer is glad to have the extra treat.

For Alan, routine use of cocaine helps him sparkle during his show, keep up his machine-gun patter, and sound enthusiastic as he delivers the same soap or hamburger commercial for the thousandth time. When he's feeling overwhelmed, he's thankful he has his six lines of coke. Alan told us during our interview with him that he isn't interested in seeking help about his cocaine use. "Cocaine is just a part of my routine," he says, "like getting up at four A.M."

Ever since he was in high school, Vinny has had a talent for making things happen. He barely graduated, but he was hands down the most popular kid in school. No party officially started until Vinny arrived. He was the one who enrolled an imaginary student at the state university using one boy's near-perfect SAT scores and letters of recommendation and getting one of the girls to write the essay for the application. It was Vinny who filled the school's fountains with Jello-O on April Fools' Day and Vinny who always kept a bottle of aftershave lotion that smelled suspiciously like Scotch in his locker.

He's now 29, a talented bartender, and still boyish and charming. He understands people; he never went to college but says he has a "Ph.D. in partying."

The owner of the bar where Vinny works knows he is lucky to have him. He keeps the place humming every night, and most of the regular customers come in because he's created a party atmosphere in which he's an unobtrusive master of ceremonies. Several regular women customers have a crush on Vinny and also depend on him to give them a rundown on the men they might be interested in and to steer them away from weirdos. No matter how busy he is he can always spot an attractive woman and deftly begin a conversation with her in the fleeting moments when he's free to talk. He usually gives her a free drink, tells her a couple of jokes, pays her a compliment. This often develops into a long-lasting pseudocourtship, with the woman coming back week after week because even if she doesn't meet a man, Vinny always makes her feel that she had a date with him. Consequently, Vinny's bar has a reputation for having the best-looking girls in town: it's the place to go, for men or women, to score.

In a rare, serious moment, Vinny told us:

"You know, I sometimes feel like the supporting actor in a bad movie. I never get the girl. The really dynamite chicks will talk to me because I really know how to make them feel good, but in the end they go for the three-piece suits every time."

His old and new friends all trust Vinny to keep on taking care of them, and they always give him cocaine. Sometimes it comes to him as a sort of tip, or at other times, a buddy or customer might snort some coke with Vinny and a woman he has introduced to this man. Friends and customers are always offering to bring Vinny in on group cocaine purchases whenever they have a good deal. "I'll split it with you, Vinny," is a proposition he rarely refuses.

Since he always has a cocaine supply around, he uses it himself at work, and he gives it to various people: sometimes to a woman he wants to get to know, sometimes to ease the first awkward moments of a new friendship. Just as some people know how to measure their drinks to stay pleasantly high without getting drunk, Vinny has learned how to measure his cocaine: two short snorts about every two to three hours keep him feeling bright, happy, and on top of the action in the bar.

Beyond supplying him with energy, Vinny's routine cocaine use does two very important things for him. Since he supplies the drug, it guarantees that he'll be the center of activity in the bar. It makes him feel desirable and magnetic. And it gives him a feeling of control: cocaine is one of the reasons people keep coming to his bar.

Cocaine maintains what Vinny calls his "attitude": jovial, sociable, energetic, and youthful. Vinny is stuck in a role he's been used to since he was a teenager: "Mr. Good Times." What he gets from the small amounts of cocaine he uses is not a high, but a feeling of being young, the way he used to feel when he was in high school. Despite his outward image as a happy-go-lucky guy who's settled in his work and has more girls than he knows what to do with, Vinny is actually a frightened adolescent who's nearing 30. His routine cocaine use is just one of the things he does to help himself avoid coming to terms with this state of affairs. Vinny has been offered an opportunity to buy into the bar; he tells us that as a result he is beginning to consider the legal consequences of using and distributing cocaine in his bar. As he begins to assume more responsibility Vinny will probably develop different priorities, and cocaine may become less crucial to him.

———

Thomas is a 32-year-old oral surgeon. He and his girl friend, Jenny, were interviewed at his office. Their straightforward dialogue tells more about his routine cocaine use than any narrative could.

"Well, I was the one who got him started on it," says Jenny. "He's always so glum and reluctant to try anything new. He'd go to the same restaurant and eat the same thing every night if it weren't for me. He's the most wonderful, sensitive person, and he's really fun once he gets going— he's just so slow to try new things.

"I thought it would be fun to do cocaine one night and

then make love. I did it once years ago with this real bachelor type—you know, big round bed, black satin sheets. It was all very sexy, but I wasn't into more than one night with that guy. I never forgot about the cocaine, though. When my friend Amy got some, she offered some to me. I thought it would be just the thing to get Thomas going—I thought he might even take me dancing. Things turn out strange sometimes, though.

"The coke didn't seem to give him much of a buzz. He got talkative instead and kept me up half the night with the long version of his psychoanalysis. He said he wasn't feeling especially high or sexy. We made love that night, but it was the usual. Don't get me wrong; Thomas is an excellent lover. He does everything technically right, but it's always so, well, it's so scientific, know what I mean? I suppose that's why he makes such a great oral surgeon—he's so precise. But just once I'd love to feel like some hot, juicy number with him instead of a woman being operated on.

"So I was surprised—no, make that stunned—when I found out three months after that night that Thomas had been using coke daily for that whole time. He never said a word to me about how much he liked that first time. Now I'm getting worried about him. He says it's nothing, that he just uses cocaine to stay alert during working hours. He hasn't even told his analyst about it—he says it's irrelevant to his therapy.

"I don't buy that. I think he knows that if he brings it up he'll have to deal with it and that he'll have to stop. And I don't think he wants to."

Thomas uses extremely small amounts of cocaine every three or four hours during his office hours. He'd heard about cocaine's wonderful effects for years from some of his fellow oral surgeons who used it recreationally. They would talk about how great it was that they could order pure pharmaceutical cocaine. One of them used his calculator to figure out how much a jar of the medical stuff would be worth on the street, given how much it's normally cut. Thomas never showed any interest, and he'd ignore their kidding about how his idea of getting high was to have a monosodium glutamate headache.

He ignored it all until Jenny gave him his first cocaine, and the next time his associates brought some out, Thomas joined them.

"It doesn't do anything for me, really," Thomas says. "It just gives me the energy I need for long hours of staying alert. You know, trying to build up a practice at this stage of my career takes real endurance. The cocaine really helps me get through those long days.

"I keep it in here," he says, crossing the room. The cocaine, in its brown glass bottle, sits among similar, serious-looking bottles lined up in one of the overhead cabinets in his examining room. "It's not so sordid, you know."

"But, Thomas," Jenny says, "I really think you ought to be more careful. You drive yourself so hard all the time and I think you're burned out from putting in too many hours. If you didn't use cocaine for energy, maybe you'd notice how tired and run-down you are."

"Look at me," he says, ignoring Jenny and giving us a serious, spectacled gaze. "Do I strike you as some kind of junkie?" He smiles.

Rob has always been a "plugger"—he's needed to push himself or be pushed by someone else in order to succeed. He desperately wanted to go to medical school and he barely made it in. He had to take an extra year of science courses and see a tutor in the evenings. In the end he knew that the reason for his acceptance was that his uncle sat on the board of one of the city's most prestigious hospitals.

One of Rob's friends has nicknamed him "Dr. Hang-dog" because Rob's expression often reminds him of a chastised hound. He looks as if he carries an unbearable burden.

He is now 31 and a resident in anesthesiology at a large teaching hospital. He seems to have to work much harder than everyone else. He's been married to Gail for five years and they have two young sons, 2 and 4, so there's little chance for him to rest at home. He loves Gail, but sometimes she makes him angry because she pushes him so damned hard, just like everyone close to him always has.

Rob does enjoy his work in anesthesiology and neurology. He faces life-and-death drama every time he walks into the operating room. But his days are long, and the nights are even longer: Rob is on duty and on call for seventy-two straight hours, and off for twenty-four. Like many other residents, he is exhausted from this schedule. He's even come close to making critical mistakes with a couple of patients, and his chief resident has hauled him out on the carpet twice this year. He knew that the strain, along with his own tendency to buckle under pressure, was getting to him. He started feeling as if he needed something to get through his shifts.

Late one night in the hospital cafeteria he poured out his heart to Cynthia, one of the scrub nurses. He was on his tenth cup of muddy coffee and still he felt drained and worn out. After listening patiently, Cynthia told him that she occasionally used cocaine to get through long surgeries; it would be just the thing, she said, for what ailed him. Rob didn't like the idea of using drugs, but he was so desperate that the next day he helped himself to a tiny bit of cocaine from the ophthalmology service's narcotics cabinet.

Rob discovered that Cynthia was right. A snort of cocaine in each nostril once every three hours or so did wonders. He felt more alert, no longer fatigued or crushed by the pressure of his work. He began using it regularly, several days a week. There was no problem keeping himself supplied: cocaine was used as a local anesthetic in ophthalmology and plastic surgery. Rob had found a way to cope.

Once he determined the exact, tiny dosage he needed to get the right effect, and once he realized that he only needed it when faced with a long case and no time to get adequate sleep, Rob devised a better method to ingest it than snorting it dry. He began mixing the pure pharmaceutical cocaine with water to create an infusion. He kept the infusion in a nasal atomizer and could easily inhale the liquefied cocaine mist once or twice during a long surgery without being noticed.

Rob began to feel more confident about his future. He saw his cocaine use as a temporary way out of his problems with fatigue and effectiveness, and as something he'd do just until he finished his residency and left his murderous schedule behind. He was aware of the risks he was taking, not only by illegally pilfering cocaine, but by risking dependence on the drug. But he was convinced he had it under control; besides, the dangers of cocaine paled before the prospect of failing to make it through his residency and into an established career.

After he completed his residency Rob came to us for help on his problems of feeling stressed. He had, as he promised himself, given up cocaine on graduation day. He was surprised that it felt like a bigger sacrifice than he imagined. "I'm always tempted to start using it again," Rob tells us. But Rob may not need to. He has made a great deal of progress in his life situation. In his therapy Rob is working at setting realistic goals for himself. He and his wife recently agreed he will take the least demanding hospital position offered to him. For the first time in many years he was able to act for himself and feel real elation. We agree that he will need to be ever watchful of his impulse to undo his success.

Mick is 27 and trains racehorses for a living.

"I don't get to ride in competition, you know. I never got a break when I was young enough. But I still have to be as good as the big-money jockeys. A horse runs like he trains, and you've got to feel like a jock to him or he won't run right," Mick explains.

Like ballet dancers, models, and other athletes who must keep strict control of their weight, Mick finds cocaine superior to pot because it diminishes rather than increases his appetite. Mick is very small, under five feet, 99 pounds, and a gentle presence. One can't help wondering how he can command a half-ton horse, but apparently he can because Mick is always in demand.

He has used cocaine since he was 13, when he started hanging around the track.

"There was always stuff around," he says, "but no one wanted to give it to me because I was just a kid. All I got was a little taste sometimes."

As Mick worked his way up from stable boy to groomer to trainer, he also worked up to a steady routine use of cocaine. It happened so gradually that he doesn't know exactly how long he's been using his tiny doses of cocaine every few hours throughout the day.

"Maybe it's been five years since I've been doing it every day," he says. "I know I've been with Jane for five years and I was doing it when I met her."

Jane uses cocaine daily, too, but not all day long for energy and stamina. She takes a snort or two with him when he comes home in the evening. They make a point of doing it before dinner, to curb their appetites, and will even do it instead of dinner if they're particularly worried about their weight. It's something they do together.

Jane has never had any problems with cocaine, but Mick had increasingly severe headaches and some dizziness several months back. He avoided seeing a doctor about the symptoms.

"I know guys who get headaches and nosebleeds from using it the way I do." He shudders. "God, I even know one guy who actually got a hole in his nose from it."

Mick admits that he was afraid of finding out that there was something wrong with him. He also says he was afraid he'd have to give up cocaine on doctor's orders.

"It would be a real inconvenience to have to stop," he says.

As he continues to speak about cocaine and the place it has in his life, he finds it harder and harder to hide his feelings about it. Yes, he says, he uses the coke to control his weight. And he's really grateful for that extra boost of energy on a strenuous day, or when he has a dawn workout and has to keep working until long after dark. But he's more worried about his health than he realized, and he finally decided to see a doctor for a complete physical.

Mick was told that he had nothing seriously wrong with him, just a sinus condition that might or might not have been related to his cocaine use. But Mick was taking no chances. He had stopped using cocaine for a few weeks before keeping his doctor's appointment. And he made it a point not to mention anything about his cocaine use to the doctor (who would have no way of diagnosing cocaine abuse without gross symptoms of damage). The doctor made no connection between Mick's symptoms and cocaine, but Mick stopped using it for six months just to be on the safe side. It was uncomfortable, and he discovered that it was not as easy to keep weight off without the drug. He had to maintain a strict diet the whole time. He found he slept more and felt exhausted on the job. Once the headaches went away, Mick returned to his former pattern of routine use.

"You know," he says, "it makes you feel so strong, there really isn't anything else like it. I just feel like I have to have it sometimes. Maybe I wouldn't *really* have to have it if it wasn't around so much. Down at the track, someone is always peddling it everywhere you look."

Mick has heard that he could avoid headaches by free-basing or injecting cocaine, but he's decided against it, for now. Instead, he rinses his sinuses by snorting a palmful of warm water after each time he uses cocaine. "But I got to tell you, those headaches were really killers," he says, shaking his head.

Mick is dependent enough upon cocaine to return to it even after a bout with painful and possibly dangerous health consequences. The fact that he hid his use from the physician is a sign that he is withholding something from himself that he is afraid to face. In the long run cocaine spells trouble for him.

The Performance User

The Social Sniffer uses cocaine for recreation; the Routine User takes it to sustain energy at work; and the Performance User uses it to bolster his low self-esteem and enable him to perform. The Performance User believes that at bottom his success is due to luck and not to his talents or abilities; that at any moment he will be discovered for "the fraud he is" and his success will evaporate. His shaky self-esteem has never matched his success and adulation.

Because the Performance User has trouble giving approval to himself, he needs more of it from others. He's tuned in to what he thinks other people expect of him. Often he's chosen a profession that exposes him to the judgment and approval of others. He's always on the line. His fear of criticism is perpetual and grows worse with each success, as his achievement exceeds his low self-evaluation.

Many Performance Users are either in the performing arts—musicians, actors, dancers—or are entertainers and athletes. Just as many, though, are ordinary people who have a difficult time dealing with the same kinds of daily performance situations we all face.

One aspect of the American dream is that we can and

should be the best at whatever we do. We should be the best at work, the best husband or wife or lover, the best son or daughter or parent, even the best at our recreation. In our culture, we learn early that it's important to be a winner.

Most people find a way to cope with these kinds of pressures, realistic and unrealistic, and eventually come to terms with their own limits. But many react to an inordinate pressure to be the best by developing an obsession on performing. They must reach perfection. Nothing less will do. Next to their vision of perfection, their own talents and resources begin to pale.

When cocaine alleviates feelings of inadequacy and gives a person with performance anxiety a feeling of power, control, competence, and self-worth, then that person becomes a prime candidate for performance use.

This is how it works. The Performance User takes cocaine because it gives him confidence. When he succeeds at something, he attributes the success not to his abilities, but to the cocaine. He cheats himself of the satisfaction he deserves. He invests cocaine with power: it has been the source of his mastery and achievement, not he. He is nothing without the drug. Performance use becomes a self-fulfilling prophecy of failure.

Many Performance Users have an M.O.—they will regularly buy cocaine, will often put themselves at risk to get it, will protect it, and will use it according to a set, comforting ritual. There may be accumulated paraphernalia—a favorite container, a secret hiding place, a silver spoon.

The amount of cocaine Performance Users take varies widely. Some need to be mildly high in order to rise to the task at hand. Others need to be "blasted" with cocaine before they feel able to perform. As the drug wears off, many of them have an intense crash. Many Performance Users take sedatives or tranquilizers to relieve it.

Performance Users have already crossed the boundaries of relatively "safe" cocaine use into more dangerous territory. They may escalate the amount of cocaine they snort or may graduate from snorting to freebasing or even to injecting the drug. This is far more than simply a switch of methods to increase the drug's kick. Though Social Sniffers use cocaine to enjoy themselves, and Routine Users take it to sustain themselves through unpleasant tasks, Performance Users do cocaine to deal with deep doubts about themselves. The intensity of the high from freebasing or injecting cocaine can mask for a moment a Performance User's most intense fear.

Jennifer is strikingly pretty. She has penetrating green eyes and a presence that fills a room. People are magnetically drawn to her. She tells us that at 35 she has finally "made it." Jennifer is a top-rated television newswoman. "What's it like" we ask her, "to be part of a dynamic news team consistently rated number one and a wife and a mother of a lively, beautiful little girl?" She really does appear to have it all.

She tells us about the constant high of being a "television personality." She talks about the excitement and challenge of trying to do it all and about her goal to become an anchorperson on the news. "But how do you find the time to combine work, your relationship with your husband, and motherhood?" we ask her. We talk for three hours about this enormous juggling act. Finally, she almost whispers that she has found a remedy for the lack of sleep and the near-total exhaustion that has ruined many a romantic evening for her and her husband. "Sex was becoming almost nonexistent for us. Our schedules practically made it impossible, and when we were finally together the last thing I felt was romantic. I just wanted to take a hot bath, put on my flannel robe, and curl up in bed. It went on like this for nearly three months. Ned said this was crazy and that I had better fit *him* into my schedule somehow. It was then we decided we would schedule in sex. Every Wednesday night, come hell or high water, we would turn off the phone and relax, have fun, and make love to each other again. It all sounded great except that when Wednesday came I was still exhausted and could barely keep awake, no less feel sexy and chatty. I took vitamins, I ate health food, but nothing worked. What I really needed were thirty-two-hour days and twelve hours of sleep —none of which was possible.

"The station was really hot on covering cocaine stories—almost two a day—and that's when the idea struck me. I casually spoke with one of our researchers who confided that she uses cocaine at least three or four times a month in order to cope with the lack of sleep and burnout after late-night shifts. I hinted around at first, but then she asked me if I wanted her to get me some cocaine. Trying not to sound desperate, I told her yes—and that I needed it before Wednesday night. I got home at about eleven-forty-five and took two sniffs before my bath. I guess the only way I can describe it to you is that I felt renewed, refreshed, and the added benefit was that I was no longer exhausted; in fact, I was even turned on. Ned and I did it in the bathtub; Ned and I did it in bed; and then we sat in the kitchen and talked and joked the way we did years ago before dual careers and motherhood.

"I have been using cocaine for about a year now—only on Wednesday—a gram discreetly dropped off before the six-o'clock news broadcast by my research assistant. It lasts almost two months and it is just the perfect solution for me—at least for now. Next year I will be anchoring more and in the field less and my schedule will resemble normality—at least for me. I don't see any reason why I'd stop using cocaine now. I wouldn't want to keep on using it, but for now I can use all the help I can get."

When Mary Alice graduated from a southern college with a major in art history and seventeen beauty-queen titles (everything from Miss Peach to Miss May Fest), she moved to New York City hoping to find a job in one of the museums or art galleries and maybe do some modeling on the side. "I was in for a shock," she exclaimed in her southern accent. "Back home I was the proverbial big fish in a little pond, but in New York I was more like bait."

Mary Alice couldn't find any jobs and to conserve money took an East Side apartment with four other women. "The great thing about living with these women was that they had 'connections to everything.' One worked in wholesale garments and supplied us all with free samples from scarves to pantyhose. One knew every restaurant owner in town, so we always got a free meal or two, and one had some connections with photographers and modeling agencies. It wasn't long before I was working regularly. Good spots, too, and fun. I did some commercials, even was an extra in a couple of movies." Mary Alice got her break when she landed a TV cosmetics ad. Suddenly she was in demand and everybody was competing to get her to sign a contract. "I knew I finally had made it . . . really made it. But the funny thing is, I didn't feel as great as I thought I would.

"I should have expected it. Winning, being the best, was never enough for little old Mary Alice. At least, not for very long. And I was getting lonesome, too. I was careful to steer clear of the old casting couch and didn't want to date any of the guys I worked with—too complicated—so I had been alone. I don't think I had more than five dates during my career climb. Here I was practically famous and feeling like it might not be worth it; in fact, I was wondering if I could handle it at all. I don't know why, but I began to 'lose it.' I mean, I got scared . . . more scared than I'd ever been in competition before. I was afraid I couldn't cut it.

"It was around this time I was having to go to a lot of promotional parties. It was good for the product and good for me too. I had seen cocaine floating around at some of those parties before, but I never wanted to try it. I didn't want to do a drug and lose control . . . be stupid or sloppy. I always hated it when I saw someone all bent out of shape on 'ludes . . . and I guess I'm prejudiced to say it but I always thought it looked especially bad in women. Also to look good you really have to take care of your health.

"Then I met this adorable curly-haired psychiatrist at one of these parties. He was just like out of the movies, pipe and all. He asked me out for dinner and I couldn't resist. He was the one who told me about cocaine . . . how it's different from other drugs. He said that you can keep it under control easily. That it makes you feel good and sexy but isn't dangerous. He really seemed to know what he was talking about. I trusted him. The next time he called me we went out, and we used some coke. He even gave me some of my own to keep. Said I shouldn't use anything off the street because it might not be pure, but that he could get me some if I wanted it. We got together three or four times a month, and he gave me coke each time. At first it just felt pleasant, nothing special. Then I noticed how when I was on it I got a break from my old self-doubt. I felt in charge and optimistic. Talk about control, I was even in charge of my appetite. Don't let this one-hundred-and-seven-pound body fool you. I have some appetite and, unless I watch it, I can finish off a quart of Haagen-Dazs without taking a breath.

"It was subtle, but I did start to count on cocaine for extra pizzazz. If you don't make eyes at the camera, it shows up in the darkroom, and I wanted to sparkle and outdo everybody in every photo and every taping session. It was important to me. Then coke became important to me. Once I had started taking it from my shrink friend, I took it from my co-workers.

"I started using cocaine for practically every modeling assignment, and finally it began to have some really bad effects. I got weepy, shaky, and difficult to be around. One day I just walked right off the set. I had a good talking to myself. I said, 'Mary Alice, you always do whatever you have to do to take care of yourself. Now what is it going to be, cocaine or your career?' I stopped taking cocaine that very day and it has been two years since I've seen the stuff up close. I'm an all-or-nothing kind of person and it is easier for me to just pass on it than try to play around with taking little bits."

For about a month Mary Alice said she felt kind of "blue" after giving up the cocaine. Although she never had depended on it very heavily, she still felt as if she was losing something. She, like many people who give up a habit they have decided is bad for them, went through a kind of "mini-mourning" period. But recently she decided that she was ready to take a new risk. She has landed a small but significant role on a hot daytime TV program.

Bobby is rising fast in the garment industry. He wholesales ladies' lingerie and is a fast-moving young man in his early thirties, perfect for the "rag trade" with his tinted glasses and well-cut suits—everything sharp. Bobby has no trouble playing the cool guy, but when he's under pressure, he goes in with a cocaine assist. For the past eight years, he has used cocaine whenever he makes a presentation to an important client. He has begun to believe he cannot make it through a crucial sales meeting without cocaine. Just to make sure he's prepared, Bobby always carries cocaine, although he uses it less than once a week. It goes into his pocket along with his credit cards, keys, and wallet every morning. Just having it puts him at ease.

"I call it my 'pacifier,'" he explains with a grin. "It makes me feel secure. I feel like I know I can be funny if I have to, or quick, or interesting. I wouldn't set foot in the office of some of my important clients without a few snorts of cocaine." Bobby doesn't worry about this. He feels he's way ahead of most people in the garment business because he doesn't drink. Most of them do. Bobby sees it this way: everyone in the business uses something to get by. They use booze, he uses cocaine.

For most of his life, Bobby had a very hard time talking to people. He'd be seized by fear, his mind would race, he'd feel as if he couldn't breathe. Until late adolescence, Bobby stuttered. But he was always easygoing; people were drawn to him, found it easy to talk to him, felt comfortable around him.

He dreamed of going to dental school, but in college he met Beth, married her after graduation, and she soon became pregnant with their first child. Her father offered to take Bobby into his lingerie business; right from the start everyone told Bobby and his father-in-law that Bobby was a born salesman.

He *was* a good salesman. The problem was that every time there was a big deal on the line, he froze inside. He couldn't think of anything to say, couldn't remember a funny line, and the thought of making conversation made him tremble. Bobby endured this agony for a year or so. But after discovering at a party that cocaine suppressed his feelings of inadequacy, made him feel in control, Bobby decided to see if cocaine's effect would help him during a sales pitch. He snorted two lines before a crucial meeting . . . he felt better; fine, in fact. He marched into the client's office and walked out in record time with the best sale he'd ever made. He charmed the guy like a snake. He was brilliant. Cocaine, Bobby decided, was for him. He made it a prerequisite for important meetings.

Since cocaine use was common in the garment business anyway, it was easy for Bobby to find a reliable source for his two grams a month. About four lines before a sales pitch gives him confidence.

Bobby does not like to admit that his cocaine use may be a problem or might ultimately be damaging to his performance, but he acknowledges its seriousness in another way: he keeps it a tightly guarded secret. He's never told anyone that he uses cocaine, not even his wife. Bobby says this is just smart thinking.

"I'm a businessman," he says earnestly. "I have an image to maintain. I can't let people think I need coke to make my sales."

That's true, but there's a deeper truth behind his secrecy. Bobby freezes under pressure without cocaine because he feels incompetent. And when he succeeds with cocaine, he cannot enjoy his success because he believes it's a result of the drug, and not his sales talents. Every time he uses his "pacifier" to make a pitch, he also feeds his self-contempt, because he feels he can't perform without cocaine.

Bobby joined an ongoing therapy group that could have been tailor-made for him. For a year every Thursday night from 7:00 to 8:30 he and eight other businessmen and businesswomen shared concerns about performance and practiced asserting themselves through role playing sans cocaine.

Alex flashes his perfect white teeth and serves up the smile that has won the hearts of many of his fans. He's tan, well built, and walks with the carefree stride of a teenager. Alex is 34, a native of Palm Beach, and has been playing tennis since he was 4. From the beginning, Alex was a winner, a born athlete, a prodigy. At 15 he was traveling the professional tennis circuit, ranking number twenty-one in the listings. By the time he was 24 he had risen to number twelve. There was still a good chance for him to crack the top ranks. Then his luck changed.

A nagging pain and stiffness in his left knee was diagnosed as mild arthritis, and while he still played a full schedule, his game faltered. The pain was minimal except in damp weather, but his doctor advised him to rest the knee, get off the circuit for a year, and follow a rigid physical therapy program.

Alex felt frustrated, angry, and challenged: "I never believed for a moment that I wouldn't be able to beat the arthritis," he says. "I mean beat it, like an opponent."

"Lots of players take time off," he reasoned. "I'll just come back better and stronger next year." Alex returned to Florida and got a part-time job at a posh Palm Beach resort as the resident tennis pro.

After a year Alex returned to competition. He entered the Boca Raton tournament in the men's singles division. Things went sour right from the start. He was matched against an old friend from his teen years. Three years ago he could have blown Mark off the court, but now he was worried. His knee had begun to act up a few days before the match and for the first time in his life he felt no rush of pre-combat adrenaline. He couldn't concentrate on the game. It was over fast; he lost miserably. The next day Alex visited a doctor, who discovered fluid in his knee.

"You're crazy to play," he told Alex. "Wait until next year. You'll hurt yourself." Alex insisted. Exasperated, the doctor drained Alex's knee and wrote him a prescription for Percodan, a powerful opiate pain-killer.

"Be careful with these," he told Alex. Alex gulped one

down and limped back to the practice court. There was another match tomorrow and he needed to warm up without pain.

An hour later the pain was gone. The Percodan was a miracle, but it had a flaw: though it made his knee feel good as new, it dulled Alex's reflexes, threw his timing off. And it killed that surge of adrenaline he needed, the competitive instinct. He couldn't raise the bloodlust or feel the thrill of the anticipated victory. His confidence sagged.

He spilled his fears to his manager, who recognized that Alex would not make it through another set in his condition.

"Go change into your practice clothes," he told him, "and meet me in the training room."

When Alex arrived in the training room, his manager was sitting on the massage table and was rolling a brown glass bottle with a rubber bulb in its cap back and forth between his fingers.

"This is a 'cocaine infusion,'" he said. "It's pure pharmaceutical, real premium, diluted with distilled water. There's about a gram's worth in that bottle. Use it like nose drops. Take one full dropper in each nostril to start and see how you feel. Go slow, but if you think you need some more, go ahead.

"Don't worry about this stuff, you can use as much as you want," the manager continued. "It's perfectly safe; you can't get hooked on it."

Alex's heart sank.

Somewhere in the back of his mind he knew that this was not the last time he'd need Percodan for the pain and cocaine to get on the court and play. Then he drew a sharp breath. It didn't matter. Nothing mattered except winning.

He measured a dropperful. It wasn't such a big deal. Everyone knew cocaine was not dangerous. He did two dropperfuls in each nostril. "After yesterday, I need a double dose," he reasoned. He strode out to the practice court. He felt like a prince. His knee felt perfect. This was even better than his own burst of power. He felt like he could punch the ball right across the Caribbean. He smashed an ace right down his partner's throat, ran him all over the court, played like a machine. He wouldn't lose to Mark to-morrow. Or ever.

The next day he drained the brown bottle before hitting the court and ran his opponent right into the clay. He could do nothing wrong; he felt like Superman, and his knee was spring-loaded. Later that night, alone, he wept in agony when the Percodan wore off and he felt the hot pain in his knee. But damn, he thought to himself, he had won.

After nine years, Alex has learned how to balance the Percodan he needs for his increasingly painful knee with the cocaine he needs to take him to the top of his form. He knows how to train to keep the knee from flaring up every time he competes, so he doesn't need to use cocaine for every match. But he takes no chances before the critical con-tests: then, it's Percodan an hour before play and half a gram of cocaine diluted in water moments before he hits the court. Even his vision seems to improve.

Alex hasn't made it to the top; in fact, he slips a notch or two each year—he's ranked number twenty-three—but he's still ranked; that's what counts. And he looks splendid. The old winning smile still does it for him. He's got a "sweet deal" going with a tennis clothing manufacturer, and he does commercials regularly. He's reconciled himself to using cocaine during matches.

"Look, I'm in good company, you know?" he said. "More than half the pros on the circuit use coke and some of them do it just like I do—to compensate for the downside of their heavy pain medication. We all get hurt, but you've got to go on."

Alex also notes that many of the other pros use cocaine for other things as well: to take the edge off the lonely nights in hotel rooms, to keep up with the pace of plane-hopping on the tour, and to make themselves feel better, since there's never time to get close to anyone they meet. Alex states that for him cocaine is just the elixir that tightens him up on the court.

Last year, Alex started therapy. He wants to evaluate his life, try to figure out where to go from here, whether to keep playing or not. He says he needs to make some changes. His happiness lasts for a few minutes on the tennis court when he's won a match and hears the thunder of the applause. But he's bored, restless, and unable to sustain a relationship with any woman for longer than a year. He's lonely, and he wants to be able to feel more and get closer to people.

In the last few months, Alex admits that he's also started taking his "medication"—Percodan chased with a blast of cocaine infusion—when he's not playing tennis.

"There's more than mere physical pain, you know," he told us sadly.

Since Alex is on tour eight months out of the year he made a contract with us to call on our telephone helpline whenever he was out of town and felt like using cocaine. In the beginning he still used cocaine a couple of times, even after his phone sessions with us. But as the month went on our conversations put time and understanding between his impulse and his action to use the drug. Increasingly he has practiced relying on friends (us and others) via phone to build up his hope and enthusiasm before a game, rather than turning to cocaine.

———

To many men, Renee is a dream-come-true. She exudes a 1950s pinup girl allure. From her big blue eyes and glossy mane of thick brown hair to her creamy skin, she looks like a doll.

But there is an aggressiveness about Renee that seems to contradict her image. She calls herself an "operator." She punctuates almost every conversation with some variation of "I can get it for you wholesale." She has a knack for producing things fast and cheap. She is an assistant producer for a popular soap opera, and she's quick to point out that she got the job because she could get anything for anybody in record time at the best price. Her aggressiveness can be unnerving, but it's the key to her success. If you need 5,000 green helium balloons in one hour, Renee will deliver.

Renee feels she must deliver in order to be liked. She believes that if she stops doing things for people, they'll reject her. She first discovered how easy it was to deliver and get approval when she was a teenager. All she had to do was let a boy do what he wanted with her and all the attention was hers.

On the set of her soap opera, quite a few of the folks—actors, technicians, even the cleaning woman—use cocaine. They come to Renee if they want a quick toot during the day. She's cultivated relationships with all the street cocaine dealers in the neighborhood so that she can step out, buy a gram for whoever wants it, and zip back in no time. She also buys cocaine for herself, but not often. Renee has been sniffing for a few years, but she usually does it with men, and usually when she's going to have sex. She has never felt comfortable, "free" she calls it, in bed with a man. She feels anxious and afraid that men will reject her if she can't deliver exactly what they want. She discovered that snorting cocaine made her feel more relaxed and less inhibited.

Recently, cocaine has assumed a more important role in Renee's life. She had stopped by the office of her veterinarian brother-in-law to say hello, and they got to talking after the office closed. Cocaine came up in conversation and Peter asked her if she'd ever shot it instead of snorted. She said she hadn't.

"I get Merck, perfectly pure. Want to try some?" he asked. Renee felt aroused by the prospect, though she didn't know why.

"I tell you, there's one hell of a rush to it," he told her. "You go right into orbit. It's like—like getting fucked in the heart. I mean, it's intense."

It sounded fantastic. Renee longed for what he was describing.

"Okay," she said. Peter motioned her to the couch in the waiting room and quickly produced a glass bottle of cocaine, a bottle of sterile water, and a syringe. As he mixed the blend of cocaine and water, a hard look settled onto his face. It frightened Renee, but the anticipation was getting to her. Her heart was racing.

"Will it hurt?" she asked.

He looked annoyed. "Just roll up your sleeve and make a fist," he said irritably. He snapped a tight rubber tourniquet around her upper arm and told her to squeeze her fist to pump up a vein. She watched, mesmerized, as he pricked

106

her skin with the needle and drew her blood back into the syringe to mix with the cocaine. He tapped some of the red solution into her arm and drew it back again. Her mouth dropped open as a wave of pure ecstasy washed over her. Before she could gasp it happened again. This rush was like an orgasm of the soul.

"Ahhhh," said Renee, eyes shut tight. Nothing could be compared to this. She settled back on the couch, filled with bliss, and vaguely heard Peter preparing a similar shot for himself. Then she felt him drop back on the couch next to her to savor his rush. When the intensity gradually began to subside, Renee felt shudders of pleasure.

Suddenly, she felt Peter's mouth on hers, his hands on her breasts. She responded instantly, not thinking at all about herself or her sister or the consequences of what she was doing. In a few seconds Peter had undressed her and they were making love. She did whatever Peter demanded. The physical sensations were good even if the idea of being with Peter was not. Renee felt desirable.

Half an hour later, the effects of the drug began to wear off, and Peter shot them both up again. They made love again three times that night.

Renee would never tell her sister about what's now evolved into a regular routine with her and Peter. About once a month they meet at his office or in a hotel to shoot cocaine and have sex. Renee doesn't find him an especially appealing sex partner, and he becomes cold and commanding under cocaine, but with the injections every half hour she can get into the sex; then she floats away on the tides of her rush.

"I have these orgasms that feel like they go all the way back to God," she says. Their cocaine use is a ritual, and Renee is beginning to worry because sex without cocaine, even with a man she likes, pales before these encounters.

A few months ago she decided to enter psychotherapy to understand some of her feelings. We were surprised to hear that Renee doesn't think her body is at all beautiful, and in fact sees it as her nemesis.

"Men like my big breasts, not me," she told us. "That is always in the back of my mind." Her eyes are brimming with tears. "I always thought I was ugly, fat, and that boys only wanted to be with me because I put out. Cocaine makes me forget my insecurities and makes me feel like the person I always wanted to be—someone who gets loved just for who I am."

⬛

Bill is a big, muscular man and his deep voice and aggressive manner suggest that it might be best to do things his way. He has worked his way up from a salesman of food products to chief distributor in his region. He is 41 and has been doing well in this high-paying spot for three years now, but he often fears that he will lose everything he's worked for.

Underneath his bravado, Bill is insecure about almost everything he does. He hides his fears even from himself. Rather than "feel" his anxiety he transforms it into aggressive or angry behavior. He's so frightened of his anxiousness that whenever we confront him about it during therapy Bill becomes agitated and will do anything—even begin to drop off to sleep—rather than talk about it.

All day long at work Bill uses his aggressiveness to get things done his way while constantly fending off feelings of vulnerability. It's no wonder that when he discovered cocaine, Bill thought he had found a way to make himself invincible.

Bill began using cocaine about six years ago, when he was still a salesman. He and the other salesmen would meet for drinks after work a few times a week and snort a few lines of cocaine. At the time, he felt his cocaine use was purely social, even though he was using it two or three times a week. Now he says:

"Even then it wasn't really recreational. I was drinking and snorting coke to reduce anxiety. I wasn't using it to give myself good feelings, but to squelch bad ones."

After a while he began to carry coke with him when he went on the road on selling trips. To fight off his loneliness and to boost self-confidence before a meeting, two to four lines would give Bill a buzz.

"I felt like I was in the locker room before a game. Snorting coke was like psyching myself to get out there and win."

As it became clear that Bill might be in line for the big distributor's job, he began to depend increasingly on cocaine to help him perform. Now he was not just confronting clients; he had to handle the big guns in the company, deal with them every day.

"I'd feel like I was going to dissolve," he says, "just come apart."

Bill's lack of confidence was apparent in his personal life, as well. After his promotion, Bill, his wife, and two teenage daughters moved to a suburban neighborhood where most of their neighbors and new friends were well-to-do and well-informed professional people. Neither Bill nor his wife had gone to college, and his feelings of inadequacy intensified whenever he socialized with his new friends.

"I actually began to study the *New York Times* every day so I'd have something to talk to them about," he told us, embarrassed. "So I began snorting a few lines of cocaine for confidence before a cocktail party or a dinner." The number of "crucial moments" when Bill felt vulnerable and out of control were multiplying. So were the number of cocaine "takes."

When his teenage daughters confronted him about money or car privileges, he felt that he could hold his own more easily if he snorted some cocaine. And when he fought with his wife, he found that if he could fortify himself with a few snorts of coke, her anger, which was devastating to him because of his low self-esteem, was less so.

For five years cocaine was his secret.

About a year ago, Bill reached the peak of his performance use. He was consuming about a gram of cocaine a week, at the rate of two to four lines each time, five days out of seven, at home and at work. One day it all came to a halt. He told us:

"Jan and I were dressing for a party, and I was in the bathroom standing in front of the mirror, knotting my tie. I stopped for a snort of coke, but I must have forgotten to lock the door because just as I was putting the spoon to my nose, in walked my fourteen-year-old." Bill's voice cracked and he looked at the floor.

"You should have seen the expression on her face," he said softly. "She ran out of the room. She was in hysterics."

His family "came unglued," Bill says. He lost his authority; his family was miserable. He considered leaving. Suicide. But his wife and daughters loved him and they approached him with a proposition. If Bill would go for help with his problems, they'd go into family therapy with him. They all wanted to save their family.

And they have.

———

Amy is 26 and has been dancing since she was 5. She was one of the special few who started with after-school lessons and continued to make a career as a dancer. She looks the part—her posture is perfect, her neck is long and graceful, her hair in a tight chignon at the nape. Her feet don't seem to touch the floor when she walks. All twenty-one years of her dance discipline are inherent in every move she makes.

Amy vividly recalls her mother patiently waiting to pick her up after school every day to take her to her dance classes—3:45 until 5:30, Monday through Friday. She says she feels as if she grew up in a rehearsal room.

She is quick to tell you that yes, she's a professional, but she's not really a dancer. She'll extend her leg and point out that she doesn't have the right legs for it; they are too short, she says. But Amy did have a tremendous amount of determination and drive. Her mother had her heart set on Amy becoming a dancer, and Amy learned all about single-mindedness and discipline from her.

Amy feels she never had enough determination, not as much as her mother wanted her to have. She has never felt that she is good enough at what she does. Adequate, maybe, but never more than that. She marvels at her success so far. No amount of hard work or applause could convince her that she is *really* good.

Amy began using cocaine about a year ago. She had an important audition for a good part, and as usual, she had been up most of the previous night worrying. When she arrived at the dance studio in the morning she looked terrible: drawn, pale, tired, and she knew she was not going to do her best at the audition. She was scared that she would fail. As she was changing into her leotard in the dressing room, a dancer she knew, auditioning for a different part, offered her some cocaine matter-of-factly.

"I always do a one-and-one before an important audition," she said. "It gives me the edge I need—especially since I'm not eighteen anymore; there are all these kids out there to compete against."

Amy knew other dancers who used cocaine just before a performance. She'd been offered cocaine in the dressing room several times just before going onstage, and she'd always turned it down. She'd never tried it once, even socially. Today, though, she desperately felt that she needed something, just this once. She wanted this part more than any other she could remember.

She accepted the offer and the other woman laid out four lines for her, two for each nostril. She took all four, and in a few minutes she was full of energy, full of life, and convinced that everything would be fine. She was brimming with confidence, and for a few moments she had an unexpected flash of insight. This feeling of confidence was truly like nothing she'd ever experienced before. All her life she'd measured her feelings about auditioning or performing in terms of being more or less uncomfortable, apprehensive, anxious. She'd never, until this moment, experienced auditioning positively. It was a revelation. She was sure the part would be hers.

Amy took a third snort in each nostril and bounded up the stairs into the studio. She danced especially well at the audition—better than usual, she claims—and got the part. Since then, Amy has continued to use cocaine several times a week, just before any performance she feels is significant. She gets her cocaine from Tania, another dancer, and buys a gram about every two weeks. She uses coke from one to four times every week, about six lines, four hefty snorts, each time. "I need to get really high for it to do any good," she says. "I want to *fly* out there." She has also started using cocaine before some practice classes.

Amy is convinced that cocaine gives her a creative edge in her dancing and that it improves her ability to perform for long periods without feeling fatigued. She also says that since she's started using cocaine she's no longer aware of the physical discomfort that limited her during preperformance "endurance classes" lasting up to five hours, which work dancers up into a peak state before they go onstage. She has discovered another bonus, too: cocaine suppresses her appetite. Her tendency to gain weight has disappeared since she started using the drug.

Amy is a very good dancer. She is talented, and it's easy to see this when you watch her move. Her talent is obvious to everyone—except Amy. She thinks cocaine is responsible for solving the one problem she thought she had—inadequate ability. She believes it improves her performance. No one else has noticed this.

———

Stan is a self-made man. He's 54, and he's a millionaire. He started out thirty years ago as a journeyman optician and gradually built up a regional chain of eyeglass stores. He began to make good money around 1970 and enjoyed some success, but years of intense devotion to his business had damaged his marriage beyond repair. His wife left him. Since then, Stan has maintained a cordial relationship with her and has always been close with his two sons. One of them recently became a physician, and Stan is even prouder of this than of his own successes.

While he missed living with his family, Stan also liked being single again. He enjoyed his work and easily fell into dating and cultivating a new social life. He keeps himself in good shape; in fact, he sometimes looks as if he's trying to be younger than he is. He tends toward the flashy and favors open-necked silk shirts, Gucci loafers, a couple of gold chains around his neck.

After his divorce, Stan began dating younger and younger women. They made him feel younger, and it was easy to dazzle them with his money. In the mid-seventies, Stan was introduced by one of his young women friends to snorting cocaine, and he took it up as a regular but infrequent practice. Around the same time, he also began to worry more about his looks and sex appeal. He found that a few snorts of cocaine would markedly improve his sexual performance. He could get an erection more easily, maintain it longer, and have intercourse more than once an evening if he had some cocaine every half hour or so. Over a period of two or three years, Stan became a sexual Performance User. Cocaine at first had improved his sexual capabilities on off nights, but now he wouldn't have sex without a couple of snorts to ensure a cocaine erection. After a few months it got to the point where he was actually afraid to make love unless he had cocaine. He began to feel that he would be unable to have sex with any of his beautiful young lady friends without the help of cocaine.

Stan had meanwhile discovered that letting people at the bars and clubs he frequented know that he had a lot of money, and also used a good deal of cocaine, made him a magnet for certain gorgeous young women and their friends. The coke was a lure and worked like a charm. Stan became a sort of local celebrity. He found that some young women were happy to go to bed with him if he gave them cocaine. As Stan's insecurities about his looks and virility increased, so did his reliance on the two things that made him feel he was "not over the hill": going to bed with beautiful women and using cocaine to attract women and improve his sexual performance.

During this time, Stan kept right on working his usual long hours at the main optical store, masterfully running his successful business. He never touched cocaine at work, not then and not even later on.

Then Rhonda, one of his 24-year-old girl friends, introduced Stan to freebasing. She cooked up a batch of purified cocaine and showed him how to heat the pipe and inhale. Then they went to bed: all the sex Stan had been having for the past ten years suddenly seemed like kindergarten, like just so much foreplay.

"It made me feel like king of the jungle," he says. "I

became a madman for sex. I could do it all night long with freebase, again and again and again."

He asked Rhonda to ask a few of her friends if they'd like to come over; he offered cocaine. There was a night when he thought he'd died and gone to heaven, as he made love to one woman after another until he had been with all four of them. This was too good to be true, and the freebase pipe seemed to him like a fountain of youth.

One night one of Rhonda's friends, Sandy, brought over a breathtaking young woman named Dee. Dee was a professional, a highly paid call girl.

"We told Dee about you and she insisted on coming," Sandy told him coyly.

"This is on the house," Dee said appreciatively. "I've heard a lot about *you*." Dee consumed more coke-smoke than any of the other girls and then showed Stan quite a few tricks he'd never even heard of, let alone tried. She even enticed one of the other girls into bed with them. As Stan watched the two women make love to each other after he'd just finished with both of them, he toked on his freebase pipe and his only thought was that this was simply too good to be true. In fact, it wouldn't last.

Dee soon introduced Stan to some of her friends: some of them were also hookers, some just hangers-on. He met some of their boyfriends, too: slick, expensively dressed men his age and younger, most of whom had no office telephone numbers and always knew the latest odds at the track. Nothing was too wild for them.

Stan led a double life. By day he worked and ran his business with usual expertise, and by night he freebased, danced, and partied with his ever-expanding group of new friends. Sometimes there were expensive dinners out, where Stan picked up the bill, followed by orgies afterward. The sex got kinkier and kinkier. A little freebase and Stan was ready for anything. Over a few months, he had begun freebasing cocaine five and six times a week, and indulging in group sex almost every night. By now he was worrying less about getting older and losing his virility than about how to keep his hands on all the cash he needed to sustain not only his but all the girls' and their friends' freebasing. At one point, Stan and his friends were consuming forty-five grams—about $4,000 worth—of cocaine every week.

Stan started to lose his grip on his routine. He began getting in late to work, and some days, exhausted, sore, hung over, deep into a cocaine crash, he couldn't show up at all. Stan felt fatigued all the time he wasn't freebasing and he found himself constantly irritated and barking at his employees. He also began to believe that some of them were following him after work, spying on his orgiastic activities, and planning to blackmail him. He began to suffer from a mild paranoia, at first intermittent, and then more constant.

He talked to his ex-wife and sons. They all told him to slow down or stop his social life altogether. They told him he was acting paranoid from too much cocaine. He believed them and began to worry that he might be losing his mind.

Strange, frightening things had started happening to him. He had a feeling that his young women friends had been setting him up to be robbed. One night two of them lured him to one of their apartments, where he had never been before, for some three-way sex. When he returned home, his house had been broken into and robbed. The same thing happened again about two months later, with two different girls. By now, some of Dee's lady friends had become Stan's cocaine contacts, able to get him better quality at better prices than his old connection had. One of them beat him on a cocaine deal, taking his money and then failing to return with the drug, claiming that she had been mugged.

At his son's urging, Stan flew to California and consulted an expert in treating serious cocaine problems. The doctor showed him horrible photographs of nasal septums eaten through by cocaine abuse, lungs damaged and scarred from freebasing, neurological damage, and bloody police photos of people who had died from violent seizures from cocaine overdoses.

"This could happen to you, too, if you don't stop using cocaine," the doctor solemnly told him. Stan was convinced that he was paranoid, that his family was right, that he was delusory, crazy, destroyed by cocaine.

When he returned home after his trip, he found the leather seats in his sports car shredded and his house ransacked from floor to ceiling. Every inch of everything he owned had been torn to pieces and sifted through for cocaine or money. This was obviously the work of his new friends. He tried for several days to contact Dee and her crowd. No one would take his calls.

Stan stopped using cocaine, cold. He threw himself into his work, barely spoke to anyone for weeks. When he checked his depleted investment portfolio, and the cash figures for the money he had skimmed off his business, Stan found that he had spent $250,000 in just under twelve months, most of it on cocaine. He realized by the time he had stopped himself he was on the verge of starting to use cocaine not only for his off-hours orgies, but during his workday as well. He shuddered when he realized that he had been on the verge of becoming a Cokeaholic.

"I was right in the middle of the biggest midlife crisis you ever saw," he says.

One of Stan's sons, worried about his father's health and now aware of the details of the past year, saw us on a local TV talk show.

"He had scribbled down the phone number," Stan says, "and he stomped into my office and slammed it on my desk. 'Call now, goddamnit!' he yelled," Stan told us, with a hint of pride and wonder. Stan picked up the phone.

He entered treatment and has been in therapy for about two years now. He is relieved that there's someone who understands the subtleties of what happened to him. He's also glad to know that he was not crazy in the way he originally thought, but he recognizes the depth of the emotional problems that led him into his crisis. He wants to learn how to feel better about himself, how to feel acceptable without using cocaine. Stan brings to his therapy the same kind of motivation and determination that helped him become a successful businessman and that has helped him recover from his severe cocaine abuse.

Elly is 38, has four children, 2, 5, 6, and 8, and is married to a fast-rising vice-president who works for a major corporation with offices nationwide.

"In the past ten years we've moved five times," she says. "It's wonderful that John keeps moving up the corporate ladder, but most of his promotions have meant a transfer, and this is kind of hard on the kids—changing schools, losing their friends. I get tired of it too.

"Every move is the same routine. Enroll the kids in school; start volunteering time though the PTA—it helps to get involved, tells me about the school system, and gives me a chance to meet people—go to the newcomers' clubs. Then I have to contract a painter and an interior decorator to get the house in shape. It's a good thing John's company pays the relocation expenses. Then I hunt down the best places for marketing and clothes for the kids. Next comes politics— meet all the right wives, cultivate the important ones, get into all the best clubs." Elly pauses for breath.

"I should be on salary too," she says. "And these days everyone wants to know what kind of job I have on top of it all." She laughs and shakes her head.

But Elly has discovered something that makes the whirl of her social and business responsibilities a bit more manageable. In the past year, she's been a Performance User of cocaine. She told us:

"About a year ago I was at a large party talking to Frances, who I hardly knew then. Now she's a friend of mine.

"In fact not only is Frances my friend now, but also my 'cocaine connection,' as they say. She is the neighborhood supplier to the 'cocaine housewives.' Anyway, somewhere between commiserating about the trouble with nineteen-and-a-half-percent bank interest rates and how neither of us can really stand aerobic dance classes, Frances mentioned that she sometimes used cocaine. I almost fell off my chair when I heard that. I always thought cocaine was a hard drug, a narcotic, but here was this sweet little woman telling me sincerely that cocaine was very nice, and that she only uses a little, and it's no problem at all, really. I looked at her

117

more closely, and she looked okay, not out of her mind on something. Then she asked me if I wanted to try some, and I don't know what came over me, but I said yes.

"We went into one of the upstairs bedrooms and locked the door, and she took out this little bottle with a spoon in the cap and showed me how to snort it. It made me feel so lively and bright. Fran and the cocaine made me sail through the party. I was in top form, witty, sexy, said all the right things to all the right people. I didn't feel anxious the way I often do. It was terrific.

"I called her up the next day and asked her where she gets the stuff. She told me she gets it from her sister-in-law and that she'd be glad to go halvesies on a gram with me if I wanted. I said yes, and now Frances and I split a gram about every month. I have to tell you that I like it. I mean I *really* like it. But I only use it when I have to entertain. I use just enough to get a glow and get rid of the nervousness—will it go right? Will I make a mistake that will hurt John's career? Will someone get drunk and will I be able to handle it?

"Cocaine makes everything go smoothly, like clockwork, better than it ever went before. I'd be a drag without it. I don't know how I ever used to get through one of those business parties without it—all the preparation, the cooking, setting up, playing hostess. It has turned something I used to dread into something that's really okay."

Elly uses cocaine about twice a month, more when there are more social functions, like during the holidays. She usually snorts two generous lines, twice during the evening, to keep going.

"I need to have the buzz to really feel like it's doing me any good," she says.

She has no problem with crashing, although once in a while she'll take a Valium to get to sleep.

"John doesn't know about it," she says, "and I'd never tell him. He does everything by the book and he'd be terrified for our reputation if he knew. He'd make me stop.

"Look, I'd never do anything dangerous or stupid like go buy cocaine on the street or go around telling my friends about this illegal thing I'm doing. It's just between me and

Frances and her sister-in-law. It's too bad cocaine has such a bad reputation. I think it's wonderful."

Elly was very interested in whether our research into cocaine abuse might improve the drug's reputation so that people like her could get it more freely.

———

Larry's mother bought him his first toy drum kit when he was 4 years old. It amazed her that such a quiet, gentle child could take such pleasure in bashing on drums and cymbals.

"That was it for me, right from the start," Larry explains. "I always had the beat, for as long as I can remember." Larry is now 39.

By the time he had worked his way through garage bands in the early sixties, rock 'n' roll groups in the late sixties and seventies, and dance bands in between, Larry had established himself as a solid professional drummer with an excellent reputation. He'd been in the musicians' union since he was 18 and had been sitting in on studio sessions almost since then. At 35, he worked regularly at top-paying jobs, playing in the pit six days a week for Broadway musicals and in gala shows at Radio City Music Hall. By most musicians' standards, Larry had it made; he was working all the time, making good money, and things looked as if they could only get better.

But there was a problem. Larry could never escape a gnawing feeling of inadequacy.

"All along, I just never believed it was me," he says. "I mean I knew I was an okay musician, but I just thought all the success was mostly luck. I kept thinking that when people went wild about my playing, they didn't know what they were listening to or that their standards were not very high.

"You've got to understand this," he says. "I sincerely believed it was all luck. Nothing more. Just blind luck. That I had nothing to do with it."

Drugs had always been on the music scene, and although Larry had sampled most of them once or twice, he didn't much like them—except for cocaine, which he had used socially perhaps half a dozen times.

About four years ago, Larry's career shifted into high gear. He had a succession of big Broadway jobs, found himself being requested by top names when they went into the recording studio, and suddenly realized that his appointment calendar was filling up months in advance. Everyone was patting him on the back and offering him work. He was a success. But the more he worked and the more praise he received, the more uncomfortable he became.

"After all," he says wryly, "since it was all luck, and I was never very good, it was only a matter of time before it all came crashing down, right?"

One afternoon, waiting for a studio session to begin, one of the sound engineers called him out into the hallway, told him he looked like hell, and offered him a snort of cocaine. Larry was tense; against his better judgment, he said yes. He was both sorry and glad he did. That day the cocaine did something for him it had never done before: it made him feel confident, relaxed, and in control. His fear evaporated, and he asked himself why he'd been so nervous in the first place. He was hot, ready to go, couldn't wait to get back into the studio. The session went flawlessly and afterward Larry was convinced the cocaine had made him play better than he ever had. He called a friend he knew used it and bought a gram. The idea was that he would only use it at the most demanding studio sessions, and then only a little bit, just to get through.

He continued to rise in his career. It seemed that the most important sessions were coming more frequently now and he was using more cocaine more often to get through them. The more he played, the more successful he became. The more successful he became, the more important every studio session and then every live job became, and the more often he felt he needed cocaine to perform adequately. Though he told no one, he was convinced that his success was directly the result of the coke. If a job did not come through, he would tear himself apart over it. Had he been found out? Was his true incompetence about to be revealed?

Going to studio sessions was sheer agony now. When

he worked, he was constantly agitated. He felt that the other musicians were competitively assessing him, looking to outdo him.

At first, he'd pull out his pocket vial of coke and pass it to the others for a taste before they started. It seemed like a good way to break the ice with those he considered top musicians. Sometimes they would grin and have one perfunctory toot with him, while he had two or three. When the other musicians gradually began declining Larry's offers, he'd just sniff up their shares as they watched him.

Over the next few months his schedule intensified. Larry was finding that the crash from his cocaine high was unbearable: sickness in the pit of his stomach, chills, sweaty palms. There was no way to avoid this during a session. Since he couldn't be snorting cocaine every fifteen minutes when he was in the studio for ten hours at a time, he began popping a Quaalude to stop his hands from shaking. He had to at least hold the drumsticks.

Larry started to slip. He showed up late for one studio session, then another. Once he failed to show up or to call for an important one-take recording. He often overslept, then dosed himself with coke to wake up. He went to sessions unrehearsed because he was spending most of his time looking for cocaine, snorting it, or trying to shake off the effects of a crash. Sometimes he'd crash in midsession and leave the studio with a track half-laid-down. Friends approached him, asked what was wrong. Gentle Larry looked them in the eye and told them, "Nothing."

After a while, his phone stopped ringing. There were no confrontations, but the work slowed down, then stopped. Larry became desperate. The only thing that kept him from feeling terrified was cocaine. He was snorting cocaine every day, ten grams a week, dealing to support his habit. He had shrunk to 120 pounds from his normally burly 195. With no resources, he had to give up his loft and return home to live with his retired parents. He was 37, broke, destroyed. He was a Performance User who had slipped into the nightmare of the Cokeaholic.

Larry's best friend tracked him down at his parents' and convinced him to enter therapy. He began to recover one step at a time. He gradually stopped using cocaine, he found a job, and began after two years to dabble at playing music again. Though he knows that cocaine will never be a casual diversion for him, he still uses it three or four times a year.

"What can I say?" he asks. "There's something about coke I just can't let go of. I suppose that when I do, I'll be 'cured.'"

The Boredom/Stress Reliever

A lot of people who use cocaine regularly say they do so either because they feel stressed or they feel a general malaise, a boredom. Although these may seem like opposite feeling states, they have the same origins. When we take a close look we see not boredom or stress but too little meaningful interaction with other people. Boredom/Stress Relievers suffer from alienation and loneliness.

When boredom or stress become the reason for aimless or even self-destructive behavior, it's actually being used as a mechanism for numbing anger, loneliness, and other uncomfortable feelings. Sometimes these feelings are so repressed that the person does not even know he has them; he feels nothing. He feels empty. He uses cocaine to alleviate his nagging "boredom," his emptiness, instead of seeking a way to get in touch with his often-frightening feelings.

Some Boredom/Stress Relievers experience an agitation—rather than an emptiness—that drowns out the emotions they don't want to feel. Following the same pattern of behavior, such a person feels himself to be "wound up," or "up-tight," to be stressed, and he will take cocaine to block out or distract him from his feelings of agitation, fear, or anger.

Boredom/Stress Relievers who live in a state of internal numbness use cocaine to induce intense, ecstatic feelings: of sexual excitement, connectedness to others, a lively emotional state in which they seem to share their feelings freely. Those who often feel agitated tell us that cocaine frees them of the inhibitions they feel prevent them from getting close to other people and understanding and coping with their emotions.

For most of us, feelings of boredom and stress are transient and will pass on their own. We usually try to make ourselves feel better by making contact with other people, telling them how we feel, and experiencing their care and support.

Boredom/Stress Relievers, however, have trouble opening up to people. It is difficult enough for them to admit their feelings to themselves. Their "real" relationship is with cocaine.

Some of the modus operandi of Boredom/Stress Relievers are truly baroque in their complexity and structure. There are special containers, special mirrors, reverent preparations, expensive paraphernalia. A Boredom/Stress Reliever who consumes copious amounts of cocaine may forge a dangerous or complex relationship with a dealer in order to be sure he can get enough "good" coke.

Escalating from snorting to freebasing is more common among members of this group, because by comparison there is a greater contrast between how they feel before and after they use the drug. Boredom/Stress Relievers are subject to repeated cocaine binges, with greater risk of serious physical and emotional aftereffects.

Even though their cocaine use often causes problems in their relationships and family lives, Boredom/Stress Relievers generally do not allow their cocaine use to intrude on their work or careers. Frequently they have achieved remarkable success at what they do. Their outward behavior may make them look like perfect role models in their field. But they run into trouble when they are faced with spending time alone, away from work, or with perhaps one other person. A Boredom/Stress Reliever can allay bad feelings by immersing himself in his work. When the workday's done, his feeling of emptiness or stress descends and he turns to cocaine. This is particularly dangerous because he is using cocaine to provide feelings he has trouble getting naturally—joy, excitement, sexual arousal, closeness, warmth, connection. Dependency is based on inducing with a drug those powerful feelings one wants to feel naturally, but cannot.

Many Boredom/Stress Relievers use sex not to forge relationships but to get intense pleasurable feelings they cannot get otherwise. So the singles scene can be a seductive and self-destructive playground for Boredom/Stress Relievers. Some people in this scene have for years sought feelings and relationships with the help of cocaine and sex but gotten only sensations. Cocaine produces sensations of power, sexuality, competence, connection, intimacy, *but not the real thing.* Boredom/Stress Relievers tend to increase the amount of cocaine they use each time to further intensify the feelings they get from the drug. Past a certain dosage cocaine can cause temporary impotence.

There are couples, too, who become Boredom/Stress Relievers and take up cocaine together in an effort to improve or resurrect their emotional and sex lives. They may be using cocaine to invest themselves with feelings for each other that they've never been able to share or express, because both of them have been unable to risk intimate contact. For couples like these, cocaine may become the major thing they "give" each other.

Boredom/Stress Relievers can use a lot of cocaine in a very short period of time. A Boredom/Stress Reliever couple may consume a gram to a gram and a half of cocaine over a period of four hours. And once they feel good, it is very hard for them to stop. Any diminishing of the cocaine euphoria only heightens the awareness of their own inner pain, and they want to avoid that at all costs. Boredom/Stress Relievers frequently binge and go two or three days in a row consuming as much cocaine as they can afford. If a Boredom/Stress Reliever couple uses a large amount of cocaine on a given evening, chances are they will get some more the next day, and the next, until the money runs out or it's time to go back to work.

The feelings Boredom/Stress Relievers get from cocaine are not as fulfilling as the real feelings they're missing. But they are intense, and when the drug wears off, the Boredom/Stress Relievers feel emptier. This feeds the compulsion to keep using cocaine, and if it continues, Boredom/Stress Relievers can end up Cokeaholics. Often, they'll use other medications, like Valium and in many cases barbiturates or narcotics, even heroin, to ease their coming down.

Boredom/Stress Relievers live in a world of ever-diminishing thrills, from cocaine and from sex, and of ever-diminishing human connections, as cocaine takes their place. They are headed for a dead end of joyless alienation.

———

At first glance it seems Laurie and Mark have a cocaine romance—a relationship in which the common denominator is cocaine. They seldom relate to each other sexually or emotionally without the drug. Cocaine was a part of their courtship and then their marriage. There are strong feelings of love and respect between them, however, and their marriage stands on firm ground. Laurie is 30, Mark is 40. He's adored her completely from the moment he laid eyes on her six years ago when he noticed her gingerly testing the water in a friend's pool in Marbella. They were in love before breakfast, before their host had even had time to introduce them.

They lived together for two years, and four years ago they married. Both used cocaine socially before they slipped into their mutual boredom/stress relief. Laurie began using cocaine when she was 17 as just one of a pharmacopoeia of drugs she experimented with over several years. She sampled everything from pot to pills, but long ago settled on cocaine as her drug of choice because she feels more self-confident when she uses it. Although she is very pretty and bright, she often feels inferior—especially around other women. She acts detached and aloof, while she's actually insecure.

Mark did not start to use cocaine until he was in his

thirties and a successful internist. He has a lucrative practice—the excellent income has provided him with a life-style he doesn't want to give up—but after ten years, he finds his work unchallenging. He's bored with his routine.

The first time he tried cocaine he realized it made him feel good in a way he'd wanted to for a long time; it filled him with optimism and good cheer. He began using it, regularly but infrequently and in small amounts, as his reward for getting through each week.

It was Laurie who initiated the couple's joint cocaine use before they were married. During the ever-increasing silences between them she began to feel a yawning anxiety, loneliness, and fear. She didn't know what Mark's silences meant and she was afraid to ask, in case she was the cause of Mark's depression. She suggested cocaine.

"I think my cocaine use also had something to do with this feeling that I 'sold out' when I decided to marry Mark," she says. "I'm used to living well, and Mark can give me all the material possessions I need to have a sense of security. But sometimes he's cold, and sometimes I'm actually intimidated by him.

"He's really a lot like my father," she says. "He's always in charge. Everything is okay as long as it goes his way. It's all right as long as I go along with him. If I don't, he 'turns off' and I'm afraid he'll actually leave me."

Their cocaine use seemed to ease the situation. Laurie felt easier around Mark, he seemed to loosen up, and there was a sense of warmth and closeness between them. She also found that he was more interested in having sex after some coke. Still, there was no growing connection between them beyond the drug's effects. Even though they talked and talked to each other on those nights when they were high, they never discussed their problems, Mark's distance, Laurie's fear, her sense that they were isolated from each other.

The cocaine rituals became solidly entrenched in their lives. Since Mark's office was closed on Tuesdays as well as the weekend, Monday evening's dinner consisted of several snorts of pharmaceutical cocaine followed by half a Quaalude to trim the sharp edges off the high, washed down with

Perrier water. They both lost weight. They would snort about a gram of coke through the evening, talk, and make love. Friday and Saturday night the menu was the same as Monday—no dinner, a gram of cocaine snorted between them, and Quaaludes. Sunday was spent nursing the awful crash, usually with Valium. They followed this routine week in and week out for about three years. Both of them avoided noting that just about all their time together centered around cocaine—getting high, staying high, or recovering from being high. Cocaine was the pastime when friends came over to Laurie and Mark's. Mark prided himself on being a connoisseur and would discourse knowingly to guests about its pharmacological effects as he offered the mirror and then handed out the Quaaludes. There was little risk involved— Mark got all the drugs through his practice, so there was no need to deal with cocaine sellers—and the expense was next to nothing. Neither of them thought their "controlled" cocaine use was a problem—they saw it as a consistent part of their well-to-do eighties life-style. They talked about it as something they were "into" for now and that they would stop doing when they got "bored" with it.

After about the first three years of regular cocaine use, Laurie found herself feeling more and more depressed on those days in between. She noticed Mark, too, was more withdrawn at those times. She had difficulty sleeping and her appetite dwindled. She dropped from 115 pounds to 100.

Mark came home one night and told Laurie he had a surprise for her—he was going to teach her how to freebase. She watched as he processed the already-pure pharmaceutical cocaine in a double boiler in the kitchen. He took the freebase, produced a new glass pipe, and showed her how to heat it and inhale the vapors. With the first hit, Laurie was almost knocked down by the feeling—warm, tingly, an all-over glow. It made her feel extremely sexual. Mark also felt a new high. He acted like a kid again—happy, funny, even silly—not like his usual cool, controlled self.

Laurie and Mark stopped snorting to freebase. They bought a special set of glass beakers and Laurie nicknamed Mark "Mr. Wizard." They were still using cocaine religiously every Friday, Saturday, and Monday night, but their consumption doubled from three grams a week to six or seven. The anticipation of waiting for those nights was almost unbearable, and the depressions in between were bleaker. Three nights a week they'd sit in their luxurious, high-tech living room on their gunmetal gray carpet and pass their freebase pipe back and forth. At these times, they felt very connected to each other. Mark didn't have to think about being an internist and Laurie didn't have to think about feeling inadequate or lonely.

"Freebasing was like taking a vacation from my head, from trying to figure things out and understanding what was going wrong," Laurie explains. "I've been in and out of therapy for eight years and I get pretty tired of being 'analytical' all the time."

To Mark and Laurie, freebasing felt better than anything they had ever known. Later they both admitted that they were terrified that they had such easy access to "bottled euphoria," as they call it. There was no built-in financial limit to how far it could go, since Mark was getting pharmaceutical cocaine for $25 an ounce. They knew they were in danger of losing control.

"Sometimes we thought we just wouldn't be able to stop," Laurie says with a shudder. "We prayed that the evening would go on and on. We completely forgot about food or sleep for three days out of the week."

Mark began getting more irritable at work, and Laurie kept getting thinner and more depressed.

The following year, Mark went to Florida for a two-day convention. The first evening he was gone, Laurie decided to freebase some cocaine alone. She looked for the Cartier snuffbox in the linen closet where they always kept it, and suddenly panicked: it was gone. Laurie flung everything out of the closet looking for it. Gone. Then she tore apart all the closets and finally ransacked the entire apartment—drawers, cabinets—hurling everything to the floor, looking for it. She found nothing. Defeated, she curled up alone and tiny in their king-size bed and wept.

When Mark returned two days later, that's how he found her. Laurie was terrified by what she'd done and how she felt. She was shocked at the intense drive she had felt for the cocaine. Fortunately, Mark was able to respond directly to her for a change. They talked to each other, horrified at what they now knew they could no longer avoid. Their lives were falling apart. The shambles in the apartment was a metaphor for what cocaine had done to their lives. They both acknowledged that they had to stop using it and find out why they needed it in the first place.

Laurie began seeing a new psychotherapist, a woman, knowledgeable about drug use. She's been with her for three years now. Mark entered therapy about six months after Laurie.

They've come a long way. Both of them have been working in therapy to learn how to "fill the empty spaces together," as Mark puts it. They stopped using cocaine at home about a year ago, but they have used it several times at friends' houses and at parties. They have an agreement not to bring cocaine into their apartment, and they've never broken it. They've begun to learn how to plan their weekends and structure their free time. They took up sailing, Laurie began classes in stockbroking, and Mark is about to become a licensed pilot.

They still feel frightened from time to time, empty and depressed at others. They aren't sure what's going to happen to them or to their marriage, but they both feel strongly about the commitment they've made to living a really good life—"a normal life again," as Laurie says—and to being more open and honest with themselves and each other.

———

Susan uses her fair, freckled, pretty looks to fool everyone. She's really a little sad and lonely, but when she throws the switch she can make you believe that she's full of zest for life, that she's a daredevil, and that she has a million friends.

Until a few months ago, she was secretary to Steven, an attractive obstetrician in his late thirties. Though Susan knew that Steven has been happily married for seven years, not long after she began working for him, she became infatuated with him. She fantasized about him, his piercing blue eyes, his tall lean body. She conjured up images of the two of them in romantic hideaways. Although Steven had never hidden the fact that he noticed Susan's good looks, he never pursued her.

Susan is pretty good at reading other people's wants and needs, and after a few months, she figured out how she could seduce him.

Susan knew that Steven had a taste for the adventurous and a rich imagination. She presented herself to him as a wild type, "kinky," sophisticated, a young woman who would try almost anything.

"I had never used anything but pot," she says, "but when I heard Steve talking about how glamorous cocaine sounded, and how he'd never tried it, I decided to make him do just that."

Susan set out to seduce Steven. He seemed flattered and curious, and her innuendos became bolder. She alluded to her frequent cocaine use. She implied that she liked group sex. She took to staying late to finish her work, to be alone with him in the office. One afternoon she made up a wild story about how she had gone out to a club, used cocaine, and then brought home a couple she had just met. She could tell Steven was turned on. She suggested they try a little of the cocaine in the office supply cabinet. To her surprise, he agreed.

Though neither had actually done it before, setting the lines and sniffing was easy. She immediately discovered that one of the drug's effects was that she felt filled with desire. She felt charged, alive, and very sexual. Steven felt the same way. There was a silence. Then Susan slid onto Steven's lap and kissed him. In a few minutes they were making love on Steven's examining table. They continued to snort cocaine, getting higher and higher. Susan was dazzled by the experience.

She and Steven continued their sexual fling. He made it clear from the outset that he loved his wife, had no intention of leaving her, and would not let their relationship grow more serious. Every ten days or so, they unlocked the cocaine, got high, and made love in the examining room. Steven enjoyed the secrecy and the clandestine thrill of it, and he also liked the cocaine, but didn't get nearly as much out of it as Susan did. For him it was fun, just a diversion. Susan's affair with Steven continued for two and a half years. For him she had created an entirely fictitious self. Steven thought she was a worldly, active, busy woman with many friends, other lovers, and a hectic, fulfilling life. Susan really had no life at all outside of her intense fantasies about Steven. She gradually dropped most of her relationships with other men. Her friends saw her less and less as she fell more deeply in love with Steven. In the middle of the second year, she began snatching small quantities of cocaine from the office cabinet and snorting it alone in her apartment and fantasizing about him under its energizing chill. It made her feel in charge, sensuous, and in control of the situation. On weekends she sat by the phone, but he called her less and less frequently. She had never told him how much she cared about him, and he was not emotionally involved with her.

Susan's cocaine-inspired escapades with Steven were the only things she looked forward to. So when Steven told her that his wife had become pregnant, and their affair was over, Susan was crushed. Reality and deep depression set in.

When Susan came for help she was terrified of attending group therapy sessions, yet she desperately needed and wanted friendship and peer support. For Susan we employed the "buddy system." We paired her with a young, shy woman named Mary who sat with her while she wrote résumés and made phone calls for job interviews. This was all part of their "treatment plan." They made up "life-improvement assignments"; Susan helped Mary find a new apartment. Susan said it was easier to follow through on activities and promises if she made a commitment to her "buddy" Mary to do so. They both got a deep sense of fulfillment from helping each other.

Susan quit her job and eventually found a better one as a junior buyer in a department store. The store is financing her night classes in merchandising. Though she understands that it's healthier for her not to see Steven anymore, she still thinks about calling him. But as the circumstances of her real world become more exciting, Susan thinks of him less and less. Susan has used cocaine twice since she has left Steven but doesn't long for it anymore. Both times, she used it with men who offered cocaine as a prelude to sex.

Ben is 42 and Sharon is 32. They have been married for three months, and for each of them, this is the third try.

"Third time's a charm. And make that a double, I hope," Sharon says brightly.

Ben is a printer. When he and Sharon met, he had been using cocaine for about five years, casually, after work with his buddies. Sharon, a nurse, had been using it for ten years. She discovered it right after her second marriage. She found that coke made her feel more relaxed in the singles scene. It turned her on, made her eager for sex, and kept her from feeling lonely or frightened when she was with people she didn't know.

Ben met Sharon at a bar well known as a place to get cocaine, while he was drinking with his buddy. The buddy was known to "carry" coke with him and to share it freely. Sharon knew him slightly and spent the evening fluttering around him and Ben, coming on very strong. She wanted coke, and Ben; she got both.

"We really got it on right away," Ben asserts. He sounds like he's in charge, but he's no more so than in his last marriage, where he was so dependent on his wife and so angry at her for it that he lost his sexual drive. Sharon is in control of this marriage, and cocaine only makes Ben feel like he's in control. Since he got together with Sharon, everything has gone her way. Every element of their "adventurous" sex life has been invented or introduced by Sharon, who uses sex to control him and make herself feel wanted.

During our interview with them, Sharon energetically dominates the conversation. She whispers and laughs and uses her expressive voice to sound sincere, or seductive, or vulnerable. She talks about cocaine and describes the first time she made love while using the drug, when she had a severe sunburn.

"It really hurt, but it was an exquisite, tingly sort of pain." She gives the impression she could go on at length about things that hurt but feel good too, but instead she says:

"Ooooh, cocaine. Ben and I just *love* coke, don't we, honey?"

Asked how they take it, Sharon and Ben glance at each other and grin. He straightens up proudly in his seat.

"Well . . . we play these little games with it," Sharon says. "We like to put it on our lips, on our gums, on my nipples. Ben likes to put it on different . . . parts . . . of me and lick it off." Here she cocks her head, waiting to see if we will ask which parts.

"Of course we sniff it too," she says. "From our navels and palms."

Sharon looks directly at Ben. "It's just delicious with sex." She turns to us. "Don't you think it's amazing that in all our relationships, even our marriages, neither of us ever found anyone we were so completely sexually compatible with?"

"I've never known a woman so comfortable with sex," says Ben. "She even talks sex better than anyone else. She tells me the greatest sexual fantasies I've ever heard. Listen, last week we were having dinner in the restaurant at the top of the World Trade Center and she said she thought we should go do it, right then, in the stairwell of the building. We skipped dessert, snorted a little toot, and went and did it. Sharon groans sometimes, and you could hear her up and down the well for fifty floors."

They are obsessed with sex, and they never have sex without cocaine. When they're not having sex and coke, they talk about fantasies about sex and coke. Theirs is a real cocaine romance: cocaine has been central in their relationship since it first began; they have only related to each other with cocaine and sex. Without the drug, Ben and Sharon might have nothing to talk about and nothing to do together. So far they have expressed little compassion for each other, little understanding or communication. They use each other to feel valuable, worthwhile, whole.

While she was single, Sharon's discovery of the wonderful effects cocaine had on her sexual behavior led her into a good deal of experimentation. She got into group sex, both with other single people at orgies and as the extra woman with couples looking for a threesome. Very soon after she and Ben got together, she introduced him to her network of swinging friends. Swapping and group sex with other couples quickly became part of their cocaine and sex pattern.

Sadomasochism is another element that often accompanies an extreme preoccupation with cocaine and sex. After a few months, Sharon introduced a game that became part of their sexual repertoire. "It's my sadomasochistic streak," she explains. She loves to scream "No, no, no!" when they have sex, while she actually means "yes." She especially likes to do this when they include other couples or singles, to see the effect it has on them. Only she and Ben know that "no" really means "don't stop" and that the code word for "stop" is "bourbon."

"People sometimes get really freaked out when they hear me screaming and begging 'No, no, no,' and Ben just keeps going," Sharon explains coolly. "That's part of the fun."

Ben and Sharon use cocaine and have marathon sex, alone or with their swapping partners, every weekend without fail. When they use it they use every bit they have. They generally buy one or two grams a week. Ben splits it with a friend at work. This means that they spend a significant amount of their income on cocaine: between $8,000 and $10,000 a year.

Between their cocaine weekends, Sharon and Ben almost never make love and, in fact, barely communicate at all.

"We both work long hours," Ben says, "and Sharon is usually sleeping when I get home."

Sharon and Ben will try just about anything. From one of the couples they have sex with, they picked up the idea of smearing a dab of cocaine paste on the underside of Ben's penis. The fellow who showed this to them said it helped him sustain an erection. In fact, the man was using so much cocaine that he had become impotent. Ben and Sharon have also tried cocaine suppositories and an anal infusion of cocaine and water.

One of their partner couples was a doctor and his wife, who injected cocaine.

"Wasn't that gross, hon?" Sharon asks. "Ben did it and loved the rush, but I wouldn't even try it." She wrinkles up her nose. "I don't want tracks. I'm no mainliner. Uggh. It makes me think of slums and addicts."

But in spite of her aversion to any suggestion of heroin or opiates, Ben and Sharon routinely use Dilaudid or Demerol, two of the most powerful opiates available, to avoid their monumentally sickening crashes. Sharon allows that it's lucky she's a nurse and can spirit the drugs out of the narcotics supply cabinet in the hospital where she works. Sharon keeps her cocaine with her at all times.

"Never know when the urge may overtake you. I keep it in this," she says. It's a gold figure of a nude woman. She demonstrates how the head screws off to reveal that it is hollow and filled with cocaine.

"We tried freebasing," she continues, "but it's too expensive. The coke disappears too fast. Besides, for me it felt more like a downer."

But she does not want to know any details about where the cocaine comes from or how much it costs. She just likes to watch as Ben pours out those straight little lines on their glass coffee table. Since Ben and Sharon cannot connect emotionally beyond cocaine and sex, they have developed rituals through which they signal to each other that they are important. One thing Ben does is pay strict attention to protocol when he makes his compulsively straight cocaine lines. Sharon is keenly aware of the equality of the lines—everyone must get the same amount, but above all she must not get less. She measures her status, especially if there is going to be group sex, by how coke is distributed. It makes her feel important.

Sharon entered therapy because of her problems related to men, *not* related to cocaine. She was referred by her physician. In therapy, Sharon's main concerns are her lack of self-worth and her difficulty trusting and feeling loved by a man. She learned early to manipulate men with her sexuality. This makes her feel powerful on the one hand, but completely helpless on the other, because she feels it destroys the possibility a man will love her for herself and not for her sexual performance. She repeatedly sets up a self-fulfilling prophecy; in the end, it always seems that "men are only after one thing."

Sharon and Ben's marriage is in serious jeopardy. They're both in therapy and this seems to be keeping them from increasing their cocaine use. But they haven't slowed down. The longer they use cocaine and sex to avoid their real feelings, the emptier and more panicky and driven they'll begin to feel.

Evie was quite articulate about how she felt as a Boredom/Stress Reliever. She started therapy because she was worried about her increasing cocaine use. Here is exactly what she said:

"It's just that I get this empty feeling—a hollow nameless kind of feeling—it's not exactly anxiety, not exactly anger, not exactly sadness. If I were sad I could cry it out. If I were angry I could yell at somebody—but it doesn't feel quite like any of those things. I come home at the end of the week to my little studio apartment and the feeling just comes over me.

"Don't get me wrong, I've fixed up my apartment really cute and I love it. I could pick up the phone and call any number of friends I know who would love to go out with me—men or women—but the only thing I know I can depend on to make me feel better is coke.

"The very first time I tried it I knew it was the *something* I had been looking for all my life. I know it's terrible but it's true, and there is nothing, and I mean absolutely nothing, that I like as much as coke.

"I know I'm beginning to go overboard. I'm using it every weekend and sometimes in the middle of the week. The thing that scares me is not how much I'm using it but the reason I'm using it. Why is it that cocaine is the only thing that makes me feel good? I know I'm going to have to give it up . . . but it's going to be very hard.

"So here I am."

Patrick and Mathilde looked like a perfect young couple. He was 24, slender, boyish, athletic. He spoke with an aristocratic air that quietly announced money and good breeding. She was 30 and a strikingly beautiful redhead, understated but stylish. Her thick French accent and fractured English were decidedly charming.

Patrick used to tend bar in a good restaurant and was working his way toward a management position there. He also wrote remarkably good song lyrics and music. He had begun to attract some interest from a number of people in the music business who spoke of developing his career. Mathilde was a free-lance interior designer whose first love was photography. Like Patrick's music, her photo work had begun to attract some attention but had yet to bring in any real money. They lived in a tiny but impeccably furnished apartment and just squeaked by on their combined earnings.

Patrick first entered therapy three years ago at Mathilde's insistence. On his first visit, he gave us quite a performance. With a smirk that was both irritating and sad, he lay down on the office couch and blew smoke rings from his imported cigarette. Then he introduced himself.

"I've been in therapy many times before," he declared nonchalantly. "So far it hasn't worked much. I never would have come here if Mathilde hadn't insisted. Begged, really."

Patrick delighted in telling us how "bad" he'd always been; he watched for a reaction after each confession of self-destructive or illegal behavior.

Patrick was the youngest of six children and was five years younger than his next older brother. His father is a wealthy corporate lawyer. All his older brothers and sisters became successful professionals.

"It's just that Mom was all used up when I came along," he explained. "She'd lost her looks, lost her health, and was depressed all the time. Also drunk most of the time. Dad divorced her, all my brothers and sisters were gone or busy with their lives, and I was left alone to take care of her. We lived in this gigantic twenty-three-room house. It was a wreck, and there were no servants.

"The other kids all had lots of friends and lives of their own. I was the only one who really loved her, so I took care of her. Sometimes I had to clean her up or dress her all by myself. I was just a kid. She really got crazy sometimes, you know?"

His mother would go from screaming at him and hitting him to cuddling him; sometimes her behavior became seductive—she would undress in front of him and pull him to her.

"Guess what?" he said. "I don't trust women. But Mathilde and I are really close. We're really good friends; we're 'suffering artists' together. The only thing we don't have is sex. I can't."

Patrick told us that he could not feel sexual with a woman he loved, and he couldn't produce any passion for his beautiful Mathilde.

"I can pick up any girl I care nothing about. The younger they are the better. I'll have a quickie after work, but I can't do it with Mathilde. It really upsets her. She understands how my mother was with me and how that makes it almost impossible for me to do it with women I respect, but she can't take it. And I feel I have to tell her about the other girls, you know. That really gets her. So we fight about that, and sometimes she'll leave me. The few times she has I get—I don't know—sick inside without her. I can't eat, I cry all the time. I throw up, I can't write music, can't go to work. I feel like I can't even breathe without her."

But when Mathilde came back, she and Patrick were lonely together instead of lonely alone. Patrick's reaction to Mathilde's leaving was not the agony of true love; it was the panic of abandonment. Patrick and Mathilde's attraction was more a deep mutual dependency than a deep intimacy.

Patrick decided to try cocaine as a cure for his sexual problem.

"I didn't really like depending on the coke, but it worked like magic for Mathilde and me," he said. "When we did it we had sex, sex, sex. The only problem is that Mathilde never had an orgasm with coke and, well, there are only certain ways I can get turned on. I'll tell you what a louse I am. Unless I had coke, and sometimes even then, I couldn't do it with her unless I covered her face. She hated it. It really hurt her that I couldn't do it unless I could kind of forget who she was. Sick, right?

"But it's better with coke. Mathilde says it's like a holiday from the suffering-artist routine. She loves the rush. It's the closest thing I can give her to an orgasm."

But Patrick needed more than cocaine to overcome his sexual and emotional problems. Walter, a car jockey, handyman, longtime heroin and methadone addict, supplied Patrick's cocaine, most of the time for free. But on one condition: that he could watch Patrick and Mathilde make love and sometimes bring his girl friend Grace along for some fun. The four of them got together every Saturday for cocaine and sex. Mathilde was disgusted with the whole scene but somehow felt compelled to participate.

"Walter was a devil. He was my best friend. Mathilde didn't like me to hang around with him because he dealt drugs, and she really didn't like him to come into the house, especially with Grace, who was always high on something. But I thought it was a turn-on when they came over and we all had sex. Grace was a real sexpot.

"Walter doesn't touch Mathilde—she'd never let him near her anyway—but he's happy to watch her with me. 'A peeg,' Mathilde calls him and says he makes her skin crawl." It amused Patrick that he and Mathilde, graduates of good private schools, alumni of the best country clubs, had linked up with types like Walter and Grace.

"He's pretty foul," said Patrick. He told us that Mathilde just endured Walter's commentary as he watched them make love: "He likes to give instructions.

"Grace is always so high, she's totally out of it. She wears those bras with holes cut out of the nipples, you know? And these fake leather panties with a zipper in the crotch? She wears them real tight. She always looks so bored with the whole thing. Never says a word to me or Walter, but she does exactly what he says, very obediently, very prompt."

Despite Walter's offensiveness, Patrick was dependent on him for cocaine, so he concocted all manner of excuses and rationalizations for his "friendship" with him: he felt sorry for him; he was demonstrating his socially liberal attitude by mixing with a lower-class loser.

Patrick told us that Mathilde always wanted them to stop using cocaine but couldn't seem to exert enough influence to accomplish it. They began snorting ten lines apiece during an afternoon when they'd have one of their "get-togethers," and afterward Mathilde would be filled with remorse.

"She'd cry and say she wanted me to 'get better' and grow up. She was thirty, you know, and she wanted to have a baby. But we both knew what a mess I was. Could you see me as a father? There was no way that she was going to have a kid with no money and me being all fucked up."

Mathilde did get pregnant, however, and had an abortion. It traumatized her. She cried for a week and was extremely depressed; so was Patrick. They were both borne down by the mess their lives were in. Walter had been trying to interest them in shooting cocaine for a few months, but Mathilde wouldn't even let him set foot in the apartment with a syringe. Then, at the peak of this depression, she decided she wanted to try injecting cocaine. For Patrick, shooting was a revelation.

"We both felt like we were in heaven that night, warm, close, safe in each other's arms. We didn't have sex, we just pressed our bodies together, and it felt like her skin would melt into mine and we'd dissolve into each other and become one. We never had that kind of closeness before from snorting cocaine.

"Maybe it was so spectacular because it was mixed with some heroin," Patrick said. "A speedball. Ever since that night, we love to shoot up. We do it at least once a week, always speedballs. Without the heroin the coke makes you very wired. I never feel warm and safe and relaxed anymore without a speedball. I don't understand why something I really need like that, that makes me feel okay inside, is against the law," he said.

"Believe me, I'd really like to be someone else. I walk around with this big ugly feeling all the time. I know Mathilde really wants to love me and I really want to love her, so how come we can't? I know I must be a rotten guy to be this way, but you don't know how awful it is to be inside my head." Patrick's veneer of coolness slipped and there was a sob deep beneath his words. His grief was beginning to show; a real feeling was about to be born. But he quickly caught himself and shifted to a casual disinterest.

"Well, it's really not all that bad," he said. Patrick's nonchalance, his disguise, was firmly back in place.

When Mathilde talked about her relationship with Patrick, there were no theatrics or melodrama. She was sharp and perceptive. She was also clearly in a good deal less emotional jeopardy than Patrick.

"Patrick is so sensitive," she said. "He is a beautiful artist and this comes out in his music. I know he does love me. But he can't give me anything, and he can't take what I want to give him.

"I am also very sad from my childhood. We are the same in that. My parents were very cruel, not showing any love. That is why I am so nervous inside all the time. Patrick and I understand each other for that.

"We do terrible things to each other. I think it is because we are accustomed to not being loved. He tells me that the other women he sees, that they are like me. One even had the same name. So why doesn't he just want to be with me? He says he needs always to be far away from me inside, with his feelings, not *intimate* with me.

"I do not care about sex and I am not embarrassed about my body. He likes to show me off in sex to his friends. I would never do that except high on cocaine. The cocaine makes me feel calm inside, and I feel together with Patrick, so I can do it. But I still do not want to. I know I do it because I don't want to leave Patrick. I am terrified of that.

"Now the more we use cocaine, the more we do not have sex. Especially the needles. Now the needle is instead of the sex. I don't understand what is happening. I have had men who were good to me, kind men who loved me, but always they bored me somehow. I am drawn to Patrick. I cannot get away. I am very unhappy, but I am stuck. I would like Patrick to get help."

Patrick and Mathilde's boredom relief quickly became

more serious cocaine abuse and then their life together collapsed. Walter stopped supplying their free cocaine. Patrick borrowed $25,000 from his father on the pretext of buying a co-op loft as an investment, and he and Mathilde used the money to buy cocaine and heroin for speedballs. Their once-weekly use of Walter's free cocaine grew into a two-month Cokeaholic binge during which they shot speedballs several times a day every day. At the end of eight weeks, the $25,000 was gone. They had both stopped working and were completely unable to function. Patrick's father discovered what had been done with his money and had Patrick hospitalized. Mathilde returned to the French countryside to stay with her family for six months.

Mathilde's withdrawal was far easier than Patrick's. When she returned to the United States, they tried to get back together again while both were "straight." But Mathilde could no longer raise romantic hopes for Patrick, and he decided to confront his loneliness by himself rather than risk ruining Mathilde's life along with his own. They divorced.

Mathilde entered therapy. After three arduous years of wrestling with the repressed rage she had carried around, she was able to free herself from her need to seek out unfulfilling relationships. Her most dramatic discovery was that rather than wanting Patrick to get better, she had actually depended on his instability and emotional inadequacies to help maintain the relationship. Terrified to trust another person, she needed to be in a situation in which she was continually depended upon. She felt "safe" with the knowledge that Patrick could not breathe or eat without her, even though she knew at the same time he would never fulfill her needs. Her gratification had come from knowing that she was depended upon and that she never had to learn how to trust Patrick.

Eventually, Mathilde fell in love with and married a divorced man with a young daughter of his own. She soon became pregnant with their child and has told us that she wouldn't dream of using cocaine again for any reason.

Patrick has been in and out of hospitals several times

since their last breakup and has intermittent bouts with alcohol and methadone as well as cocaine, although his worst drug episodes now entail once- or twice-yearly Cokeaholic binges. He says he is committed to solving his problems, however, and is deeply involved in therapy. He has also cultivated a supportive relationship with his father and older brother. He says he's beginning to believe that one day he might be able to have a successful marriage. He has not lost his sense of irony, though. Patrick has always liked very young women and he's recently decided that he might as well make the best of it.

"Most of these young girls I go out with are usually just a little more emotionally mature than I am," he explains. "So I figure that at the rate I'm going, by the time I'm forty I should be able to keep up perfectly with a nice, conservative eighteen-year-old."

For Patrick, getting straightened out will be a long battle. He will have to struggle to maintain successful relationships, and it will be difficult for him to learn that he can find trust, love, and comfort in people as easily as he knows he can find them in cocaine.

The
Cokeaholic

The Cokeaholic is the most extreme cocaine user. He is the person possessed, the media cliché: the Hollywood producer who burns hundreds of thousands of dollars on cocaine; the rich playboy who systematically excavates his family's fortune and liquidates his investments to buy it; the successful lawyer who empties her savings account to feed her cocaine craving; the middle-class housewife or career woman who turns to shoplifting, embezzling, or prostitution to get money for the drug. It helps to be rich if you're a Cokeaholic, but you don't have to be. We've seen factory workers, middle-class professionals, housewives, and businessmen all suffering from extreme cocaine abuse.

The Cokeaholic has lost all control of his cocaine use; his health, relationships, and career are in serious jeopardy. He will consume the drug at a phenomenal rate; snorting, freebasing, or injecting every bit he can get his hands on until it is gone, and then immediately concentrating on how to get some more. He'll continue to do this until his money runs out, he can't get more cocaine, or until he's physically unable to sustain the assault of the drug without sleep or food to recharge. His binges can last for weeks or even months. It's not unusual for a Cokeaholic to consume several grams a day and to spend tens of thousands of dollars. These intensive, all-or-nothing binges are usually associated with Cokeaholics who shoot or freebase their cocaine. They use a huge amount of the drug each time, craving the intense rush. The high wears off quickly, and the crash is extremely unpleasant. The Cokeaholic immediately consumes more coke to cut the crash and is shortly using the drug more to avoid the horrible effects of coming down than to stay high. There are just as many Cokeaholics who snort a gram or more every day without fail, and who remain high almost all the time, but are able to function better than a freebaser or cocaine mainliner.

Any type of cocaine user can quickly become an abuser, especially if he freebases or shoots the drug. This has less to do with cocaine's effects than with the Cokeaholic himself.

Although no one knows exactly why it is that one person maintains a low or moderate level of cocaine use while another suddenly becomes a Cokeaholic, we do see patterns. Just the right mixture of circumstances: life stress, underlying psychological illness, social encouragement to use the drug, and ready access to cocaine can ignite and rapidly produce a full-blown Cokeaholic. We often see Cokeaholics who started bingeing after a painful career or love loss. We find Cokeaholics among people who have difficulty forming strong, trusting relationships. They are often people who have trouble enjoying themselves. And very often they have had sexual problems that preceded their cocaine use, such as premature ejaculation, lack of orgasm, or impotence.

Cokeaholics are often severely depressed, though they may not recognize this. A Cokeaholic may be extremely successful at his work but will feel a profound lack of fulfillment, worthlessness, and an overwhelming but often unrecognized rage. He may be very good at satisfying other people's needs while being unable to satisfy his own. He frequently suffers from low self-esteem even when he appears to think quite a lot of himself. And he also suffers from compulsion.

Cokeaholics are locked into a powerful compulsion.

Compulsive behavior is always a repetition of behavior that once gave pleasure. The same behavior is returned to again and again, even after the original gratification has been diminished or even eliminated.

Several factors combine and trigger the Cokeaholic's descent into destructive chaos:

1. an emotional proclivity for the cocaine-derived gratification
2. the subtle forces of learned behavior
3. the emergence of the self-perpetuating use-crash-use-again cycle

A Cokeaholic has lost all control. He cannot break his addiction without professional help. At the root of cokeaholism is cocaine's extraordinarily reinforcing high: euphoria, omnipotence, power, strength, control, joyousness, ecstasy. The cocaine high is one of the most, if not the most, powerful chemical reinforcers. No other drug delivers such intense feelings.

Cokeaholics often tell us the drug delivers feelings they could rarely conjur without it. They want to experience these feelings as often as they can, for as long as they can, as intensely as they can. When the drug wears off and they begin to crash, their reasons for wanting more cocaine are twofold: they want to cut the horrific sensations of the crash and they have a compulsion to feel that euphoria again.

This need feeds the "paradise lost" syndrome. Binges are indescribably pleasant for all Cokeaholics when they first indulge in them, and they will revel in the sense of relief and profound reduction of anxiety the cocaine gives them. But sustained use of large quantities of the drug often result in intensely unpleasant effects as well: anxiety, jitters, remorse, depression, impotence, and psychotic states such as paranoia. Though one would think the Cokeaholic would stop using cocaine when he felt these effects, he does not.

Because they have discovered in cocaine a deep satisfaction and pleasure they have never had before, they will subject themselves again and again to a now-unpleasant cocaine high, hoping to recapture the "paradise lost" that they first experienced from the drug. They will often pursue this lost euphoria while feeling tired, sick, nauseated, and thoroughly miserable from the effects of cocaine.

Faced with his unbearably overwhelming compulsive cocaine use, the Cokeaholic may begin doing things he never would have done in his precocaine life. An honest person may look you in the eye and lie if it means getting or protecting his cocaine; someone with no criminal tendencies or background will steal or embezzle. For some, there are eventually no limits at all to what they will do.

At some point all other sources of strength—close relationships, friendships, career—rank second to cocaine, which rapidly becomes the only source of gratification in the Cokeaholic's life. Cocaine becomes his only source for resolve, optimism, confidence. The very qualities he needs now to stop his Cokeaholic behavior are weakened by the drug, and this works to sustain his cokeaholism. He looks for strengths and can find none without the drug and is so terrified to try to do without it. This in turn increases the amount of stress in his life, thereby aggravating two of the primary factors that make him susceptible to cokeaholism in the first place.

The Cokeaholic often feels certain of only one thing: he can maintain control by taking cocaine. The more he uses it, the more he demonstrates to himself that he is in charge of how he feels, while the rest of his world collapses around him.

He feels that everything is working against him and he cannot help himself. A Cokeaholic must often surrender to his behavior until something beyond his control stops him: physical collapse, running out of money, losing his access to cocaine, arrest, hospitalization, or death.

He may insist that he loves cocaine, but he's actually terrified of what's happening to him. Of course, he doesn't want to feel that terror, and the way he avoids it is to use more cocaine to distort his feelings and emotions, substitute his fulfillment from cocaine for his fear.

What makes cokeaholism such agony, both for the

Cokeaholic and those close to him, is that in some way he is actually aware of what he's doing and is often torn by terrible conflicts: on one hand, he wants to stop, is terrified of what's happening to him, and begins to hate himself for what he's doing, and on the other, the compulsion drives him to continue the abuse; as a result he'll often become hostile to anyone who tries to help him.

But on some level, the Cokeaholic wants to be stopped. Time after time our Cokeaholic patients have told us that after they were arrested or had to be committed to a hospital, even strapped down to a bed or into a straitjacket, they felt profound relief that a force stronger than their compulsion had finally rescued them.

The expense of cocaine does impose a built-in limit for all but the wealthiest Cokeaholics. But the Cokeaholic gets around this with a binge-and-retreat cycle. He might binge day and night for a few days to a week and then recover for weeks or months, only to binge again. Some will sustain a binge for months, by alternately increasing and decreasing the amount of the drug they use. Most abusers who seek treatment do so within the first six months of the onset of their compulsive cocaine behavior, sometimes because they've pushed themselves to the point of physical or psychological collapse, but more often because they've simply run out of money or can no longer make enough money to pay for the amount of cocaine they need.

At the peak of his abuse, the Cokeaholic will often begin to display signs of psychotic behavior, due in part to the chemical effects of the drug but in some cases to underlying psychological predispositions tapped by cocaine. He may begin having delusions. He may become paranoid; some Cokeaholics are convinced people are out to get them, and carry weapons. Others concoct elaborate telephone ring codes in an effort to predict who is calling before they pick up. Many have hallucinations; the most common is that there are thousands of tiny insects—"cokeroaches" or "coke bugs"—crawling either on or under the skin. The skin itches and they will scratch at the bugs they imagine until they bleed.

The Cokeaholic has tuned out most of the rest of his life.

His dealer, with whom he will go to any lengths to stay on good terms, is his most important human contact, more significant than his wife, husband, lover, child, brother, sister, or parent. His feelings are all cocaine-related or -induced. Often he doesn't sleep, doesn't eat. He lives for the cocaine euphoria and the talkative, powerful, fulfilled self that emerges after his cocaine rush.

But following the rush is always the crash, more severe for the Cokeaholic than for any other user. Again, this is due in part to the chemical effect of the drug, but it's also due to the fact that during the crash the Cokeaholic is faced with the neglected emotional problems he avoids by using cocaine. No matter how wonderfully high a Cokeaholic may feel after a puff or shot of cocaine, he knows he's due for that sick, shaky feeling, that unbearable depression, that deep panic, the anger and irritation that comes when the rush is past. This often takes place as soon as ten to thirty minutes after the last dose, so the Cokeaholic is on a perpetual emotional roller coaster.

In treatment, many Cokeaholics have told us that they'd rather give up anything but cocaine; and a sorry number of Cokeaholics do pay for their compulsion with their relationships, careers, and sometimes their lives. But we have seen and treated many Cokeaholics who have conquered their drug problem with courage and hard work. We have worked with Cokeaholics and their families to discover and encourage each individual's resources and inner strengths. Cokeaholics can and do recover!

━━━━━━

Frank, Linda, and cocaine were like a bomb about to explode. But neither they nor anyone else realized it until it was almost too late.

Both 32, they began using cocaine occasionally about six years ago at parties with their neighbors. Their introduction to the drug could not have been more innocent. Frank is a housewares salesman in a department store and Linda is a housewife, and when they'd get together with friends, other middle-class parents whose children were in the same school with their two young daughters, someone would often lay out a few lines of coke on a mirror and pass it around after a few drinks. Frank and Linda liked it; in fact, they liked it much more than either of them ever allowed the other to see, but they both limited their use to parties.

They never discussed their instant love for cocaine with each other, although for both of them the drug released intensely special feelings of power, competence, and optimism. Frank and Linda seldom shared such profound feelings with each other. Although they had been married since they were 21 and seemed to be a contented couple, over the years they had developed a great deal of anger toward each other.

Instead of being in tune with her emotions and needs, Linda intuits others' needs and acts in the way she hopes will satisfy them. She will often behave as if she were in a good mood, if she thinks that will please Frank. No one ever has to ask Linda to do this—she has practiced it since she was a child. She learned that unless she took care of her parents by pleasing them, they often subtly withdrew their affection, filling her with fears of abandonment. Consequently, Linda now lives to satisfy other people's needs, while she is filled with her own unmet needs and ungratified desires. She was ready for the rush of gratification, confidence, and fulfillment she got from cocaine.

Frank is a perfect complement to Linda. He is self-centered, with no patience about waiting for anything he wants. When he's struck by a strong desire, he must indulge it now or else become enraged. He becomes frustrated easily. Frank is so self-absorbed that he hardly notices how his behavior affects other people. From his point of view other people, especially Linda, should give him what he wants when he wants it.

With their perfectly matched neuroses—she's the giver, he's the taker—Frank and Linda are bound together but unable to share. When they each discovered the gratification in cocaine, they retreated into their own private pursuit; they sought a way to assert their independence from each other.

It took a long time for their cokeaholism to emerge. Their social use gradually increased, and after three years they were using cocaine every weekend without fail with various groups of friends, consuming about a gram between them. Midway through the fourth year, things started to get out of control in different ways for each of them.

"I see now that we went out of our way to avoid noticing our own and each other's coke problems," says Linda. "At the time, it seemed very important to keep it all very private. It felt like the only thing I had for myself."

Linda developed into a clandestine Cokeaholic who needed to snort cocaine every day, several times a day, just to get through her normal routine, like the alcoholic housewife who knocks down three or four martinis per day, every day, just to get by. Frank, on the other hand, developed into a Cokeaholic binger who would drown himself in cocaine for days on end and then stay away from it for weeks.

For Frank it started at their weekend parties when the coke was gone. He would always find an excuse to leave for a couple of hours so that he could cop more cocaine just for himself. "I was so obvious, now that I look back on it," he explains. "I don't see how I expected anyone to believe me."

In fact, their friends didn't, but no one ever wanted to acknowledge what was going on. They would make nervous excuses for his behavior, and Linda would pass it off as if good old Frank was always on the go for something or other.

Linda's developing cokeaholism paralleled Frank's. Because of her chronic, underlying depression, the days in between their cocaine weekends became intolerable for her. For almost six months she nursed a powerful drive to get her own cocaine, but she was afraid to do it. She built up her courage by accompanying Frank and their friend Will a few times when they went to buy it. She shuddered as they drove into the run-down ghetto neighborhood where the coke connection lived. Frank and Will would disappear up a narrow hallway in a crumbling apartment building while Linda waited, and return fifteen minutes later with the cocaine.

"For weeks I walked around with two hundred dollars in my purse, trying to get up the nerve to go to that place alone.

"I took the money out of my secret bank account," she explains. "The day before I got married, my mother took me aside and told me to start an account of my own. 'You never know when you might need your own money,' she told me. 'Men are unpredictable. You can't trust them.' It's funny. It was me I couldn't trust," she says.

"I had saved exactly $8,317.46 over nine years of marriage, nipping tens and twenties out of grocery money and household expenses."

Linda finally bought herself two grams of cocaine. She was surprised to find that she had to stand on line with half a dozen other middle-class people before she was allowed to slip her money under a bolted, steel-jacketed door and then give her request through the peephole. When she got home, she secreted the two foil packets in her jewelry box.

"I don't know," she says. "As soon as I closed the drawer, I got this overwhelming feeling of security, which I hadn't felt since I was a kid."

Next morning, Linda was struck suddenly with the awareness that she was monumentally bored with her routine.

"I knew what was happening," she says. "I had the coke in the drawer, and I knew what it would do for me. I allowed myself to get depressed enough to feel I had to do something about it."

So after the kids were off to school Linda snorted a few lines and, fortified with a good buzz, floated through her morning cleanup. Two hours later she had a few more lines and dispensed with the afternoon chores, and then a few more toots two hours after that, and a couple more to get dinner prepared. Frank was in a foul mood when he came home, but after Linda did a couple of more toots in the bathroom he seemed almost agreeable. Around 1:00 A.M. her last dose wore off and Linda was overcome by depression. She swallowed a Valium and went to sleep. Next morning she couldn't wait to get the kids out of the house so that she could sniff up her first lines of the day.

Linda quickly worked her way up to three grams of co-caine a week. The whole world seemed lovelier, and all she had to do to maintain her happy existence was to re-turn to the run-down tenement and parcel out some cash. First, she returned weekly and dropped $100. Very soon she was returning twice a week and leaving behind $100 each time. Soon she started to lay in supplies for the future, just to make sure she wouldn't run out. Within three months she was sliding $500 per week under the steel door. Her $8,317.46 had dwindled to $1,200, and there was no end in sight to her desire for cocaine. By now she couldn't face the thought of a single day without six to ten lines of coke and a Valium at night. It was no longer so much fun, either. The clear, wonderful buzz she used to get now gave her a head-ache, and the exciting heart racing now felt suspiciously like the palpitations of anxiety. Her nose was always stuffed. In fact, she was now snorting the coke not so much to feel bet-ter as to avoid the nauseating, terrifying crash and then the numbing depression she knew was waiting for her after six to eight hours without the drug.

Linda kept this up until her bank account was empty, but running out of money only made her panicky for some new way to acquire her cocaine. One afternoon while she was standing on line in the smelly hallway where she bought her coke, a nice-looking, expensively dressed fellow in his mid-thirties, standing behind her, teased:

"What's a nice-looking girl like you doing in a place like this?" He suggested that they pool their money to buy co-caine for a better deal. Linda agreed and arranged to meet him there a few days later to repeat the joint purchase.

"I knew right away where it was going," she says wryly. "One thing very quickly led to another. He took me out for a drink, then to his place. Before I knew it I was in bed with him, and not long after that, he'd be picking up one or two of my grams for me if I'd go to bed with him." She curls her lip in disdain.

"He was a fence for stolen goods. Handsome, but a real snake. I was being pretty slimy then too," she says ruefully.

This man suggested that if her money was running out,

she could make some extra money by shoplifting and credit card scams.

"With that innocent doll face, you're a natural," he told her. "And I can move the goods and get you cash. Simple."

He taught her all the tricks of the trade. She was a sharp student. She learned how to bleach out the signature from a stolen credit card and substitute her own, and quickly learned how much she could charge without a store running a check on her. She also practiced stealing large, heavy objects. She hobbled around her bedroom for weeks wearing a full skirt and holding a telephone book between her thighs until she could do it with relative ease. Then she went to department stores and substituted small TVs and stereo equipment for the telephone book and minced out with hundreds of dollars of cocaine money between her legs.

"I was crazed, like some kind of fiend," Linda says. "I was a prisoner inside my own head. After a shoplifting spree, I'd come home, hit my private cocaine stash, and then pace back and forth over this one spot on the bedroom rug. I actually wore the rug out; there's a threadbare trail there."

In fact, the kick from stealing began to feel almost as good as the high from cocaine, and she continually upped the ante. First she'd snort some coke, and then make her heist, going for bigger and bigger goods, returning to the same store several times a day. Shoplifting actually became a secondary addiction for Linda, and she became as compulsive about it as she was about her cocaine use. One day a department-store floorwalker spotted her on her third trip of the afternoon.

He escorted her to the security department, where she was grilled and humiliated and scared to death. Her last dose of cocaine wore off and she began to shake, sweat, and hyperventilate.

"I was scared shitless, and the crash only made it worse," she says. "They must have thought that I was going to freak out. So they didn't call the cops. They gave me a warning and sent me home. That was it for me. Coke or no coke, I wanted no part of jail."

Linda immediately cut her cocaine use down to two to

four lines a day, only a few days a week, and was able to sneak enough out of the grocery money to pay for it. She felt like hell, but she held on and stopped seeing her helpful gentleman friend.

Meanwhile, Frank's behavior had become much more erratic, but as long as Linda could get high and feel secure and protected, she hadn't noticed what was happening to him. Now she couldn't help but see. He was spending two or three evenings a week down in the basement den with the door shut, and he was unwilling or unable to talk when he emerged. He often spent several days in a black depression. He was missing work at least one day a week, sometimes more. He'd been on the job a long time and had seniority with many sick days to cover himself, but still, it was unlike him. She did not find out until a little later that while she had been evolving into a shoplifter and having her "affair," Frank had discovered freebasing.

"I was up to two or three grams a week," Frank explains. "The freebase I'd get from one gram would do me for an evening, but I'd go on a binge. You know, start Wednesday, keep doing it Thursday and Friday, and then it would be the weekend and I'd go with Will or someone else to get my 'official' weekend coke to snort in company. In between it was murder—the crash was just awful—I'd get the shakes, chills, diarrhea. I was furious, angry as hell all the time, even at work."

These were the least of Frank's problems, though. He soon discovered that while high on cocaine, he developed intensely paranoid thoughts, psychotic delusions he believed were true. He'd believe the phone was tapped, or that someone in a car across the street was watching the house, or that Linda was in league with their neighbors to systematically drive him insane. Everyone became an enemy. When he'd snort coke with company (he never freebased except alone; it was his private pleasure, as Linda's coke use was for her), he'd believe that when he turned his head away from the drugs for a second, that someone had quickly substituted phony or diluted cocaine for the real drugs there a second earlier.

"When I'd come down, I'd wonder if all that was a delusion, if I was making it up or if it was all happening," he explains. "I stopped using coke for two months, no binges at all, and sure enough the parnoid stuff disappeared."

Frank needed to be sure, though, so he decided to "test" his conclusions with a cocaine binge. After the first hit on the freebase pipe, the paranoia flooded through him. Again he believed it was true, true, everyone was engaged in plots against him and his cocaine. It couldn't have been the coke that caused it, he reasoned.

"The feelings were just too real," he says now in wonderment.

He immediately stepped up his cocaine use to four and then five grams a week. By the end of six months he had spent the entire family savings, about $10,000, along with a $20,000 home-improvement loan, all on cocaine. He was irritable all the time with Linda and the children, even when he was not high on coke. Linda had begun asking him to go for help, but that seemed to do more harm than good. Anything could set him off. One day Linda said he looked tired. This became the stimulus for a devastating paranoid fantasy.

"It was crazy," he says. "I was afraid Linda was slowly murdering me, putting poison in my food. I was convinced she was, that my whole family was trying to kill me."

Frightened for his life, Frank threw a butcher knife at Linda and fled from the house. He jumped into the car, gunned the engine, and screeched out of the driveway, plowing up the lawn and bouncing off a few of the neighbors' cars before he got to the highway. He jammed the gas pedal to the floor and roared down the road at ninety until the fear subsided. This kind of maniacal driving fit became his outlet for paranoid rages seven or eight more times over the next month or two.

"Looking back, I suppose I knew it was better to chance wrecking the car or myself than maybe killing Linda," he says.

His luck finally ran out, though. One night he ran off a curve in the highway and rolled the car over into a stand of trees. He was not injured, but the ambulance crew that arrived insisted on taking him to the hospital emergency room for a quick check. There, the intern who examined him spotted some of the signs of cocaine intoxication and began to ask the right questions. Shaken, heading into his cocaine crash, and finally aware of how badly he wanted something to stop him from his cocaine binges, Frank told him everything, broke down in hysterics, and later promised Linda to go into therapy with her.

At the time we interviewed them, Frank and Linda had been in couples therapy for eight months and neither of them had touched any cocaine. They'd begun to learn to communicate with each other and examine the problems that were destroying their marriage. Linda took a part-time job in the cosmetics section of a department store, and she found it helped build her confidence and reduce her depression. Frank insisted that he was really all right, that it was the cocaine that drew him in against his will like nothing else could have, but he has begun to acknowledge that the real reason for his abuse is related to deep psychological problems. Whenever either of them feels weak, ready to go get some coke, they reevaluate their life together and survey the wreckage that they're trying to clear up—the tens of thousands of dollars lost, the violence, Frank's brush with death in his car accident—and they remind themselves that any life has to be better than the one they had before.

Heads turn when Tina walks into a room. She is 23, five feet eight, 115 pounds, and stunningly beautiful. Her eyes are brilliant blue with a touch of green.

All her life Tina has known the power of her physical appeal. She learned to charm people to get her way before she was 2 years old and has been remarkably successful at it. But her beauty has also worked against her. Her mother envied her and had difficulty giving Tina the praise she needed. She was also obsessed with cleanliness and couldn't tolerate little Tina's normal child's share of mess and disorder. She scrubbed, wiped, and mopped after Tina everywhere, and her obsession imbued Tina with an exaggerated sense of her own disorderliness and a vigilance about uncleanliness. Her continuous disapproval made Tina feel inadequate.

Her father burdened her with another problem: he showered little Tina with compliments, but only for her prettiness. He rarely praised her for being smart, or kind, or honest, or accomplished. Tina recognized that his praise was excessive and began to doubt it. Most of all she became acutely aware that Daddy needed a pretty child or he'd be unhappy. She got the message: take care of Daddy by being pretty, and he'll take care of you.

The result is a breathtakingly beautiful woman who knows how to use her looks to get whatever she wants, but at bottom never believes she is all that attractive. She is constantly on the alert for the first signs of deterioration in her physical appearance.

Tina began part-time modeling when she was 15, and as she matured she rapidly acquired a succession of charming suitors. Then, during the last half of her senior year in high school, she met George.

Everyone was baffled because George was not Tina's type. He had no dash, no style. He was overweight, sloppy, had little money, and drove a noisy, rusty old Volkswagen. George never took Tina anywhere nice, like her other boyfriends had; in fact, he hardly took her anywhere at all. Yet he seemed to exert some phenomenal pull on Tina. He was the first boyfriend whom she did not overpower; instead, he was in charge and Tina meekly did his bidding. It was only much later that she finally understood the magnetic power George seemed to have over her.

"I always got everything I wanted with my looks, but I was never sure of myself. I had no self-esteem at all and I was always waiting to be revealed as a worthless fraud. I'd go over my modeling photo contact sheets with a magnifying glass and see nothing but imperfections. My friends didn't understand. They'd say I was the most beautiful girl they knew.

"But George would see," she explains. "When I said my

face was too flat, he'd notice I was right. If I said I was fat, he'd suggest I lose another few pounds. I felt like I belonged with George—he knew about me what no one else knew, the terrible things, all my doubts, my fears, my real self. I needed him."

George had tapped into Tina's deep ambivalence about herself, her crushing lack of self-worth. He was magnetic to her because he responded directly to her feelings. It did not matter that the feelings were negative and often did not coincide with reality.

George made his living selling marijuana. He liked cocaine and eagerly used it whenever one of his pot connections threw some his way. Tina never had a taste for drugs and refused them when George offered them to her.

"He really loved his drugs, though," she says. "He never really offered me any, if you know what I mean. It was just a gesture. He never wanted to share them."

When Tina graduated from high school she landed a secretarial job in Manhattan and moved into a tiny, expensive apartment. Her parents were dead set against it.

"It wasn't like they cared so much about me or anything," she explains. "They just always wanted to control me."

Her secretarial job and occasional modeling work barely paid the rent. George, meanwhile, was now dealing exclusively in cocaine and making money. He bought a new car, new clothes, and he began to give Tina money, too.

For three years Tina continued her modeling career and George expanded his drug business. He now drove a Mercedes and gave Tina wads of money whenever he saw her, but she wanted something else.

"I wanted to get married," she told us. "I mean, we'd never even lived together. I told George, I insisted." She began to sob. "That was when he told me he was already married to someone else. He had been since he met me. The bastard. But he said he would get a divorce; he swore he'd be free in six months."

George pleaded with Tina to let him put her up in an apartment. It was a perfect arrangement—she would be free to do what she wanted, while he paid all the expenses, and he'd have a safe place to keep his large stash of cocaine. Thinking this was a prelude to their marriage, Tina accepted the deal and moved into a glass-walled high rise twenty stories above the city. Her "job," George explained, would be to keep a low profile and, above all, keep her mouth shut about what was under the platform bed—rows and rows of metal containers and plastic bags of cocaine, hundreds of thousands of dollars' worth neatly packed into shoeboxes.

Tina began to feel isolated. George came over only to pick up or to deliver cocaine and to give Tina her weekly "pay" of $500. He never came to socialize, seldom made love to her, never took her anywhere. He'd breeze in, perhaps snort a few lines of coke, always offering some to Tina, who always refused. Tina had quit her job, she never invited her friends over because she felt funny having them up to what she thought of as her "kept woman's" place, and she rarely even saw George now. She became more and more depressed and blamed herself for all that was wrong. She searched for the reason she had failed. Was she losing her looks? Was she too fat? Was she getting old? She was all of 22.

One day she decided to help herself to some of George's damned cocaine. She set up a few lines for herself as she had seen him do so many times and snorted them up. As the drug's effects hit her, Tina underwent an immediate transformation for which she was completely unprepared.

"I had never liked drugs," she says. "They always made me feel sick. But this, this was—I don't know how to describe the first time. It was like I was flying, like the glass walls of the apartment fell away and I soared out over the city. I hadn't felt so good in months—in my whole life really. I felt like I was finally perfect—my body was perfect, I felt courageous, powerful, gorgeous."

Tina knew nothing about cocaine, though she was sleeping on over half a million dollars' worth of it. About an hour later, she simply dipped into some more, just before crawling into bed to watch the "Late Show." The next morning, she woke, showered, and immediately went to the shoebox for another four lines. George would never miss it; he said she could have some. And besides, it made her feel wonderful. Tina used cocaine every day for a week, snorting four to six lines whenever she wanted some. She quickly fell into the cocaine abuser's cycle—get high, crash, take some more to stop the crash, get high, crash, take some more.

"I couldn't tell you how much I was using," she says. "All I can say is that one day I never touched the stuff, and three days later I was using a lot of it, all the time."

By the time she saw George and mentioned that she'd been getting into the coke, strange things had already started happening to her. No one had ever told Tina about cocaine's nasty side effects—paranoid thoughts, delusions —so she didn't recognize what was happening. George took little notice of her, as usual, and brushed aside her odd questions.

"George, look at my teeth," she asked, forcing a wide grin. "Are they turning a funny gray color? George, I think there's a bad smell coming from me. Do you smell it? George, do you think I'm too fat?" George was too busy to answer.

Tina was in a state of cocaine paranoia. Her teeth had not changed color and she did not smell. She'd sit in the apartment, stoned on coke, now examining her teeth in the mirror, now bathing three and four times a day to rid herself of her imaginary odor. Soon she began to believe that her old friends were talking about her.

"They think I'm some kind of whore to live like this with George," she thought, panicked. Then she began to wonder about him. Had he deliberately set her up, surrounded by all that cocaine, just so she'd start using it? Why would he do that? And why did her teeth seem to be getting darker and grayer? Would they turn black?

By Tina's third week of constant cocaine use, she found that even if she used enough to avoid her crash and slept only when she literally collapsed, she began to feel profoundly depressed while she was high on cocaine. She would feel "wired," intensely agitated and depressed at the same time, a common result of ingesting excessive amounts of cocaine over a sustained period. In her depression she counted her flaws. Her gray teeth were what she hated most. She made an appointment to see a dentist.

"I want you to pull them all out," she told him. After an examination revealed not even a cavity, he naturally refused her request.

Tina stomped out of the office. Systematically going through the "Dentists" section of the Yellow Pages, she pursued dentist after dentist over several weeks, until she finally found one who complied: he pulled all of her perfect teeth and hurriedly fitted her with a set of upper and lower plates. For twenty-four hours Tina felt relieved. She had trouble keeping the dentures in place and her mouth hurt, but at least these artificial teeth wouldn't turn gray. Whenever the horror of having no teeth descended on her, she'd snort some more of George's coke to forget.

Then Tina was faced with another delusion. She seemed to be covered day and night with thousands of tiny, itching insects. No one had told her about coke bugs, and in her state she wouldn't have believed them anyway. She gouged her arms and legs with her long nails, scratching, trying to take out the bugs—they were driving her mad. They were so small they were virtually invisible, but they were everywhere, on her, in her clothes, in the bed. Tina called the exterminator every week for three weeks. Each time the fellow looked at her strangely, sprayed, and left. Finally, in a panic of itching, she called her friend Ruthie and told her to rush over right away.

Ruthie, who had not seen Tina in about a month, was appalled at what she saw. Tina looked like a skeleton. She was horrified when Tina told her what she'd done with her teeth.

"Oh, that's nothing," Tina insisted, dragging her friend around the place by the arm. "It's these goddamned bugs that are important." Her friend was amazed as Tina stood there scratching herself. She made her friend look under the bed, in the kitchen cabinets, in the closets. "I know you can't see them, but they're here," she insisted, now drawing blood from her lacerated arms. "They're all over. They're driving me crazy."

"There are no bugs here," her friend insisted. "It's the cocaine that's making you itch. You're killing yourself, Tina. Please promise me you'll stop."

This was not what Tina wanted to hear. "Yes, yes," she promised and hustled her friend out the door.

Tina continued to use coke every day for about two more months. The bugs got worse and worse, Tina's arms were covered with sores from constant scratching, and her weight fell to 90 pounds. She almost never left the apartment and George had stopped even cursory conversations with her when he came by. One day she went out to pick up some juice; when she returned half an hour later, the door to the apartment was swinging on its hinges, the lock and door-jamb shattered by a crowbar. The entire place had been ripped to shreds. Even the carpet was sliced up. Her belongings were dumped everywhere. And all of George's cocaine was gone. Someone had obviously been watching her comings and goings.

"I was crazy, but not that crazy," she said. "I packed up some clothes and got the hell out of there and went to my grandmother's."

But this was not the end of Tina's cocaine use. She still needed it, the more often the better. She couldn't bear how she felt without it. She borrowed money from friends, from her grandmother, from business acquaintances. She begged her friends who used it socially to give her cocaine whenever they had some. Then she started to steal money for coke. She hung out in singles bars where she knew there was co-caine and went to bed with men who offered it to her. But without George and the easy access to his coke, it was hard to continue, it took too much of her time.

"I stole all my grandma's jewelry and hocked it to buy coke," she says, her voice cracking. "I felt awful about it, but I just couldn't stop myself. I needed that coke to feel okay again. Actually, without it I felt I wanted to die. Once I got up there with it, I just couldn't face coming down."

Tina stopped only when all her means for getting cocaine were exhausted. She finally collapsed, so physically and emotionally shattered that she had to stay in a darkened room for the first week. Ruthie had been waiting in the wings and showed up to nurse her back to some semblance of health.

"Ruthie became my mother for two weeks," Tina explains. "She sat in that room with me and held me, rocked me like a baby, reassured me, fed me. She took two weeks off from work to do that. She saved my life." Ruthie helped Tina find a therapist and then drove her to therapy twice a week for the first month to make sure she got there.

At this point, Tina has been in therapy for six months and is holding her own. In fact, she's healthier than she's ever been. And she has no illusions about her experience with cocaine.

"For me, cocaine was poison, almost death," she says. "There's nothing good in it for me. This is all I got for it."

She passes her hand across her lovely face and lowers it to her lap. It is a mountebank's gesture. In her hand she holds her false teeth, upper and lowers. Her gorgeous model's face is now completely collapsed upon itself; it is the face of an old woman with the skin of a young girl. Thanks to cocaine, Tina's beautiful white teeth and perfect smile are gone forever. Tina, like many recovered Cokeaholics, is less tempted to return to using cocaine because the negative consequences are so painfully remembered.

You'd never guess that Mickey grew up on the streets. He has none of the bravado or harshness that sometimes gives away street kids who have made something of their lives. He's sensitive and caring and always has time for other people's problems.

Mickey sustained some significant losses early in his life. His father and both his grandparents died the year he was 5. His mother could never support them and never remarried. Mickey remembers always being poor. He got his first job at 7, sweeping out a neighborhood candy store, and never stopped working. He learned early that he could count only on one thing: what he went out and got for himself. He also learned that though he might have sad or angry feelings, the trick was not to display them. He could go home and cry, but outside, he had to be cool, to hustle, to find odd jobs while he was in school.

Although he was dogged by feelings of inadequacy, hurt, and anger, he came across as assertive and confident because that got him what he needed: money, respect, and some control of his life. In fact, he was never comfortable acting aggressive, and no matter how successful he was, he always felt that everything he got was only temporarily his. Because of his history of loss, he felt a constant need for vigilance; at any moment everything might be taken away.

Mickey managed to get into college on an academic scholarship and while he was there he fell in love with a lovely—and extremely wealthy—young woman named Laura. Just as he had risen above his spirit-crushing origins, she had risen above being a spoiled upper-class child. Laura had soul, and she and Mickey immediately fell in love. They married right after graduation.

"I really had no idea about what I wanted to do after college," Mickey says. "I'd always been into electronics, and one day when Laura asked me what I wanted, I told her about my fantasy—I said, 'I'd like to own a chain of stereo equipment stores.' This was back in the early seventies, when that concept was just getting hot. 'Okay,' she said. 'How much will it cost?' I looked into it and came up with the numbers—nearly two hundred thousand dollars just to open the doors on the first one. Two weeks later Laura presented me with a bank letter of credit. She'd sold off some of her investment portfolio to raise the money. 'After all,' she said, 'someone's got to support me in the style to which I'm accustomed.' So I went ahead and did it."

Although Laura raised the initial money, Mickey made the business go, and within two years he'd expanded the first store into a chain of six and was taking home $250,000 a year.

"Not bad for a kid from the streets, eh?" he says. "I'd never been more than a hundred miles from home before, and now we were vacationing three or four times a year in Barbados, Europe, Saint Bart's. I had everything."

Mickey treated himself to a silver Porsche 911S and a wardrobe of custom-made clothes. His business was cruelly demanding—he spent fourteen- and sixteen-hour days at the stores, with no days off, for two or three months at a time. When he would find himself reeling from the pressure, he would jump into his car, head onto one of the parkways, and drive out his tension. He was also aware that he was feeling more than just the tensions from work.

"There was always that lingering feeling that anything might happen. I mean, here I was, poor, struggling, and then boom—I met Laura—and then boom—I have this business and suddenly I'm rich. It was too weird. I felt like I was living on borrowed time, like everything could evaporate as fast as it had materialized."

Although he loved Laura and their marriage was good, he began to feel dependent on her; it terrified him. His work, his love, it was all related to Laura. Though it was he who had made the business into a thriving success, he could never shake the feeling that he was somehow at her mercy, not in complete control of his life. He felt more tension; he began getting headaches and back pains. Laura was aware that Mickey seemed to be spending more and more time in his car late at night, roaring around the highways trying to "ride it out."

Mickey and Laura first tried cocaine at a friend's house. They both enjoyed the sense of euphoria, the way the evening seemed to sparkle. When the cocaine was finished, everyone was ready to take a Valium and go to sleep. Everyone, that is, except Mickey. Mickey had made a discovery: he knew he'd like the feeling from the coke without the company. The high had made him forget about everything: the tension, the stores, his sense of dependency on Laura. The cocaine made him feel in control and instantly dispelled the nagging insecurity he had felt since he was 7 years old. He felt safe. Protected.

For a month, Mickey thought about that splendid coke-induced state. But he never tried to buy the drug; he suspected that cocaine might be very dangerous for him.

Sometime later, Mickey met Bobby, one of their neighbors, in the hallway of their apartment building. Bobby invited him into his apartment. Once inside, Mickey discovered that although Bobby was in the music business, he supplemented his income by dealing a few ounces of cocaine a week to pay for his own supply. Mickey and Bobby snorted up half a gram in about an hour, and Mickey bought a gram to take home with him.

From the next morning on, Mickey began to use cocaine daily. Instead of his morning coffee, he would start every day with a short walk down the hall to Bobby's place, where he'd buy one gram of cocaine for $125. He never bought more, never less. That was how he controlled his cokeaholism. He quickly developed a rationing system whereby he'd dole out cocaine to himself through the course of the day. He even doodled the equation on his note pads at work:

2 lines = Ignition on
4 lines = Energized
6 lines = Supercharged
8 lines = All systems go—feeling no pain—anything is possible.

"It was very crazy," he told us, "but for the first time in my life I felt like I was completely in control of everything. I could control my emotional state to the nth degree; it was just like fine-tuning the carburetor on my Porsche. I could predict exactly how I'd feel in half an hour just by varying my dose."

Mickey used a gram a day, seven days a week, for about six weeks before anyone noticed. He went to work religiously and functioned pretty well; he felt like a dynamo and he kept up his most important connections. But his employees and managers noticed that for all his running around, things were not getting done. They picked up the slack without comment.

Since Mickey's long hours kept them apart during the week, it was on the weekends that Laura first began to notice his strange behavior. She saw that he was eating less and had trouble waking up in the morning. She noticed that he seemed to want to spend more time alone.

"I knew all the time I was right on the edge of completely losing it," Mickey says. "I knew, and I was scared shitless, but goddamn, I just felt so good. So I tried to cut down, but that didn't work. Then I told myself I'd have one last weekend fling—I'd snort my brains out Saturday and Sunday and then quit. But I was back at Bobby's door at eight A.M. Monday morning."

Mickey slid into compulsive, uncontrolled daily cocaine abuse. Laura confronted him with it. He tried to convince her that he had it under control; she kept after him to stop. They had fierce battles about his constant coke use. She tried reasoning with him, threatening him, coaxing him, but nothing worked.

Within three months he was snorting at least eight thick lines at a sitting, consuming two or three grams per day, Monday through Friday. Saturday and Sunday he'd crash. Every Friday he'd promise Laura that this was the last time, but it never was. Laura would awaken three nights a week at 2:00 A.M. to find him missing from their bed, out driving to cope with the crash.

"The crash was brutal, unbearable," Mickey says. "I'd fire up the car and just burn down the road. I'd go two hundred miles before the sun came up. I'd drive all night to fight it off, but after a couple of months that wasn't enough. I needed something more." Desperate, Mickey tried everything to make himself feel better—Valium, codeine, Sominex, it didn't matter.

"It was a good thing I was making so much money. I was dropping fifteen hundred dollars a week on coke and pills, but I never got to the point of skimming money out of the business to pay for it," he says.

Mickey would stop using cocaine for one day, and in the midst of the crash he'd be flooded with remorse and feel committed to stopping for good. But the coke was so close— right down the hall. All he had to do was to see Bobby and all his insecurities and fears would vanish.

After about four or five months, Mickey rose one night at 2:00 A.M., left Laura a note saying he was out driving off his crash, packed a change of clothes and three grams of cocaine, stuffed $1,500 in his pocket, pulled his car out of the garage, and headed west. He had no idea where he was going to go. As he roared through the night, he went over and over his situation. He couldn't face what he had become. He knew he needed help, but he didn't know where to get it; he wanted to stop using cocaine, but the idea of letting go of that incomparable high was unthinkable. He was afraid to face Laura, afraid of what was happening to their marriage. He didn't know if they could ever make it right again. He was afraid to go to work. He was afraid of everything. He was even afraid to stop the car, and somewhere in the middle of Pennsylvania, he opted not to. Mickey decided to drive to Los Angeles.

"God knows what I was thinking," he says. "All I knew at that point was that driving always helped me with the crash, with getting rid of tension, with sorting things out. Anything was better than facing what was back in New York. I snorted all the cocaine I had in about forty-eight hours, and the crash really hit me somewhere in Colorado. By the time I got to Las Vegas, I felt like I was having some kind of breakdown. I couldn't stop crying, couldn't drive, couldn't sit, couldn't stand. I called Laura."

Relieved to know at last where Mickey was, Laura talked him home, state by state. He'd drive until he thought he would fall apart, and then stop and pick up the phone and she'd tell him everything was all right. By the time he got home two days later, she had found a therapist for him, and for the next three weeks, Mickey didn't go to work, or even leave the house, except to see the therapist.

"I knew the big thing was the temptation, you know?" he says. "I was afraid to go out because I thought I'd go right back to Bobby's and start all over again. That was all I could think about when I was alone. After the third week, I told Laura to find us another apartment, right away."

Within ten days they had moved.

"I was right," he says. "Once I was out of there, I wasn't thinking about coke twenty-four hours a day."

Mickey and Laura struggled to save their marriage. About six months later, Mickey had one more intense bout with cocaine, but it lasted only two weeks and he hasn't touched any in three years. His life has changed a good deal. He's learned how to get angry and not turn it inward on himself, and he's recovered some of his old self-sufficiency and drive. He and Laura still lead an energetic life and Mickey is constantly alert to temptation that might lead him to another relapse, but he figures that as long as he never touches cocaine again, he'll be fine.

"It's just too dangerous," he says, and he has remained true to his word. He has a thriving business and a happy home.

━━━━━━

When Missy was a little girl in Michigan, she believed her father was magical. He took her everywhere with him—to ball games, on fishing trips, even to work sometimes. She was his pride and joy. Their relationship was truly special. "You are a princess," he'd tell her, "and that makes me a king." Missy idolized him.

One day when she was 9, Missy came home from school to find her mother in hysterics. Missy's father had just been arrested for embezzling from his real estate firm. The little girl was devastated. Her father was convicted and sentenced to prison. From then on, Missy's mother spoke of her father as if he were anathema. Because of their financial situation, Missy and her mother had to move, so Missy lost all her friends as well as her father. She felt as if it were her fault that everyone she loved except her angry mother suddenly had been taken from her. And her mother shackled Missy with an agonizing demand: she insisted that Missy tell people that her father was dead.

Missy did not grow up feeling very sure about anything except that deep down she always believed that she was responsible for her father's downfall.

When she was 16, Missy discovered alcohol. When she drank with her high school friends she was the one who always had to be carried home unconscious. Drinking made her forget her bad feelings. She did not drink every day, but when she did it was often to excess.

Still, she did well in school and went on to college. In her freshman year she met an older man (he was 35) and fell deeply in love with him. She knew from the time she met him that he was married, and although he was loving, he made it clear he was not sure he wanted to leave his wife and children. Their affair continued throughout Missy's college years. Though there were many men her own age who were interested in her, she elected to stay with James, who reminded her of her father.

After she finished college she landed a good job as an assistant buyer for a department store in Lansing. But when James's company told him they were transferring him to their main office in New York City and he swore to her that when he was settled there he would leave his wife, Missy quit her new job, packed up her belongings, left all her friends and relatives, and followed him to Manhattan.

She was lucky enough to quickly land another department-store buyer's job and she found a cramped and prohibitively expensive apartment. But she was miserable in New York. James's business and social life had picked up, and she saw less and less of him. New York seemed like a cold, frightening foreign country. The people were aggressive, loud, and competitive. She had always had difficulty making friends with other women, and she had no friends at all in New York. She felt stranded and alone as she watched her relationship with James disintegrate. She settled more and more deeply into depression. She had no support network, no one to talk to; she was completely alone. She began to drink and to remember how she felt when her father went away. She had fleeting thoughts of killing herself if James deserted her, but she pushed them out of her mind.

Missy decided she needed to get away. On impulse, she booked a trip to a Club Med in the Caribbean and flew down with a group of singles. Her first night there she met Bret. He was young, charming, and handsome, a wholesale stationery supplies salesman on his way up the career ladder, he said. He swept her off her feet.

From the moment they met, he seemed awed by her, almost worshipful. He showered her with compliments and gave her his total attention. After six months of feeling neglected by James, she gave herself up to her whirlwind affair with Bret.

By the third day, he had brought up the notion that they might think about getting married. He said he'd never been so involved so fast before. Missy was surprised, but it also made her feel wonderful—accepted, rescued, special, the way her father had made her feel. Bret squired her around the resort, proudly, protectively, bought her gifts, and during their two weeks together Missy became more and more comfortable with the idea of staying with him.

But by the time their plane touched down in New York, Missy was overcome by a surge of nauseating depression and agitation. It increased as soon as she kissed Bret goodbye and hailed a cab for home. He had said nothing about when he would call her. Her apartment seemed like a prison, and she realized that except for Bret, she knew no one in the entire city whom she could call. She sat alone in her apartment, unable to move, unable to cry.

Just when she had convinced herself she would never see him again, the phone rang. When she heard Bret's voice on the other end, she thought she might sail through the roof with joy and relief. Yes, he could see her; yes, whenever he wanted, wherever he said. Missy felt as if she'd been given a reprieve from death row.

She and Bret instantly became a couple and he filled all the emptiness in her life. He was eager to be with her all the time. No one but her father had ever paid so much attention to her. She ignored the occasional suspicion about his intensity. Anything she wanted, he bought for her; anywhere she wanted to go, he took her.

He began talking seriously about marriage. Missy was delighted when he proposed. She accepted immediately. Their sex life had always been satisfactory, but as they prepared for bed on the first night of their honeymoon, Bret unpacked a small drawstring bag that he had tucked in a corner of his suitcase.

"I want you to wear these," he said, as he laid some objects out on the bed. At first Missy was curious despite Bret's coldness, but then she became apprehensive. He was carefully, ritualistically, laying out a satin garter belt, crotchless panties, fishnet stockings, a pair of patent leather stiletto-heeled pumps, all black. There was also a bottle of cheap perfume and a small collection of theatrical makeup—dark rouge, blood-red lipstick, turquoise eyeshadow. The last thing he unpacked was a can of hairspray. "I want you to look like a real whore," he said.

Dressing up for Bret might have been fun if he had been playful, but he was rough, almost mean.

"Go ahead," Bret said, motioning toward the bathroom. Missy gathered up the things and shut the door behind her. She was beginning to feel frightened. The stockings scratched her skin. She lightly dabbed on the makeup, trying to be subtle, and touched only the smallest drops of the awful perfume behind her ears. She passed up the hairspray, slid her feet into the stiletto heels, and opened the bathroom door. When Bret saw her he was furious.

"No, no!" he shouted, exasperated. "I want you to look like a real whore," and he made her put on more of the lipstick and heavily paint her eyelids. He rouged her cheeks until they were a deep, ugly red. Then he teased up her hair into a ragged thatch and sprayed it stiff with the hairspray. All the while she sat perfectly still, mystified and scared. Then he poured a pool of the cheap perfume into his hands and doused her all over with it. Missy thought the smell would make her vomit.

He marched back out to the bedroom and sprawled on the bed.

"All right, Missy," he said. "Play it up. I want you to shake your ass and act like you're making five bucks on this deal."

Missy did as best she could. She felt like she was being raped; Bret didn't make love to her, he brutalized her. He turned her from position to position, manipulated her as if she were a manikin, and gave curt, abusive commands. He demanded that she utter obscenities. Bret was a stranger to her—she hated him. When it was over, he slept like a baby. They had brought a bottle of Scotch into the room with them, and the only way she could get to sleep was to slug down burning drafts of it.

The next morning Bret apologized. Missy was too exhausted and frightened to question him; she feared that if she complained he'd abandon her and she'd be left completely alone.

During the honeymoon, Bret's behavior continued to change. Besides the sexual dramatics, which he insisted on every night, his attentiveness turned into possessiveness. He would not let Missy out of his sight for a minute. He stopped wanting to spend money on her. He told her she was spoiled beyond belief. He was a different Bret from the one she knew before they were married.

Missy felt more and more lonely—she still had not made any women friends—and she and Bret fought all the time about money, about sex, about everything. He never wanted sex unless she dressed up like a dime-store hooker. She began stopping off after work for a drink just to prepare herself to go home. She wasn't ready to give up on the marriage, but it was getting harder and harder to participate in Bret's kinky sex routine; she was having trouble going through with it even after a few drinks.

Bret was aware of this. He decided that Missy needed a little something to make it easier for her to comply with his demands, loosen her up, make her less inhibited, and he thought some cocaine might do it. He'd used it a few times and it had been a sexual turn-on for him. An old buddy of his was a coke dealer, so it was easy to get some. The buddy, Phil, suggested that for sex, freebasing would be just the thing. Phil showed Bret how to set up the freebase and the pipe and sent him home with the equipment and two grams of cocaine.

Bret took a toke from the pipe and handed it to Missy, and after her first inhalation, it seemed that she had stepped into a completely different dimension. All her loneliness, fear, depression, evaporated. She felt ecstatic, like a child, completely safe, just as she had with her father when she was 5 or 6? It was magic. Bret let her smoke a whole gram by herself over three or four hours. Missy went to get the hooker paraphernalia herself, dressed up, and again threw herself into the role for Bret. She didn't care what he wanted her to pretend to be. She was in heaven, and she barely noticed the sex with him. She was enjoying her own private ecstasy.

When she woke up the next morning, Missy was filled with an all-consuming dread and a burning desire for more cocaine. She enticed Bret into giving her the rest of the coke from the night before by promising a sexual performance unlike anything he'd ever seen before. Bret quickly realized how to get what he wanted, and for a few weeks he brought home enough coke to last a whole weekend. But Missy was way ahead of him. From the first day, she wanted cocaine all the time, every day. Nothing had ever made her feel that good, and when she stopped using it and the crash came, it was like a visit with Death. She felt not only all the physical effects, the shaking, jitters, paranoia, but also a hopelessness so overwhelming that she thought she would surely die from it. Nothing helped but more coke.

She begged and begged Bret for more, but after two weeks he refused to spend the money. Missy quickly wiped out her bank account buying grams from Phil, and when she had no more money, she offered herself as payment. He took her up on it. As long as he'd let her freebase at his place and give her some to take home, she'd perform any sexual act he asked for and any his friends or clients might ask for too, if she happened to be there. It didn't matter; she could feel nothing but the wonderful cocaine bliss anyway.

After a few months, Bret was frightened by Missy's behavior. She was rarely home. On several occasions, he'd come home while she was freebasing and she was so high she didn't even recognize him. She was buying and consuming nearly a gram a day, every day, plus the extra she got from Phil once or twice a week. Her habit was costing about $500 a week. She had quit her job because she could no longer get out of bed in the morning, but she'd found a way to keep herself supplied. In fact, Bret had shown her the way. She had learned her hooker role so well she had started playing it for real. Now, in the evening, she would have a drink or two in one of the better bars or hotels in town. A snort or two of coke beforehand and she'd be ready to go. The out-of-towners paid the best. And she could make her week's cocaine tab in two nights and not feel a thing.

One evening she was complaining bitterly to Phil about how Bret kept bothering her, insisting that she was going overboard with cocaine and that she should stop. She was sick of it. Phil had always liked her; Missy was completely established at Phil's place within forty-eight hours.

For four or five months, Missy did nothing but freebase or snort cocaine most of the day. All Phil had to do was keep her supplied and she did whatever he asked. He worked her into his dealer act. Before Missy, he'd titillate his upper-class clients by holding court on a pillow with a loaded Walther 9-mm automatic pistol enthroned on a smaller cushion next to him. They loved the theater, and now he added Missy to it. He outfitted her in negligees and sat her on a cushion on the other side of the gun. The customers liked that even more, and when they found out that part of Phil's service included a short session in the bedroom with Missy at no extra charge if their purchase was large enough, business improved about 300 percent.

But after a while, cocaine began to take its toll on Missy. She'd become more of a drain than an asset to Phil.

"She looked like hell," he says. "Her eyes were sunken and she must have weighed about ninety pounds. She looked so wasted she was starting to scare off some of my customers. And sometimes when she was crashing, she'd get into this horrible depression, cry for hours and hours, even when I'd give her some Percodan. She'd tell me all this stuff about her childhood and her father. I thought she might be losing her mind, you know?"

Phil decided she had to go. He decided to tell her one night after the end of his business day, at around 1:00 A.M. He put away his sample tray and set the pistol on the top shelf of the closet. He sat down on the living room couch next to Missy, who was blissfully sucking at the freebase pipe. She didn't even flinch when he told her she'd have to leave.

Exhausted, he lay back and started to doze off. Missy wandered into the bedroom, leaving the freebase pipe behind. Half an hour or so passed and, more asleep than awake, it occurred to Phil that Missy hadn't come back for another puff. He knew she must be far into her crash by now, deep in despair. Why wasn't she back out here smoking or crying? His lazy thoughts were shattered by the ear-splitting blast from his pistol in the next room. For a moment Phil did not believe what he knew had happened. He ran into the bedroom. What he saw when he flicked on the light made even his granite drug dealer's heart flop over in his chest.

"She was on the bed, in a negligee, you know," he says. "Everything looked normal from the neck down. But her brains were all over the wall."

Handsome and engaging, Ed is a 35-year-old former stockbroker who used to make $200,000 a year in the market. He seemed to have it made, but despite his sumptuous apartment, fine clothes, and savvy with money, Ed's inner world was not a very happy one.

If we had asked him back then if he felt lonely, inadequate, afraid, or incompetent, he would probably have laughed. But these were in fact the dominant emotions that shaped his life, even though he had repressed them. He could never maintain a lasting or fulfilling relationship with any of his friends or with the beautiful women he dated. In a way that was all right with him, though, because getting involved with someone made him feel trapped, stifled, and sometimes on the verge of panic. He was happy to take a woman out, wine and dine her, take her to bed, but he always cut her loose when things got complicated.

Ed had always felt like the black sheep of his family. "I was the one who never did quite as well as my two brothers," he says. "Looking back, I see that I didn't do so badly either, but my parents always made it seem like I just never measured up somehow. When I got a ninety on a test, one of my brothers always came home with a ninety-six. It seemed that nothing I did was ever good enough."

Both his older brothers had preceded him through junior high and high school, where they made reputations as powerhouses of athletic and academic talent. By the time Ed got to junior high he felt handicapped by their reputations, and he refused to compete in the popular sports, as they had, and instead chose the track team. He got by with B's and C's instead of A's, and he hung out with a more rebellious crowd of kids.

The truth was that Ed had drawn the short straw when family roles were handed out. By the time he was born, his two older brothers were already the aggressive achievers, and the family needed an easygoing soul to counterbalance his hard-driven father and brothers. From the beginning, Ed's parents unconsciously began to reward him for being easygoing. His parents could not tolerate his bad moods or expressions of unhappiness or anger—they would withdraw from him. Ed was in training to be the "nice" son, not for his benefit, but for everyone else's. Whenever he expressed discomfort or emotional pain, his parents would distract him rather than respond with support.

By the time he was about 7, Ed knew that he had to maintain a facade of never needing help, always being able to get along on a minimum of attention, and of never, but never, expressing pain. In the end, he stopped allowing himself ever to feel his pain, and from the moment he began to repress it, the seeds of his depression grew.

Despite being "not so brilliant," Ed's best subject in college was chemistry, one of the toughest courses. His interest in chemistry fed his desire to play with his moods with drugs, which became almost a hobby for him. He kept a copy of the *Physicians' Desk Reference* and read a lot of the popular literature on drugs: pills, marijuana, LSD. Even with his consuming interest, though, he did not develop anything like a drug problem. He functioned more as a connoisseur of mood-altering substances, not an abuser.

Significantly, while both Ed's brothers went on to medical school, Ed chose not to do so, even with his strengths in the sciences. He became a stockbroker and quickly earned success. By the time he was 28, he had his own office and was a young hotshot.

The first time Ed tried cocaine, it was like turning the corner and bumping into the girl of his dreams. After his first few snorts he felt omnipotent; in fact, it was the first time he could remember that he had ever felt such a clear sense of mastery, power, and control. These were the emotions he had always wanted but could never feel. Still, his use of the drug did not become dangerously excessive. He used it socially, and something told him not to buy coke for himself. That is until Kathy, a woman he had just started seeing, introduced him to freebasing.

Ed and Kathy had used cocaine at parties and she knew he liked it, so she decided to give him his own freebase kit and some cocaine for his birthday. Ed liked Kathy—smart, vivacious, she was always ready with a new kick. She prepared the coke for freebasing and handed the pipe to Ed.

"When the first toke hit me, it was all over," Ed says.

He smoked all the coke she gave him, almost four grams, all day long until it was gone. Kathy thought it was funny that he seemed to shut out everything in the room but the pipe, including her. After she left for the evening, Ed sat alone sucking down the purified cocaine vapors and spinning away on his high.

He says, "I felt I was rushing at a thousand miles an hour yet standing as still and light as a feather. There was nothing like it. Nothing. It was the peak."

The minute the cocaine was gone Ed knew he wanted more. When the crash hit him he thought that if he didn't get some more right away he might not make it through the next day.

He called Kathy and, true to his past, did not communicate his agony from the crash or his intense compulsion for more coke. He only said he liked it a lot and wanted more. She put him in touch with Ronnie, a reliable dealer she knew through friends, and taught him how to appraise cocaine, buy it, and boil it down for freebasing. On his first trip to the dealer, he purchased five grams for $500 and invited Kathy to stay with him for a weekend.

"I thought it would just be a kick, an indulgence, a fantasy, a few days of getting zonked to the hilt and fucking our brains out," Ed says, still full of amazement years later.

"We started on a Friday and didn't stop for four straight months."

They smoked up the first five grams by the end of Saturday night, and Ed went back to Ronnie for another five. He and Kathy skipped work on Monday and went back to the dealer for another five grams. By Tuesday, they were back again, having neither eaten nor slept since Sunday, and this time Ed handed over $1,000 for a larger supply. This lasted until the following Saturday, when Ed and Kathy took Valium and slept until late Sunday afternoon.

"That crash, my first real, full-scale crash coming off a binge, was beyond description," Ed says. "It was like I had every terrible feeling I'd ever felt all at once. I felt angry, depressed, terrified, frustrated, lonely, you name it. Plus I had the shakes and couldn't even keep down a cup of tea. Kathy and I agreed we should stop completely and go back to work Monday."

Ed went back to his office, but all he could think about was cocaine. Tuesday night he went back to Ronnie's with another $1,000 and didn't return to work until the following Monday. Kathy had virtually moved in with him by the middle of the second week, and by the middle of the third, he had his freebasing down so that he could fit in one full day and two half-days a week at the office working while he fought the crash with Valium and brandy.

"For the first month or so, all we did was freebase and fuck," Ed said.

Robust, athletic Ed began to show signs of his cocaine abuse. He was thin, pale. Kathy, too, became wasted. Their eyes were hollow and bright, and they were obsessed with the ritual of putting the cocaine into the double boiler, cooking it, smelling the ether, transferring the base to the pipe, heating and finally sucking it in. It was like a tribal ritual. Holy: it even sent them to heaven. They lived for the pipe; every rush was better than anything on earth, better than orgasm, which it in fact soon replaced. Ed started having trouble maintaining an erection, but it didn't affect him as much as it once might have. Neither he nor Kathy cared much about sex anymore.

By the end of two months, Ed's business began to suffer, but he didn't notice; in fact, he seemed not to care. He had freebased his way through about $50,000 of his $100,000 in stocks, investments, and savings. He had started out buying good quality cocaine by the gram for $100, but soon learned that buying in quarters and half-ounces assured higher quality. His coke now came in $700 and $1,400 weights.

Ed's dealer Ronnie was a 25-year-old M.B.A. candidate who sold coke to pay his tuition. He looked very ordinary, but underneath his preppy sport coat he always wore a .357 Magnum in a shoulder holster, and in his apartment he kept two ferocious Doberman pinschers he had taught to attack on command.

Whenever Ed came to visit, Ronnie was hospitable, an accommodating salesman, like most coke dealers. He would offer him a tray of cocaine samples complete with razors, mirrors, and spoons so that Ed could taste the wares. Ronnie himself did not partake. Always calm and unhurried, he would give Ed plenty of time to choose. During one visit there was an unexpected knock at the door. The Dobermans sprang to attention, ears erect, teeth bared. Ronnie calmly reached into his jacket and pulled out his gun. Ed froze with fear, his heart racing. Ronnie carefully cracked the door, pistol at the ready. It was a careless friend who hadn't had the good sense to telephone first. Ronnie relaxed, but Ed had a fleeting thought: "Maybe this is a warning to me."

Small insights like this were of no use by this point, though. Ed needed cocaine and that was that. The changes in his appearance and behavior had already signaled his family that something was desperately wrong. They were badgering him to go for help, his physician brothers offering the names of psychiatrists. Ed ignored them. What did they know?

At the same time that they encouraged him to go for

help, Ed's father would also help him out of the increasingly frequent jams he found himself in. Ed, the child who never needed any help, was making up for it with a vengeance. His father had twice lent him money. His $100,000 in savings had dwindled to $10,000 and Ed was amazed at how fast this had happened. In just four months, nothing else mattered anymore as much as cocaine, and he seemed to spend all his time pursuing it. He had stopped showing up at his office and had lost most of his clients. Once he offered Ronnie his Rolex watch if he'd add some extra cocaine into a sale, and he had even begun to sell several grams a week himself to ensure his own coke supply.

Ed and Kathy had long since left behind them the intense pleasures of freebasing. They now used cocaine more to avoid the horrible crash, to avoid coming to terms with what had happened to their lives, and to keep on searching for the beautiful euphoria they remembered from the first weeks of their cokeaholism. Ed had begun to be bothered by the psychotic episodes that almost inevitably follow such intense cocaine abuse. He believed that people were watching him, whispering about his cocaine use on the street, and plotting to steal his drugs. He saw shadows on the walls that weren't there and sometimes he heard the phone ring, picked it up, and heard nothing but the dial tone. Instead of realizing that he'd hallucinated the phone ringing, he was positive that someone was calling and hanging up to harass him.

Under pressure from his family and frightened by the psychotic episodes, Ed began therapy about this time (an atypical act for someone so deeply addicted). The only effect it had on him initially was that it kept him at the binge level, maybe helped him cut back a little. He was still bingeing for a week to two weeks at a time.

"I hadn't really made a commitment to therapy, though," he says. "I went, but I was trying to figure out a way to keep freebasing, not to stop. My goal was to get to where I could freebase without going broke. It took me months before I could even admit that I really had a problem."

By now, he and Kathy were bingeing for a few days, stopping for a few to crash and douse themselves with Valium, brandy, and whatever else they could lay their hands on, and suffering until they could afford more. They both looked like specters. One night as Ed and Kathy sat in his apartment freebasing, he realized that passing the intensity of the rush back and forth through the pipe was the closest they ever came to making love now. Besides, when he looked at her she didn't arouse much desire. There was almost nothing left of her; it would have been like making love to a ghost.

Ed watched as Kathy inhaled deeply from the glass pipe, her blue eyes dreamy and fixed, the way they always were when she took a toke. Ed took the pipe from her and sucked on it, then sucked on it again, getting higher and higher than he'd ever been before. From across the universe he gestured to her with the pipe and asked her if she wanted another hit. She didn't answer. "She must have caught a good one last time," Ed thought.

A few minutes later, when the edge was off his last toke, Ed realized that Kathy was still sitting in the same position with her unblinking eyes open, one hand on her thigh. Her head was cocked at an odd angle and there was a thin glitter of spittle at the corner of her mouth. She was dead.

Ed automatically did what he always did when he was in deep trouble. Trembling, he phoned his father. When his father answered he cried out: "Daddy, help me. Something's wrong with Kathy. I think she might be dead."

Ed's father rushed to his son's apartment. When he got there he found Ed standing in the shadows just beyond the door, his eyes empty. His father took a deep breath and walked into his son's bedroom. Nothing could have prepared him for what he saw.

The room was a shambles. On a chair, slumped and staring down at the floor, was Kathy. Ed's father had never seen a corpse before. Kathy was gray. He touched her. She was cold. He felt nauseous, but pulled himself together. There was no time to be sick now. He had to help Ed. He turned to see his son curled up on the floor under his rain-coat, crying.

The next morning, Ed's father admitted him to a private psychiatric hospital.

"I went where the rich junkies go," Ed told us wryly. "After the police left and took Kathy away, the doctor came and sedated me. They said I fought, went wild, screamed for coke, but I don't remember any of it. All I remember was waking up a few hours later in that emergency room, strapped down with leather restraints like a madman. I would have thought that I'd have been panic-stricken, but instead the most profound, unbelievable sense of relief flooded over me. I felt safe. I was so thankful that somehow someone, something, had taken control of me and stopped what I was doing.

"I spent six weeks in the hospital and the first two were absolute hell. I crashed for the whole time. The medication they gave me helped, but I would have done anything, and I mean anything, to get some coke. After my head cleared I started thinking about what happened. I thought about Kathy and decided her death was all my fault. I thought about the money I'd lost, one hundred thousand dollars in less than six months, and my business shot completely to hell. Depressed doesn't even come close to how I felt."

Ed finally made a commitment to therapy when he came out of the hospital. He came to us three times a week and lived at home with his parents. We involved his family in the early stages of his treatment not only to get their cooperation and let them know what was going on so they could better support him, but because they were acting as "enablers," doing things to help him to continue his cokeaholism. His father's lending him money was a perfect example. They were also failing to be firm with him and were afraid to tell him how they really felt about his behavior.

Although he experienced many episodes of backsliding, at the end of four years of intensive therapy Ed has finally overcome his cokeaholism. He has really made it. He gave up stockbroking and started his own retail business, and has learned to deal with major traumas in his life without slipping back into cocaine abuse.

"I really never thought I'd be able to do it," he says. "Even when things were going well I didn't want to stop therapy. I was scared to death that the minute I did, my abuse would all start all over again. But I did it. I did it. Every once in a while I look back at the past couple of years and I repeat those words to myself. 'I did it.'"

*A*ll of the people you've just read about initially used cocaine for the thrills or the promised energy. Not *one* expected to become a problem user. Although they heard about the dangers involved in using cocaine, not *one* believed anything would ever happen to him. But the destructive forces of cocaine abuse, whether gradually or suddenly evolved, are *always* unexpected. Anyone who begins to use cocaine regularly, frequently, or in large amounts is headed for trouble— or is already there. The self-help section you are about to read tells how to put "the brakes on" *before* skidding completely out of control.

Part III

Coping and Quitting

Risks and Dangers of Cocaine

The most popular mythology about cocaine contains several misleading beliefs; the most dangerous is that cocaine is harmless. People tend to believe that although one can get very high on cocaine and even get sick, it is difficult or impossible to take an overdose. Many users also believe that no one ever died from cocaine use.

These beliefs are false. Cocaine is toxic; people do overdose on it; and they do die. The death rate from cocaine overdoses and other cocaine-related fatalities rises steadily every year, following the increase in numbers of cocaine users. The dangers of cocaine, based on laboratory studies and clinical reports, have been known for many years. But as with any drug that emerges into widespread use, the real extent of its danger becomes apparent to us only when researchers and clinicians begin to discover new patterns. Now, along with the new understanding of cocaine's potentially fatal dangers, there is a growing recognition of the serious chronic medical disorders that can result from its frequent use.

There is no hard-and-fast figure for what constitutes a lethal dose of cocaine. In humans it is generally accepted that one gram ingested all at once or over a short interval is lethal, but this only means that if a gram of cocaine is ingested, the odds of death are extremely high. The fact is that cocaine fatalities usually occur from far smaller doses. The fatal dose varies according to individual and to situation. Its toxicity is affected by the combined interaction of the way it's ingested (snorting, shooting, or freebasing), a host of immediate environmental factors, and the variations in each individual's tolerance to the drug from day to day. Since the sheer amount of the drug is often not the determining factor, it cannot be made any safer by merely reducing the amount taken in any given snort, shot, or freebase toke. There's also a strong indication from research that regular cocaine users tend to develop a sensitivity to the drug, making smaller or usual doses more lethal. In many cocaine deaths, in fact, an experienced user, familiar with the amount he needs, has taken no more cocaine in his fatal dose, or on the day he died, than he may have been using for months or years. Far from being better able to handle the drug safely, habitual cocaine users may be more likely to die from it.

It is unclear which method of ingestion—shooting, freebasing, or snorting—is the most likely to result in cocaine overdose. Surveys by the Dade County, Florida, Medical Examiner's Office revealed that of those who died from cocaine overdoses, the highest blood concentrations were found in people who took the drug orally. They were people involved in drug-trafficking who swallowed small balloons or condoms filled with cocaine, which burst. These cases were highly unusual, however. The next highest concentration was found in the blood of people who had snorted cocaine. The lowest concentration was found in those who had injected the drug.

Recent findings explode another pervasive and dangerous myth: the notion that snorting is entirely safe or significantly safer than other means of ingesting the drug. This is completely untrue. All data on cocaine deaths show that snorting is *at least* as dangerous as shooting and freebasing, and possibly more so.

No matter how the lethal concentration is reached, a cocaine overdose death is horrifying. Cocaine overdose victims do not die peacefully. Death comes from an overstimulation of the central nervous system, followed by a collapse of either respiratory or heart function, or both. Someone who suffers cocaine overdose resembles a person having a violent grand mal epileptic seizure, which comes on suddenly and usually without warning. People who have seen a friend or acquaintance die from a cocaine overdose usually report that after the person snorted, shot, or freebased, he appeared fine for a while. Then suddenly he was wrenched by violent seizures and within minutes died. Someone in this sort of seizure may bite into or completely through their lower lip or tongue or fall against walls or furniture. The end is often bloody as well as violent.

There are other effects that accompany or precede this kind of death, notably a phenomenal rise in body temperature, often to as high as 110 degrees. Fatal seizures may be preceded by lesser, nonfatal seizures. Frequently a person will have a short, nonfatal attack, get up and have some more cocaine, and then have a fatal seizure.

There is also a species of partial overdose that many people apparently experience without recognizing. This mild overdose should be a signal for a user to *stop using cocaine immediately* and see a doctor as soon as possible. Here is a description of this reaction by noted experts Patricia J. Morningstar and Dale D. Chitwood:

> There is, however, a middle level of overdose that many [cocaine users] are not aware of. The symptoms are a general malaise, sweating, and a "funny" feeling, but they are not perceived as severe. [We] think that what is happening is that a lot of users are not perceiving those symptoms as being signs of overdose, and so what people experience as a sudden unexpected onset [of cocaine seizure] . . . may in fact be due to people's failure to recognize the symptoms of moderate-level overdosing before they have a more severe reaction.

Beyond the overdose death, there are also sudden deaths indirectly induced by cocaine. The drug's stimulant effects and vasoconstrictor action place a tremendous strain on the heart and circulatory system, so that anyone with a history of heart disease or high blood pressure is at great risk when using it. And there is a particular danger for younger people who may not yet have seen any symptoms of heart problems, so-called silent disorders, which may become fatal weak points under the influence of cocaine. Deaths have resulted from acute myocardial infarction (heart attack), severe arrhythmia (irregular heartbeat), embolism, or massive and fatal stroke. After a binge, sleep-deprived coke users can fall into an unnaturally deep sleep, especially under the influence of drugs they may take to ease the crash. This deep unconsciousness, combined with anesthetized tissues and muscles at the back of the throat from snorting or freebasing, can cause the individual to suffocate in his sleep or to choke on mucus or vomit blocking his lungs.

Since cocaine can promote brain seizures, anyone prone to them is risking his life each time he uses cocaine. A seizure can be fatal. Cocaine can even override anticonvulsive medication like Dilantin and induce seizures in epileptics.

Finally, there are the compound risks when cocaine is used in combination with other drugs, as it often is, since cocaine users take tranquilizers, hypnotics, barbiturates, or narcotics along with cocaine in order to take the edge off the high and soften the crash. Lately an old drug-user's "treat" has been rising in popularity among cocaine users who inject. This is the "speedball," a combination of cocaine and heroin. It can make the user very high, and can kill him. Speedballing is what killed John Belushi. Sometimes the user will die when the heroin action camouflages the cocaine action: he overdoses on cocaine and has a seizure and sometimes he will die of respiratory arrest, not experiencing the effects of the heroin, which would normally signal overdose.

Few people realize it, but the mixture of alcohol and cocaine is also a speedball, and many people freely drink while using cocaine without giving any thought to the possible outcome. A rising number of fatal automobile crashes have resulted from this combination. Cocaine may mask alcohol's effect, and a person who feels he is sober and alert becomes intoxicated when the cocaine's effect wears off. Standard postmortem examinations test for alcohol only and not for cocaine, so many cocaine-related traffic deaths are attributed solely to drinking.

Excessive or frequent cocaine use can lead to many other nonfatal but serious conditions. Depending on the route of administration, the dose, and the frequency of ingestion, high levels of cocaine sometimes result, not in an even more euphoric state, but in a sharp reversal of the pleasurable effects. A cocaine high can turn into a physically and mentally debilitating anxiety attack, complete with hyperventilation and other panic reactions. It can also result in intense irritability, sometimes leading to uncontrolled outbursts of anger and violence. Cocaine use can culminate in episodes of acute paranoia, psychotic paranoid delusions in which people believe they are in danger, or are being threatened or plotted against by people they know or by mysterious strangers. There can also be hallucinations—auditory, visual, and olfactory—resulting in violent, destructive, and even suicidal or homicidal behavior.

Most women these days are aware of the dangers of using drugs while pregnant or nursing, but some of them feel cocaine is not dangerous because it seems to last such a short time and pass out of the system so quickly.

Unfortunately, they are wrong. When ingested by the mother, cocaine acts on the nervous system of the unborn child. It is not safe to use at any time during pregnancy. Observations of the newborns of chronic cocaine-using mothers showed the babies to be exceptionally jittery and tense.

We've also encountered nursing mothers who believe they can keep the cocaine from reaching the nursing infant by waiting awhile after they use the drug and pumping out a bit of their breast milk before they nurse again. This procedure is simply too dangerous. The rule for cocaine and pregnancy and nursing is simple: cocaine should never be used.

A 1983 survey of cocaine abusers seeking treatment at a New York cocaine helpline uncovered these statistics: 93 percent had experienced "minor" psychological consequences from their cocaine use, 56 percent had experienced major psychological consequences. Eighty percent reported feeling run-down and weak, 58 percent reported sleep difficulties. Forty-seven percent experienced paranoid episodes, 18 percent felt violent after taking cocaine, and 16 percent had had hallucinations. Sixty-seven percent said cocaine use had made them irritable and short-tempered, 65 percent reported gloominess or bad moods, 64 percent reported anxiety or restlessness. Forty-four percent reported loss of sex drive, 55 percent said their cocaine use made them feel lazy and un-motivated. Thirty-six percent reported difficulty concen-trating, 35 percent experienced confused thoughts, and 33 percent had memory problems from cocaine use.

If your cocaine use has resulted in these problems, read on.

Looking for the Reasons

People who are in trouble with cocaine almost always use the drug in cycles, and there are periods when they are aware that they have a problem and that they need to stop. Some people are able to stop on their own, some will need outside help. Whether you want to stop yourself or you want to help someone else stop, this section has been written for you.

With the exception of the Cokeaholic, who is totally out of control, almost everyone who develops a problem with cocaine can call on his inner strengths to stop using it. This holds true for anyone from the Social Sniffer, who feels he's begun using too frequently, to the Boredom/Stress Reliever, who will have to work hard to find substitutes for what cocaine does for him. We've seen that, in most cases, people will take care of themselves when they need to, *if* they know how.

Quitting cocaine isn't easy. It takes effort and discipline. Some people have a relatively easy time. For others it is extremely difficult. The important thing to remember is that it can be done, and in many instances it can be a rewarding opportunity to learn new ways to gratify yourself, to expand your repertoire of recreational activities, and to create new variety, spice, and pleasure in your life.

Step One—Acknowledge the Problem

The first step toward quitting cocaine is recognizing and accepting that your use of it is a problem for you. There may be no dramatic life-threatening crisis that results in a broken marriage, bankruptcy, or a ruined career; a cocaine problem can involve simply spending too much money, missing a few days' work, or your use may be causing friction at home.

You may find it easy to acknowledge that your cocaine use is a problem, or you may find it difficult. It pays to remember that taking this first step need not involve declarations of guilt, shame, or self-recrimination. The fact that you want to stop or limit your cocaine use is the first positive step. Many people who use drugs are ambivalent about stopping. There are some who come into treatment with a hidden agenda; they want to continue using cocaine but learn how to escape the negative consequences. If you feel you want to stop, stay with this feeling. Trust your instincts, relax, and try to feel comfortable about learning what you need to know to accomplish your goal.

If you feel anxious about trying, or you think that you'll need some very special or complicated formula to quit, keep these facts in mind.

■ High success rates for self-motivated quitting hold for all the common dependency and addiction problems, including overeating, alcohol abuse, gambling, and even heroin abuse. Take smoking, for example.
■ Between 1965 and 1974, 29 million Americans stopped smoking cigarettes.
   95 percent of them did it completely on their own;
   2 percent of them did it with the help of formal
   "stop smoking" programs.
■ Most people do not need elaborate or expensive therapy regimes. Most people do what they need to do to stop. You will, too.

All the following methods work. The only thing you have to do is pick the one that's best for you and get started. Your choice will depend on your needs, on the style and severity of your cocaine use, and on your intuition about what will serve you best. The hardest part is holding on to your progress over time, and that, too, is something you can learn.

There are two simple principles that never change:

1. The longer you stay away from cocaine, the easier it is to stay away from it.
2. If you give in and use it again (and you may), remember that it's not permanent. One relapse does not undo all you've accomplished. You quit once, you can quit again. So if at first you don't succeed, stop, stop again.

Step Two—
Locate Your Motivation to Quit

To quit cocaine successfully, you've got to pinpoint exactly why you want to stop. Be as clear about your reasons as possible, because when the going gets tough and you ask yourself "Why should I bother?" a good answer will help you get through. You won't be able to give up cocaine until you find your own good enough reason to do it.

Stick with *your* reasons, not necessarily the reasons other people might give you. Although friends, lovers, or relatives may tell you to stop using cocaine, stopping for someone else will not work. If requests by others touch you, use them to look for your own reasons to stop. Only your own motivations will lead to success.

One of the best ways to discover your motivations is to make a list. Be creative with your list and it will work best for you. Try not to censor what you include. List the little reasons, right along with the dramatic ones. It's the truth of your motives that counts, not their grandness. Making this list is an exercise in learning how not to kid yourself.

We find that people often have categories of motivations like this:

Health. Am I feeling run-down from cocaine use? Does cocaine give me a headache? Stuffed nose? Is it ruining my appetite? Am I losing weight or turning to junk food and sweets when I do eat? Am I having trouble sleeping? Is cocaine use weakening my performance in other recreational areas like jogging, tennis, or other sports?

Money. Am I spending too much money on cocaine? Do I spend more on cocaine than I comfortably do on dinner out, sports gear, or clothes? Am I spending money on cocaine that I should be spending on other things or on other people like my spouse or children?

Psychological Consequences. Does using cocaine make me jittery or anxious? Do I get irritable while high on cocaine or afterward? Do I feel depressed while high or afterward? Is the crash extremely unpleasant? Do I feel bad about myself because of my cocaine use?

Career. Is cocaine use affecting my work in any way? Am I missing work because of it? Am I using it at work? Are other consequences of my cocaine use causing stress that hurts my work? Am I jeopardizing my reputation, my license, my job contacts? What would happen if I were arrested?

Relationships. Is my cocaine use causing any problems in my marriage, love relationships, or family life? Am I fighting with my spouse or lover over my cocaine use? Is my cocaine use causing me to become secretive or untruthful with those close to me? Is my cocaine use having any bad effects on my children?

Any sort of list will do. Use what feels right to you and don't make value judgments. If one of your motivations for stopping cocaine is that you believe it is hurting your tennis game, write it down. Just be straight with yourself.

Another sort of motivation list involves making a catalog of all the negative consequences you see. Write down what you have to lose by continuing your cocaine use, or what you think you've already started to lose: career, love affair, marriage, health, friends, money, whatever you know is true. This way you will be giving yourself a kind of aversive conditioning—linking unpleasant associations to the drug or drug-related thoughts. This list can remind you of the price to be paid if you continue using cocaine. When you see the sum of what it's costing you, you'll know why you want to stop.

One basic motivation for wanting to quit cocaine is a desire to take better care of yourself. Abusing drugs is a form of self-neglect. This lack of self-care can be an acquired habit or the result of never having learned how to take care of yourself from the start. Either way, all motivations to stop using cocaine involve reevaluating your priorities for taking care of yourself—learning to eat well, exercise, relax, build self-esteem, and effectively communicate your needs to others so that they can be fulfilled.

Step Three— Discover the Reasons You Use Cocaine

Once you know why you want to quit cocaine, your next step is to discover why you use it. This is essential because how you quit depends on why you use it. When the reason for using is eliminated or weakened, the desire for cocaine will diminish.

As with finding your motivation for quitting, it's often helpful to use a list. Think of the occasions when you use cocaine. For instance, do you tend to use before you go out or while out on a date? Do you tend to use while you are with a group or when you are alone? Do you tend to use cocaine in conjunction with sex? List the occasions and then ask yourself why you opted for cocaine on those occasions.

Don't be surprised if a pattern emerges. All of us follow some patterns and finding them is helpful in finding the remedies. Once you discover *when* you use cocaine and answer *why*, you'll be ready to find new ways to give yourself appropriate substitutes for cocaine.

Here are some common reasons why people use cocaine, along with suggestions to achieve alternate, desirable effects without the drug. We've set them up as you might.

Occasion	Reason
■ Sex, seduction.	■ Enjoy the ritual of setting up and sharing the lines. Shared, creative preparation for sex.
	■ Enjoy setting up the mood, like the thrills and anticipation that come with this.
	■ Enjoy the feeling of specialness that coke adds to the occasion.
	■ Enjoy the aura of excitement coke adds—coke is associated with wild sex—uninhibited, playful, really going all the way.

A sexual encounter is a popular occasion for using cocaine. But there are an infinite number of alternative ways to set up the same conditions for pleasure: ritual, shared preparation, a mood of anticipation, specialness, excitement, surrendered inhibitions, and passion.

Use your best asset—your imagination. Cocaine is limited. Your imagination is unlimited and the results it can produce are endless.

For example, create the aura of ritual and shared preparation by inventing your own. Dress up in whatever special, sensual, or provocative clothes turn you and your lover on. Create a sexy mood. Together, prepare an elaborate, special dinner with foods you find sensuous and serve it in romantic settings—crystal, silver, music, and plenty of flirting, teasing, and touching. Take a bubble bath with your lover by candlelight. Use scented soaps and perfumes and take turns massaging each other's body with lotions or oils. Anticipation, specialness, excitement are what you're after.

The most important thing is to be creative. Talk your fantasies or ideas out with your lover. You may hit on a few you'd like to try together. There are many excellent books that cover these techniques for making your sex life more exciting. Pick up one or two and go over them together. They're full of good ideas for making sex without cocaine just as exciting as sex with cocaine. We've spoken to dozens of people who invented their own ways of enhancing sex without using cocaine.

■ One woman covers her bed with black satin sheets and then entices her husband into a warm bath filled with rose petals.

■ Another couple prepare a romantic meal and have dinner in the nude.

■ A number of couples tell us that using a home video center to play erotic material in the privacy of their bedrooms is a sure cure for bedroom boredom.

Anything is possible, and whatever you think will help probably will: mirrors, strobe lights, making love in a new environment—in the sand, in the mud, in front of a fire-place, in your office with the door locked. The possibilities are endless. All you have to do is imagine them.

Occasion	Reason
■ Parties, social gatherings, special occasions.	■ To be more sociable, to talk more easily to people. ■ To accentuate enjoyment, add to relaxation already in progress. ■ To have more fun while having fun.

It's often hard to sort out using cocaine to enhance plea-sure from using it to avoid having negative feelings, so try to be straight with yourself about this. Go back and take a look through the stories of the five types of users if you're not sure how to classify your cocaine use.

Generally, people who use cocaine only to add to real pleasure will find it relatively easy to quit once they recog-nize the potential dangers of a drug once considered safe. The simplest thing to do is to increase other activities that enhance good times, like eating, drinking, socializing—all in moderation. This is usually enough. People who use cocaine this way and let go of it usually find that they don't miss it much.

Occasion	Reason
■ When I'm with my lover, girl friend, boyfriend, husband, wife.	■ To have sex. ■ To have a good time together. ■ It's what we do together.

If your reason for using cocaine is strongly linked to your involvement in a love relationship, if you use it almost exclusively with your mate, lover, or a romantic attachment, and if it seems that cocaine use is an important part of that relationship, you may be involved in a cocaine romance. Carefully evaluate your situation. Ask yourself some questions: do you have a good time with this person *without* cocaine? How often do you see this person and *not* use cocaine? Does it require a special effort for one or both of you to spend time together without the drug?

If you see that you really cannot have a good time with your current lover without using cocaine, or if you almost always use coke when you are with this person, the drug may be playing too important a role in your relationship. You'll have to sort out exactly how much of your attraction is to the person and how much is to cocaine. If you want to stop using cocaine, you can enlist your partner's cooperation, but if he or she won't cooperate, you'll either have to severely limit the time spent together or end the relationship. It may sound drastic, but *you* have to make *your* own well-being the priority. The first order of business is *you*.

Occasion	Reason
■ At work, after work, during recreation.	■ Tired, need energy. ■ Exhausted from busy schedule—need stimulation to keep going for leisure activities.

If you use cocaine as an energizer or rely on it to wake

you up, organize your energies, and keep going, it can mean one of two things: either you need to find safer substitutes to energize yourself or you need to slow down because you're pushing yourself too hard.

When you're tempted to use cocaine for energy, don't simply deprive yourself and sit there fighting temptation. Do something for an energy boost. Go for a brisk walk, do some strenuous exercise, even jump into a quick shower when the urge to use comes over you. Do what you need to perk yourself up.

Acquiring the ability to meditate, or learning deep-relaxation techniques, or how to catnap will help you restore energy. Fatigue is often the result of tension, and these tension-reducing exercises will often do the trick. There are books that teach you relaxation techniques, and there are also classes you can take. Seek them out.

You'll discover which of these approaches works best. You may find that you simply need more rest and a less frenzied pace, not the stimulation of cocaine to keep your body from noticing that it needs rest.

Occasion	Reason
■ Angry. Tense, nervous. Anxious before needing to perform. Stressed, fed up, overwhelmed.	■ Cocaine makes me feel better—more relaxed, calmed, confident, capable of dealing with stress, more in control.

If your reasons for using cocaine are primarily connected to reducing stress, the first thing you have to recognize is that cocaine does not solve problems or help you deal with them effectively. This is an illusion created by the drug's short-term psychological effects. You—your talents, abilities, and strengths—will solve these problems, not cocaine.

It will probably be easiest to stop when things are going well and the stresses on you are at their lowest. Be aware that when you do, it is likely that at the next moment of crisis or high stress the temptation to use cocaine will come upon you full force. Don't let this take you by surprise and overwhelm you. Instead, prepare for it so you have alternatives.

The best way to do this is to find and practice other outlets and use them instead of cocaine when you feel stressed. Use your imagination here and do what seems natural to you. Don't be shy—the goal is to reduce the level of stress and discomfort so you feel better. Whatever works is the right method. Here are some methods a few of our patients have used.

■ Betsy started jogging every morning after the kids were off to school.

■ John goes to the health club and swims twenty vigorous laps. He does this even if he has to leave the office during the day and work late that night. It keeps him from using cocaine.

■ Lucy jumps into her car, rolls up the windows, turns the radio on loud, and drives around and screams at the top of her lungs for a while. No one can hear her, and she feels wonderful afterward without using cocaine.

■ Arthur has sex more frequently during periods of high stress.

■ Patricia calls her "buddy" (the buddy system is often very effective) and talks out her anxieties. Pat was a Performance User who used to think she couldn't go on without a few lines of coke to kill her fear.

The choice of stress-reduction methods to substitute for cocaine depends on what works best and longest for you. Experiment with different techniques until you find one that works. The shelves are full of books on stress reduction and coping with stress, and you may find some helpful suggestions in them.

Occasion	Reason
■ No specific time, or almost anytime.	■ Habit.
	■ I don't particularly want to do it—I just don't know how to stop, or I'm afraid it will be too difficult.
	■ I don't really enjoy cocaine that much anymore. I just don't like the crash, so I use as long as I can to avoid it.

As in all habits, people often continue to use cocaine more out of habit than for pleasure. Time after time, smokers will talk about how cigarettes were pleasant at the outset but have not been for a long time, yet they're still unable to stop smoking. Habitual overeaters will stuff themselves in spite of nausea. Cocaine users will sometimes continue to use the drug habitually even after the pleasure has diminished or reversed.

If your reason for using cocaine is habit, your first goal is to break the habit pattern—disrupt the automatic repeated use. If your cocaine habit is grounded in repeated use to avoid the crash, then your job may be somewhat harder because you will have to ride through the crash before you can develop methods for staying away from cocaine. There are many ways to do this—keeping lists, keeping journals, substituting other habits like running, substituting other pleasurable activities, calling a buddy when the urge strikes, doing something to distract yourself, such as going to the movies. One excellent way to start is to take a vacation—but leave your cocaine at home.

Quitting Cocaine

Some reasons for using cocaine are easier to deal with than others. Generally, people whose reasons for using have to do with enhancing pleasures, improving normal sex, or giving them energy have an easier time quitting. People who use cocaine to remedy uncomfortable psychological states— anxiety, anger, stress, lack of confidence—tend to have a harder time. While it's easy to learn a new technique for gaining more energy through exercise, for instance, it is difficult to learn new ways to experience and then adjust your inner feelings to a point where you don't need cocaine to do it.

People who use cocaine for psychological reasons must generally stop "cold turkey." Trying to cut down usually won't work. The good news is, once they quit, their ability to resist temptation is often very strong, since they'll remember the discomfort and want to avoid having to quit again. The difficult part is that this person will have to work very hard to find and learn to use other kinds of psychological satisfactions as a substitute for cocaine. He will have to give up the good feeling of cocaine while he searches for and then learns to use the replacements for the drug feelings.

This can mean a long, difficult period, but there are techniques to help him through, and if he's willing to use them, he can usually succeed.

Principles of Quitting

All techniques for quitting cocaine involve the same principles that effectively correct the overuse of anything—from alcohol to excessive eating, from sex to gambling. Most of these principles are centered on one fact: the excessive use of anything, including cocaine, usually indicates that you have the need to get more out of your life. Overuse of cocaine usually indicates that you're not getting enough enjoyment from other areas of your life, so you're relying more and more on cocaine's effects to supply those things. Consequently, efforts to help you quit are based on showing you how to cope with life's discomforts without cocaine and encouraging you to develop a wider range of life-enhancing activities. The principles are as follows.

Find Your Strengths and Resources and Learn How to Use Them. Overusing cocaine is not a sign of weakness; rather, it is a sign that you're not using your strengths to maximum advantage. For instance, most likely your curiosity made you try cocaine in the first place. You can use that curiosity and your pleasure-seeking tendencies to explore new avenues for fulfillment, without cocaine.

Structure Your Life So That You Can Get More Out of It. Many people fall into overusing cocaine because they have not paid attention to organizing their time, particularly their leisure time, so that it gives them the satisfaction, excitement, and relaxation they want. Cocaine becomes an easy way to fill the gaps and avoid boredom. You can learn to plan your time so that you are able to do the things that are really important to you.

Set Limits for Yourself and Others. Many of us do not know how to say no as often as we'd like, to ourselves or to other people. Limit-setting is not easy—it involves will-power, being honest with yourself about when you do or don't trust yourself, and it involves feeling clear about what you want to do, no matter what anyone else may say or do. Setting limits means saying no to peer pressure, when everyone at the party is having cocaine and urging you to join them. And it means saying no to yourself when it feels easier to give up.

Set Goals and Achieve Them. Many of us don't know how to help ourselves succeed by setting reasonable goals and then rewarding ourselves as we reach them. Instead, we force ourselves toward unreasonably high standards over too short a time and don't allow ourselves to enjoy the fruits of our successes as we progress. Quitting cocaine involves working toward reasonable goals and giving yourself credit for reaching them when you do.

Discover the Value of Exercise. Exercise can really reduce depression and diminish tension, both the kind that people take cocaine to relieve and the kind that builds up while you're trying to quit using the drug. It works as a good substitute habit for cocaine-using and increases your energy level, so if you use cocaine for a boost, exercise can help you stop. Research has shown that vigorous exercise causes the body to release powerful chemicals called endorphins that combat fatigue, "blue" feelings, anger, tension, anxiety, and stress.

Restore Your Health. Using a lot of cocaine puts a tremendous strain on your body. Even if you are not dehydrated or underweight after a run on cocaine, you may be generally malnourished. Not only do people tend to eat poorly when they are abusing cocaine, but the drug tends to use up extra amounts of certain nutrients and chemicals your body needs in order for you to be healthy and feel well. In particular vitamins C and B_6 are often found to be low, and some chemicals in the brain (neurotransmitters needed to maintain normal mood states) can be depleted. Therefore, it is a good idea to make a concerted effort to drink enough fluids, eat well-balanced meals and take vitamin supplements to help your body restore itself.

There is some evidence that tyrosine, a naturally occurring amino acid, may help the body resynthesize some of the depleted neurotransmitters when there has been an abrupt discontinuation of chronic cocaine use. We are concerned that tyrosine, available in health food stores, may become a popular home remedy for crashing, with negative results. In some cases the use of tyrosine may just delay people from stopping their cocaine use and getting the help they need, leaving them in even deeper trouble. Also, tyrosine can elevate blood pressure and may be especially dangerous for some individuals with incipient heart conditions.

Cocaine use can interrupt normal sleep cycles and people are often tempted to start relying on sleeping pills. Taking drugs to fall asleep, however, has its drawbacks since the tolerance to the drowsiness caused by sleeping medications can develop very rapidly, and you can compound the problem by becoming dependent on drugs that don't even help you get to sleep. Getting back into your regular sleep cycle may be as simple as strictly adhering to your precocaine schedule, going to bed sleepy or not and rising promptly until your natural sleep rhythm is reinstated. Taking drugs and using elaborate measures on your own to recover isn't usually wise or necessary. If you need that type of intervention you require medical supervision. It is amazing how quickly people regain their health and stamina just by eating sensibly and getting sufficient rest.

Learn How to Give Yourself Good Feelings. One thing held in common by almost every person who overuses or abuses drugs, from the slightly out-of-control Social Sniffer to the most extreme Cokeaholic, is that they have little ability to make themselves feel good by themselves. It may be that they never learned how. People overuse drugs because the drugs give them the kinds of good feelings they cannot give

themselves: thrills, satisfaction, excitement, triumph, anticipation, gratification, well-being. To quit cocaine you'll learn
how to exercise your imagination, your fantasizing skills, so
you can make yourself feel gratified by your own pleasant
fantasies. You can also learn to evoke for yourself the feelings that you've been using cocaine to supply. If you've been
using coke for the sense of excitement and thrills it gives
you, for instance, you can learn to do thrilling things instead—sports like skiing, hang gliding, skydiving, scuba diving. You can give yourself risk-based thrills through
psychological challenges too—apply for a new job or initiate
conversations with attractive people you find exciting.

Reach Out to Other People. Keeping all your feelings inside will just make you feel worse. This is as true for the
casual user who wants to quit as for the Cokeaholic. One
reason people slip into overusing cocaine is that they haven't
shared their feelings with those people who care about
them. The drug helps them push those feelings away and
allows them to act like nothing's wrong. Try to start talking
about feelings to people you love. Don't be afraid to ask for
help and support from the people who love you.

Is it possible to talk to your husband, wife, lover,
brother, sister, or parents? Your friends? Talk to your therapist if you have one. Quitting cocaine is much easier if you
don't try to do it in a vacuum. Find someone with whom you
feel comfortable and whom you can trust. You must feel free
of possible consequences so that you can talk honestly and
openly.

Methods for Quitting

Every one of these techniques is designed to illuminate your
behavior so you can change it. Each one will take you on a
small voyage of discovery where you may learn something
about yourself that you never realized before.

Think of quitting cocaine as a challenge, not a self-imposed hardship or an exercise in self-denial. See it for what it is—an exercise in self-discovery, a kind of treasure hunt for new strengths and abilities, an expansion of your capacity to enjoy yourself.

Keep a Log Book. In quitting cocaine it is very important to be concrete about what you want, what you're doing, why you're doing it, and how you're doing. Avoid being vague or abstract. Don't tell yourself you're stopping cocaine because it's bad for people; say you're stopping because you believe it's bad for *you*. Be personal, focus in on your own immediate needs and desires. Try not to think or talk about cocaine in terms of "everyone" or "no one"; talk and think about it in terms of "I" and "me." Don't say you think life is better without cocaine; say *"My* life will be better without cocaine."

In the same way it helps to be concrete about what you're trying to accomplish and why. Written lists and plans are extremely helpful for sustaining your quitting regimen. They will not only help you think out exactly what you want to do, but will also help you keep up your momentum when the going gets difficult, or when you feel you're losing it.

One of the best ways to make use of lists and plans is to keep a "Coke Book," a formal log that contains all you need to sustain your quitting program. The Coke Book can be a combination portable life raft, first-aid kit, security blanket, and companion, depending on when you need it and how you use it. It helps you to keep focused. It gives you something to fall back on if you feel shaky or low on willpower, and it provides you with a record of your progress so you can see how well you're doing.

You can tailor your Coke Book to your own personal needs and style. If, for example, you associate using cocaine with fast living, money, chic behavior, and self-indulgence, you can put those same attributes into your Coke Book. Buy yourself the finest, most exquisite blank book you can find. Go for leather covers, handmade paper, and gold-leaf rule if you think it will make you feel good. Spend a hundred dollars or more if that's what you think you'll need. It's only the price of a gram of cocaine. If you feel that once you've quit you'll want to eliminate all traces of your coke use, perhaps you should purchase an inexpensive spiral notebook that you can ceremoniously toss away when you're finished. Maybe one of those black-and-white composition notebooks will work for you if it reminds you of homework and discipline. Use your imagination, have fun, and go with your intuition.

Here are some suggestions for things to put into your Coke Book. Start by writing *Three Things to Remember at All Times.*

■ The reason I continue to use cocaine is because I don't know how to stop. *(Not* because I'm weak, immoral, emotionally ill, or a bad person.)
■ Cocaine doesn't really make anything better—but stopping will.
■ My body will restore itself to health very quickly.

Write Down the Date You've Picked to Stop. Have a good time with this. Pick a special anniversary—the day you got married, the day you graduated from college, the date you started your own business, the day you got your first paycheck, whatever has meaning for you. Pick your birthday or your lucky number. If you begin your regimen by quitting cold, then you can look back to this date and measure how long you've stayed away, for reinforcement. If you've decided instead to cut down progressively, then this target date will be something to look forward to and work toward.

Two Parallel Lists of the Pluses and Minuses of Your Cocaine Use. A sample list might look like this:

Good Effects	**Consequences**
■ Euphoria	■ Too expensive
■ Energy	■ Crash is very uncomfortable
■ Talkative	■ Tired the next day

Lists of the Pluses and Minuses (continued):

Good Effects	Consequences
■ Feel control	■ Sometimes get anxious, jittery
■ Feel creative	■ Good ideas on coke don't look so good the next day
■ Feel confident	■ Sinus irritation
■ Sociable	■ Headaches
■ Feel sexy	■ Depressed the day after

A List of Your Motivations for Quitting. Here's a hypothetical list.

■ Afraid of becoming addicted or dependent on cocaine.
■ Afraid of damaging my health.
■ It sets a bad example for my children.
■ I'm trying to get into or stay in good physical condition.
■ I want to take control of my life.
■ I want to save the money I'm spending on cocaine for something else: vacation, car, clothes, ——————.

A Catalog of Dreams and Assets. Here is an example of one person's "Dreams and Assets List."

Dreams
■ To live a long, full life.
■ To be wealthy.
■ To see my kids grow up—to be a grandparent.
■ To become powerful and successful in business.
■ To have control over my life; to do the things I want to, my way.

Review and revise the list at the end of three months.

One way to develop your Dreams List is to create a "Dream Picture" for yourself. Here's how to do it.

Lie down or sit in a comfortable place. Give yourself music or silence, whichever is more soothing and relaxing. Close your eyes and create a visual fantasy with yourself at the center of it. Imagine that you are actually fulfilling some of the things on your Dreams List. Be as descriptive, graphic, and detailed as you can be. Envision exactly what you are doing, whom you are with, where you are, what you're wearing, what the weather is like, what you're thinking, eating, or drinking, how you feel. Keep it going for as long as you can. When you're satisfied, write down the details and events of your Dream Picture in your Coke Book.

Revise and update your Dream Picture at the end of three months along with your Dreams List. Do the same at the end of six months, one year, and five years. Keep up with the changes in your life.

Assets. What Do I Have Going for Me?

- Baby/child/children
- Wife or husband
- Family
- My job
- Good personality
- Sense of humor
- Looks
- Brains
- Car
- Friends
- Good health
- Perseverance
- Courage
- Ambition
- _____

It sometimes helps to juxtapose your Assets List with a list headed "What I Have to Lose." Many of the assets will find their way onto that list, but you may find there are new entries as well.

Keep a Running Diary. It's helpful to keep a diary of your progress, but don't make it an unpleasant chore. A few sentences a day are all you'll need, so if the idea of keeping a diary puts you off, rule the diary portion of your Coke Book into squares about two by three inches so you need to fill in only a few lines. That way you won't be intimidated by an empty page.

Since the first three months of quitting are critical, we recommend that you make an entry in your diary every morning, afternoon, or evening for every day of this period. Write in the book once a day, but do it every day at the same time. The structure will help you to keep it up. If you think it will help, write down your feelings whenever you feel the urge for cocaine as well. You can also use the diary to keep a record of your quitting progress and refer to it for some confidence-building if you feel that things are going too slowly. If you're cutting down toward stopping, for instance, record each time you use cocaine and the amount you use. Refer to the record often, and work toward lengthening the time between each use and diminishing the dose each time you use. The written record will be proof that you can do it or evidence that you need to revise your plan.

Keep your Coke Book with you at all times—carry it wherever you go, and write in it whenever you want to.

Find Successful Role Models. Find people you admire who do not use drugs, who used cocaine and quit successfully, or who did something similar, and learn what you can about how they did it. Most of all, know that other people have succeeded and that you can too. Identify with them and seek to do what they did.

Talk to people you know and respect who have successfully stopped cocaine or who have quit smoking cigarettes or demonstrated that they're successful and disciplined dieters. If you know anyone who has triumphed over a drinking problem, seek him out and find out how he did it. Look to people around you who are strivers, achievers, and dreamers and do as they do.

Your role models do not have to be people accessible to you. You can choose celebrities you admire or important figures in business, politics, or the arts. Richard Pryor is an excellent role model. So are John and Mackenzie Phillips. All of them came back from serious cocaine problems. Jason Robards, Jr., the actor, had a serious drinking problem for thirty years and succeeded in quitting alcohol. There are examples all around you in newspapers, television, and magazines. Read the biographies or autobiographies of people who successfully quit cocaine, alcohol, or other drugs—you'll discover that other people have gone through what you're experiencing. You'll find these books readily available in your local library or bookstores.

List your role models in your Coke Book and note in a few words why you chose them.

Find Your Cocaine Cues and Learn to Avoid Them.
This is one of the most important ways to help yourself quit.

Whenever you feel the urge to use cocaine, stop, take two steps back, and take stock of what's happening. Give yourself time to think; leave the room and lock yourself in the bathroom if you must. Where are you? What activity are you involved in? What time of day is it? Whom are you with? What did you just finish doing or what are you just about to start? Where did you just come from or where are you just about to go? What feelings do you have?

The point is to discover exactly what cues in your environment—activities, places, people, or especially your own feelings—are directly connected with the onset of the urge to use cocaine. Try to be very precise when you answer these questions for yourself. For instance, if the urge to use cocaine suddenly comes over you when you meet, see, or think of a particular person with whom you often use it, then you know that person is one of your cues. You may need to avoid him or her, at least until you feel strong about resisting the urge to use cocaine.

If you pay a little attention to doing this, you'll quickly discover that you have quite a few cocaine cues in your life: a large stack of work that has accumulated on your desk, for instance, a particular disco or bar, or getting ready for a date. Perhaps your cue is making an entrance at a social gathering, whether or not someone actually offers cocaine. Your cocaine cues can be music, smells, or sights. They can be internal: a particular feeling, like anxiety in a social or performance situation, a memory, a feeling of low energy.

The idea is to spot your cocaine cues, take note of them, and then avoid exposing yourself to them unnecessarily.

You might even start a record of cocaine cues in your log book. Watching the list evolve can be instructive. You'll begin to see patterns and associations in your life that you never knew existed.

It is *not* a good idea to simply note your cues and then continue to expose yourself to them. Don't enter into a battle of wills. You have nothing to prove to anyone, and if you do this, you'll only be fighting against yourself, since if you lose, you'll end up defeating your own endeavors to quit cocaine. What's the point? Instead, try to use your cocaine cues to make quitting easier for yourself, and the best way to do this is to avoid them when you can, or remove yourself from them when they occur without warning.

Stay away from old haunts where you used cocaine— clubs, discos, bars—leave the party when someone brings out the drug, turn down dates with people you know will offer you cocaine. You'll have to make an effort to stay away from any cocaine relationship.

You may have to give up some things or people in order to move on and get more out of your life. For example, if many of your cocaine cues exist on your job—if the people who offer you the drug are there or your urge to use is sparked by work situations—you may have to revise or even leave your job and find a new one. You may also have to suspend or actually end relationships that are deeply connected to your cocaine use—friendships, sexual liaisons, even love affairs. Anyone who uses cocaine in front of you when they know you want to stop is not your friend. If you're trying to quit and your partner is a cocaine user and doesn't want to stop using, you may have to think about leaving the relationship. After all, if you care enough about yourself to stop using, and your partner won't share that goal, how can the relationship be good for you?

In some cases, where there are serious cocaine problems associated with cues in your home environment, avoiding them may even involve relocating to leave cocaine-using neighbors, roommates, lovers, or even your spouse. No one says this will be easy. But you'll have to do whatever is necessary for self-preservation if you want to stop using cocaine badly enough.

Remember that you can never locate and avoid *all* of your cocaine cues. The conditioning link between the subtlest cues and your urge to use cocaine is deep and powerful, often completely below awareness. *Always be prepared for the surprise urge from a hidden cue.* A surprise cocaine cue can pounce on you from out of nowhere. Without warning, you may suddenly be seized by a strong urge to use some coke. You may be amazed that something extremely subtle can set you off—an image that flashes by in a television commercial, something said by someone, an image on a poster or billboard, a smell, a song, seeing someone using cocaine in a movie, or seeing cocaine from an arrest displayed on the news. Going on vacation and finding yourself with nothing to occupy your mind can do it. Running into an old friend you used to use cocaine with can do it. Any holiday, birthday, or celebration on which you used to use cocaine can do it.

Don't panic. It's perfectly all right to feel the urge to use cocaine. Just remember that you can have the desire without actually needing to use the drug. One of the best ways to cope with this situation is to break the association between your cocaine urge and using the drug. The way to do this is to substitute an activity for cocaine-taking, and when you feel the urge—whether from a surprise cue or one you recognize—immediately go to the substitute activity instead of cocaine. After you do this enough times, the cocaine urge will be reduced and the urge for the substitute activity will become stronger.

Substitute Habits. You probably know people who quit smoking cigarettes and coped along the way by fingering worry beads or a trinket and dealt with the need to keep something in their mouths by chewing toothpicks or gum. These are substitute habits and they can help you get past the initial, most difficult, phase of breaking a harmful pattern. In most cases, a quitting smoker loses the need to continue chewing gum or toothpicks after a few weeks or months. This is often the case with substitute habits—they fade out after a time. Cold showers, brisk walks, and black coffee as substitutes for cocaine won't do it forever. Other substitute habits, the ones that bring benefits or pleasure, may be continued for long afterward. Exercise or a new hobby are substitute habits that often prevail long after a bad habit is overcome.

To locate some potential substitute habits, you can use your Coke Book again. Make a list of activities that give you pleasure, as cocaine does; or that dispel tension, as cocaine may do for you; or that make you feel more energetic, as cocaine might; or that improve your mood, if that is what you get from cocaine. Examples of these might be lovemaking or going to a movie or buying yourself a present for pleasure, exercise to get rid of tension or energize yourself, dancing or listening to music to change your mood. If the structure of your cocaine use gives you pleasure—shopping for it, testing it, bargaining for it, setting up the schedule by which you use it—then adopt something similar to take the place of that structure. Embark on a special diet, for instance, that requires a similar kind of ritual, preparation, and involvement. Begin a structured and planned health routine. Do whatever suggests itself to substitute for using cocaine when the urge strikes.

Don't be inhibited about following through with your substitute habits. Don't pay attention to what anyone else thinks, either. They are not trying to quit cocaine; you are. If you're at a party and someone brings out cocaine and you feel the urge to use, and your pleasure substitute is going to the movies, then leave and go to a movie. If your substitute activity is jogging, do that. If you need to carry your running shoes and gear with you everywhere just in case the cocaine urge strikes, then go ahead and do that.

Eliminate Your Access to Cocaine. Since ease of access is crucial to problem cocaine use, one of the easiest ways to help yourself quit is to remove your means of access to the drug. You'll partially accomplish this by spotting and avoiding your cocaine-using cues. By staying away from old haunts and from people you used cocaine with, you'll be limiting your access also. But you can take even further steps to accomplish this. Once again, your Coke Book can be helpful to you here. Start a running list of ways that you have access to cocaine and try to come up with creative ways to remove those means of getting the drug. Here are a few examples.

Access	Solution
■ Jimmy always has cocaine, offers it to me to use or to buy.	■ Avoid Jimmy.
■ One of my clients always offers me cocaine.	■ Drop client. Give client to someone else temporarily. Tell client you're trying to quit and ask him to help you by not offering cocaine.
■ My checking account or savings account. As long as I can get to the money, I'll buy cocaine.	■ Put someone you can trust in charge of your money. Let this person control your bankbook or checkbook.

Do whatever you need to do to limit or eliminate your access to cocaine.

Learn New Ways to Deal with Stress. If you use cocaine to ease anxiety, stress, or nervousness, you need to find new techniques for dispelling tension. Exercise can be helpful here. Join a health club and go every day, no matter what. Avoid predictable sources of stress in your daily life, situations that put you on edge, people who set you off. Learn how to meditate, or learn biofeedback techniques. Book regular time in a "relaxation" flotation tank. Take up yoga. Run, swim, or roll up the windows of your car and drive around screaming until you feel better. Learn to box. Learn karate. Wash your car, mow the lawn, do something that makes you sweat.

There are things you can do to keep stress from taking too high a toll on you. Make sure, for instance, that your diet is well balanced. Make sure you eat three meals a day and get at least eight hours sleep a night. Make sure you're getting enough vitamin C. Drink orange juice and plenty of water. Remember that sex is a great tension release. If you don't have a partner, then fantasize and masturbate.

Once again, you can use your Coke Book here. Make a "Stress List" of sources of stress in your daily life. On the opposite page, make a list of ways to combat or avoid each stress or to deal with the situation to make it less stressful.

Structure Your Time. Some people fall into using too much cocaine because they don't structure their time. They find themselves with unplanned hours to kill, and cocaine—searching for it, arranging for it, bargaining, buying, setting it up, and using—supplies a structure to their time. They continue using it because they have no other structure to compete with the seeking-and-using cycle. Seeking and using replaces productive work, or productive leisure, or both. To quit cocaine, you may have to impose a structure on your time that shuts out the seek-and-use cycle.

A job can be the most powerful and satisfying time-structuring device known. In fact, all the studies of people trying to stop using any kind of drug show that holding a job is one of the most effective methods for success. This holds true whether or not the person needs the income from the job. Even if you are being handsomely supported by a husband, wife, trust fund, inheritance, or investment portfolio, working will help you quit cocaine. A job is far more than just a way to earn a living. It structures your time, provides a sense of focus, gives a feeling of purpose and self-worth. It gets you out of the house if you're depressed and makes every day more meaningful. It doesn't matter if you don't find the job of your dreams right away, just as long as you keep occupied.

If you're working, then you can set about structuring

your time. There are several ways to do this. One is to make sure you plan ahead. For instance, know by Wednesday or Thursday what you'll be doing Friday evening. For the initial stages of quitting, leave nothing to chance—the urge to use cocaine can seep in to fill any time gaps you leave, so plug all the holes in your calendar.

This does not mean you have to have big doings or a wild social life to account for every minute of leisure time. All it means is that you've committed yourself for most of the free time you have. For instance, you can go to the movies Friday night, go food shopping Saturday, visit a friend Saturday night, read the paper Sunday morning, go to brunch in the afternoon, balance your checkbook and pay your bills in the evening, and catch up on your reading at night. It helps to write down your schedule. If you don't keep a date book or wall calendar for your activities, make use of your Coke Book to keep a record of your scheduled activities so that you know what you're supposed to be doing when.

Sometimes it is difficult to analyze and arrange your leisure time, so here's a helpful list of questions to ask yourself. Write down the questions and answers in your Coke Book.

- How do you spend your spare time?
- What activities do you enjoy or look forward to?
- Are you an indoor person or an outdoor person? A day person or a night person? (Use the answers to help you choose activities to structure your time.)
- How much time do you spend alone? (Be specific.) Do you like being alone or is it a source of unhappiness? Do you use cocaine alone? (If you like being alone, fine. But if you don't, and if you then use cocaine to feel better or make the time pass, take note of this and make it your business to spend time with other people.)
- What sports or other physical activities have you excelled in? Would you like to pick these up again now as a way of structuring leisure time?
- What do you do for exercise now? If you don't do anything, what do you think you'd like to do?

- What hobbies or pastimes have you had or think you might like to try?
- When do you feel bored? Be aware that these are probably the most important spots to fill with activities.
- Before you started using cocaine, *what did you do when you were bored or had nothing else to occupy you?* (If your answer is that you used some other drug, even alcohol, then you've got to concentrate especially hard on finding alternate activities. If not, ask yourself if you can begin doing again what you used to do.)

Here are some general suggestions for structuring your leisure time.

- Find a buddy to plan activities with, or find several, one for each planned activity—jogging, going to the theater, going to museums, shopping.
- Take a class. Classes are good scheduled activities. An aerobics or exercise class, for example, will kill two birds with one stone: schedule your time and give you the anti-cocaine benefits of exercise. Take singing lessons, dancing lessons, or piano lessons. Take a drawing or painting course. Take a cooking or sewing class. Audition for a play. Go back to school, start working on another degree or, if you never started, begin working toward one.
- Plan to do all the things you've been meaning to do for a while: refinish a piece of furniture, learn to use a computer, plant a garden, start spring cleaning now even if it's still January.

Just make sure you schedule everything ahead of time and stick to your plan.

Set Goals. Setting goals not only adds structure to your life but also provides you with a very concrete way to measure your progress. It keeps things from becoming abstract and keeps you focused on what you're trying to accomplish. These goals should apply not only to aspects of your cocaine use but also to your basic aims in life. Once set, they will give you the incentive to keep at it.

You can use goal-setting to implement all the other quitting methods. If you substitute running for cocaine, for instance, don't simply say, "I'm going to run instead of using cocaine." Give yourself something to work toward—"I'll run half a mile when I feel like using cocaine and add a quarter of a mile a week until I reach two miles."

Setting goals can take any form that works for you. Be inventive. You can set goals relative to your cocaine use—for example, "I'll use cocaine until my three-day weekend and then stop completely." (We've seen again and again that the best method is to stop cold.)

Use your Coke Book to keep lists of your goals. Also keep records of your progress toward achieving your goals, and most important, when you reach a goal, give yourself a reward for making it. Take yourself out to dinner, buy yourself a present, think of an activity that gives you pleasure. Rewarding yourself when you achieve what you set out to do is extremely important.

One very good way to set goals is to figure out the amount of money you usually spend on cocaine and keep careful track of how much of it you are saving week by week. You can use your Coke Book to do this. When you reach one of your goals, use the money to buy yourself a special reward.

Rewarding yourself each step of the way is crucial. As we've pointed out again and again, one of the most basic reasons why people overuse drugs is to get the kind of good feelings they never learned how to give themselves without drugs. One way to start to learn how to give yourself good feelings is to begin rewarding yourself when you reach your goals. In fact, you can even write down the specific reward you'll give yourself next to each goal on the list in your log book.

Learn How to Give Yourself Gifts and Good Feelings. Aside from rewarding yourself for reaching your goals, there are many other ways to learn how to make yourself feel good. Go back to the Dreams List in your Coke Book, for instance, and remind yourself of what you're trying to accomplish in life. You may want to make another list of intermediate dreams, a "Wish List" of things you can accomplish or acquire over the short term—like a particular piece of clothing, a particular achievement at work or at home—not far-reaching goals, but ones that will give you more immediate pleasure. Go back over your list of assets and remind yourself of your strengths and good qualities when you feel shaky, lack confidence, or are frightened.

Make out a calendar for the next three months and mark on it any special anniversary dates that have particular meaning for you. Be sure to reward yourself in some way when they come around. Another way to reward yourself is to work to change what displeases you about your appearance. If you're out of shape, get into shape by starting an exercise program. Not only will looking better reward you, but exercise will also serve as habit substitution, help you structure your time, and reduce stress. Exercise solves a multitude of problems. In addition to getting in shape, update your wardrobe. Make an effort to make yourself feel good by paying special attention to looking as good as you can. If getting dressed up for ordinary occasions makes you feel extra special, then do it.

Also, go back to the list you made of the positive effects you get from cocaine—elation, sense of control, excitement or thrills, sense of mastery—and make a new list of things you know you can do to give yourself similar feelings, *without* cocaine. If you can't think of anything, then use your imagination. Write down what you *think* will deliver that effect, and then see how close you can actually come to achieving the feeling. Here are some basic guidelines for making yourself feel the kind of good feelings you get from cocaine without the drug.

■ If cocaine gives you a feeling of excitement, then take up activities that will give you the same kind of adrenaline rush. The rule is that if you want thrills, do thrilling things. Take a positive risk. Take a raft down the rapids, go flying in an air chamber, learn to ski, try dirt-bike motorcycle racing. Get your kicks from action, not drugs.

■ If cocaine makes you relaxed, removed from what jars

your nerves, "floating," think of "otherworldly" kinds of experiences like deep-sea diving, snorkeling, isolation tanks, lying under a lonely open sky feeling the sun or watching the stars, or just relaxing in a darkened room with a white-noise machine. Try taking a shower while sitting in the bathtub as it fills up—this can be both relaxing and stimulating at the same time.

■ If cocaine gives you a sense of mastery and control, then use a list to explore what you do or might do to get those same feelings, and pursue that. What do you do well? Do more of it.

■ The same goes for any other feeling you get from coke: sexual arousal, confidence, clarity of thought. Use lists and the Dream Picture method to discover how you can get those feelings without drugs.

Do whatever you need to do that will give you pleasure, as long as it has nothing to do with cocaine or drugs.

Keep Ugly Reminders Available. Some people are able to keep themselves on a diet by constantly reminding themselves of how awful they looked when they were overweight. They'll take an unflattering photograph of themselves at their heaviest and tape it to the refrigerator door. Every time they're tempted to cheat on their diet, the photo is there as an ugly reminder of the cost of giving in to temptation. This may sound crude or comical, but it really works. Linda decided not to replace the worn carpet in her bedroom after she quit cocaine. Instead, she lets the threadbare path remind her of how agitated the drug had made her.

Some of the people we've told you about have permanent ugly reminders about what cocaine use cost them. Every time Tina takes out her false teeth at bedtime, she's reminded of what cocaine use cost her. One patient of ours contracted a massive infection in her arm from shooting cocaine with an unclean needle. Most of the muscles were removed from her arm in order to save it. Her withered, ruined arm is a constant ugly reminder of the damage caused by her drug abuse.

In choosing an ugly reminder you can use anything that will keep you from forgetting the damage cocaine may have done to you. You can, for example, gather all the overdue or unpaid bills you may have accrued if you bought cocaine instead of keeping up with your expenses. Frame them where you'll see them every day, or keep them in a safe place and, when you're feeling weak, take them out and go through them. You can do the same thing with a canceled bankbook if you've emptied a savings account to buy cocaine or with checks you may have cashed to buy the drug. One patient of ours pawned an antique watch for money to buy cocaine. He was never able to reclaim it, so he carried the pawn ticket around with him as an ugly reminder.

If your cocaine use has resulted in any visible damage or change in your immediate environment, don't repair it right away. Leave it to serve as an ugly reminder. Some people who freebase, for instance, are prone to dropping their lighter or blowtorch and starting small fires at home. If you've done this, leave the blackened remains around as ugly reminders. If you've dented the car while high on cocaine and you can manage to postpone repairing it while still driving it, do it. The dent will be an ugly reminder.

One of our patients carries in his wallet at all times a plaintive, agonized note written to him by his teenage daughter, begging him to stop using cocaine. If you lost your job because of cocaine, keep your last pay stub or your unemployment application around as an ugly reminder. Anything will do, as long as it works.

Do *not*, however, use cocaine as an ugly reminder. Some people have the notion that if they carry cocaine around with them, it will remind them that they're trying to quit. This is a bad idea. In this case, cocaine will serve not as a reminder but as a temptation. Remember that you are not quitting cocaine in order to prove your willpower to yourself or anyone else. You are quitting to do what you know is best for yourself, your health, your peace of mind, your work, your future.

Reach Out to Other People. Quitting cocaine without en-listing emotional support from anyone is difficult. No one can quit for you, but other people may be able to help you feel better while you're doing it. They can give you love and support and can listen to you. Talking about how you feel when you're quitting can be a good substitute activity for using cocaine. It is also a good way to develop the habit of making an emotional connection with other people in order to feel better.

Reaching out to people is something you can think of under the heading "Learning to Give Yourself Good Feelings." Contact, connectedness, the feeling that someone else is on your side and interested in your success are wonderful gifts to give yourself. Perhaps the best feeling you can treat yourself to is that of caring and kindness for others. Thoughtful deeds and making an effort to help someone else can make your own troubles less painful.

There are many ways to reach out to other people that will help you quit cocaine and stay away from it. Some of these ways are very structured, like the buddy system, therapy, or self-help groups, and some are free-flowing and natural and happen normally in the course of friendship. In studies of people trying to stop using alcohol and heroin, or even cigarettes, a significant relationship with a nondrug-using person is an important factor in a high success rate. An alcoholic whose spouse is not a drinker has a much higher statistical chance of succeeding than a similar alcoholic who is alone or whose mate has a drinking problem. The close emotional link with someone who does not use drugs lends many kinds of strength to the person trying to quit. This important nondrug-using person doesn't have to be a husband, wife, or lover. He or she can be a roommate or a close family member. All that matters is that the relationship is important in your life.

The Buddy Principle. An effective support for quitting cocaine is to find a "quitting buddy." If you've never done anything like this and it sounds strange to you, read on. The buddy system is one of the best ways to quit any habitual behavior. It is successfully used in cigarette-stopping groups, in Alcoholics Anonymous, and many similar situations.

Whom you pick to be your buddy is important—whether it is a friend, a brother, sister, or grandparent, an aunt or uncle, your minister, your doctor, or your attorney. Pick whoever works for you. Follow these guidelines when you choose your buddy.

■ Do *not* pick someone who uses drugs—cocaine or anything else.
■ Pick someone who you know will be strong enough to say no.
■ Make sure it is someone with whom you feel you can be open and honest.

Look around at your circle of people. Pick as a buddy someone who seems to get what he or she wants out of life, who seems to have his or her act together, someone you admire and respect.

It may not be a good idea to pick a mate, lover, or parent as your buddy, since there is often too much emotional heat there to allow for the objectivity a buddy needs.

You may feel embarrassed or self-conscious about asking someone to be your quitting buddy. Don't let those feelings prevent you from finding your ally. Be straightforward with the person you've chosen. Tell him or her that you're going to quit cocaine and would like help. Explain how the buddy system works and ask your friend to participate. Most people like to be needed and may even feel flattered to have been chosen. Asking someone to be your quitting buddy can be taken as a compliment. It shows that you trust that person's judgment and admire his or her character and strength.

Having found a buddy, the first step is for you to agree that the basis for your "partnership" is quitting cocaine; that's the priority, that's the goal. This is an opportunity to make clear, completely understood mutual agreements with another person. Your buddy must want to be there for you should you run into trouble while quitting—if you have a cocaine urge and want to talk it out instead of using, if you feel depressed about quitting, if you backslide and need to confide—anything at all. The idea is to have a shared sense of purpose with your buddy and to know that he or she wants to help you succeed. Telling all the world about your cocaine use won't get you the response you want, but talking about your cravings to your buddy will give you the support you need.

Make sure you can call your buddy twenty-four hours a day if you really need to. When you do need to call, don't hold anything inside you. That may be the reason you overused cocaine to begin with. Whenever you feel the urge to use and can't succeed in beating it with any other methods, call your buddy. Do it right away, as soon as you feel the craving. Do not ignore the first signal hoping it will pass—by the time you prove how strong you are, you may already have given in.

Integrate your buddy system with your everyday routine. Make a regular weekly schedule for checking in with your buddy, say once in the morning and once at night, every day. Exercise with your buddy if you can. Plan other leisure activities with your buddy if that is possible. Discuss your schedule, your goals; ask for your buddy's opinion and participation.

Change Friends and Make New Ones. Make a conscious effort to cultivate new friendships with people who do not use cocaine. They may have a lot to offer you. Pay particular attention to how they make themselves feel good without cocaine.

Avoid cocaine-using friends whenever possible. It does not pay to reach out to users when you're trying to quit because they increase odds that you will backslide.

Make Contracts and Keep Them; Renegotiate Them as Time Goes By. Contracting is a very powerful way to help yourself quit cocaine. It can be used in many different ways.

Whenever you set goals for yourself and then work toward them, you're contracting with yourself. You can also contract with yourself by setting limits and then abiding by them. For example, no cocaine during sex, cocaine on only one weekend day, no more than four lines. These are all examples of contracting with yourself. Since it is easier to break contracts with yourself, it is often more effective to make contracts with other people.

You can contract with your buddy or with someone close to you, a friend, spouse, relative, or lover. The point of contracting is to give yourself a concrete limit to abide by, a clearly achievable goal to attain, a line that you agree not to cross. Contracting makes you take responsibility for what you are doing, and if you break the contract, you will know that you did it, when you did it, and how. This will help you see how to be more successful at keeping your contracts in the future. Here are some suggestions for contracts to make while quitting cocaine.

With Yourself

■ The next time someone offers me cocaine at a party I'm going to say, "No, thanks, it gives me a headache."

With Someone Else

■ Arrange alternative activities to cocaine, to be planned for when cocaine becomes available. Contract with a friend, for instance, that you'll call her and plan a dinner out whenever anyone who offers you cocaine calls and wants to get together. Refuse the cocaine caller and honor your dinner contract.

Most contracts need to be renegotiated from time to time. If you fail to honor one of your agreements not to use cocaine with yourself or with someone else, don't punish yourself for it. Don't bathe in guilt or self-recrimination. Renegotiate the agreement. Accept what you did or did not do, take responsibility for it, and then make a realistic agreement. You'll keep it this time. Go on with your quitting program.

It may be that your being unable to keep the contract says something about the agreement. Sylvia had promised to do sit-ups for twenty minutes instead of giving in to the impulse to snort cocaine. When her new lover offered it in the bedroom she gave in rather than crawl out from under the cozy covers to do exercises. Was your contract unrealistic or too difficult to reach at this point in your quitting program? Did you push yourself too hard too fast? If so, reevaluate the terms of the contract so that it suits you and your individual needs.

After you've been on your quitting program for a few weeks or months, you may find the contracts too easy to honor. This probably means you're doing very well and may need to renegotiate the terms in order to make them more challenging. If you've contracted with yourself or a friend not to use cocaine more than once a week, for instance, and you've adhered to that for three months—up the stakes. Contract not to use more than once every month. Keep challenging yourself. Renegotiate your contracts after three, six, and nine months, until you feel you have achieved your goals.

One way to help yourself stick to your contracts is to set up specific penalties, agreed upon beforehand, for breaking your agreements. The purpose of the penalties is not to punish yourself but to remind yourself that breaking the agreement costs you something important. If there is a penalty for backsliding, it will become associated with an unpleasant outcome. This is a simple form of aversive conditioning. Written contracts with a list of written penalties work very well here, and your Coke Book is a good place to keep them. Sign and date both, and if you contract with your buddy, ask him or her to do the same.

Penalties can include denying yourself something significant—giving away a pair of treasured baseball or theater tickets, for example, or running an extra three laps every day for a week while your buddy sits and watches.

Self-Help Groups. Sometimes quitting cocaine is easier if you ally yourself with other people who are trying to do the same thing. This is the principle of most of the stop-smoking groups and also of groups like Alcoholics Anonymous, Narcotics Anonymous, and Pills Anonymous. A self-help group offers powerful support, a sense of being safe among other people who understand what you're going through because they have experienced it themselves. A self-help group can also help you stay on the track if you backslide. Most self-help groups will not downgrade you if you relapse (they know backsliding is a predictable part of quitting) and will encourage you to get started again and again. Self-help groups are also an unlimited source of buddies.

Over the past few years, cocaine self-help groups have been sprouting all over the country. These groups work along the same basic four principles as Alcoholics Anonymous: acknowledgment of cocaine as a problem to other members of the group; confiding; sharing of tragedies and successes; and a structured supportive environment that keeps members focused on quitting. Self-help groups will not quit for you, but they can offer immeasurable support. Some of the groups, like Cokenders in California, are focused on breaking the cycle of regular use with a concentrated one-week course held in a country retreat. Most programs charge fees; a few, like Cocaine Anonymous in Los Angeles, work like AA and cost nothing.

If there is no self-help cocaine group near you, you can look into the possibility of starting one yourself. Many community organizations will be willing to assist you in the formation of a much-needed group. In addition many regions have information clearinghouses that keep lists of self-help groups in your area, or they know where to get information on how to form your own group. Schools and churches will often aid in setting up such a group, or they may know someone who can help you.

Stop Using Cocaine for at Least Three Months; Avoid the Relapse Binge Trap. In quitting cocaine, or anything else for that matter, the first three months are crucial. It is during this period that the old habit patterns are strongest and require the most effort and concentration to break. During the first three to six months the tendency to *relapse* and *binge* is at its peak for every kind of health habit program. That includes dieting and dental care as well as kicking cigarettes, alcohol, or drugs.

But you can avoid the "Relapse Binge" trap if you know how. Here's how it works.

The first thing to remember is that the odds are high that you will relapse at least once during this time. Don't be too hard on yourself *if* it occurs. You'll succeed at quitting much more easily if you understand that you're testing your new limits. Give yourself permission to fail *after* it happens. If you relapse, *don't make it more than it is.* Try to avoid falling into a self-punishing frame of mind, because that is where the Relapse Binge is waiting. Don't use that one time as proof that you can't succeed at quitting. Many people immediately feel defeated, beaten, inadequate after they give in and use cocaine again. The reasoning runs like this.

"After five weeks [three months, four and a half months] of quitting, I *still* used it again. I guess I can't stay away from it, so I might as well just start using it again now."

The person gives up all the gains he's made, surrenders to his cocaine urge, and in short order he's binged or gone right back to where he was before he started quitting.

Don't do this to yourself. If you relapse, remember that all it means is you didn't make it through that *one* time. What about all the other days when you succeeded? And what about tomorrow, when you can continue quitting? Go right on with your quitting program. Give yourself a reward each time you return to your program. You're going to make it!

At the end of three months of no cocaine, give yourself a substantial reward for your success. If you've relapsed but always returned to your quitting program, then give yourself a reward (*not* cocaine) for sticking to it. Give yourself a reward for quitting cold or for cutting down substantially. Give yourself a reward for any progress at all.

The methods we have outlined work for most people.

Pick the ones that work for you and use them, combine them, modify them to make them better. If you're a Social Sniffer, Routine User, Performance User, or Bordeom/Stress Reliever, you can probably use these techniques to quit cocaine. But if you find you are always saying that you are going to quit tomorrow, and tomorrow never comes, then it is time to seek some professional help.

Help from
Professionals

Seeking help is not a sign that you are weak; it is the intelli-
gent, take-charge response to a problem you want to solve.
Wisdom is knowing that you are facing something beyond
your control and being brave enough to seek assistance from
someone who can help you. A painful stomachache that
does not go away is cause to see a doctor. If you knew the
pain was appendicitis, you wouldn't try to remove your own
appendix; you'd go to a competent surgeon. The same kind
of logic applies to a cocaine problem you can't tackle on your
own. Find a professional with the skills to help you.

Professional help can be found in three types of settings:
private psychotherapy, outpatient drug-abuse programs,
and inpatient hospital care. There are many different kinds
of psychotherapy, but all involve working with a trained
therapist whose aim it is first to stop cocaine use, then to get
at the underlying causes for it. Outpatient drug-abuse programs offer medical services, counseling, or therapy, while
inpatient hospitals that are equipped to deal with serious cocaine problems handle patients who may require detoxifica-
tion, withdrawal, and the reestablishment of physical and

psychological health. Hospitalization is usually followed by some form of therapeutic support.

Psychotherapy

If you opt for psychotherapy, the most important thing for you is to make sure that you choose a qualified therapist. You must find someone who is knowledgeable and experienced in treating people with drug problems.

This is crucial because drug-abusing or addictive behavior must be handled in very specific ways, and the truth is that most therapists, whether psychologists or psychiatrists, are not trained, experienced, or knowledgeable in these techniques. There are also many therapists who have negative attitudes (based on old and deep-rooted clinical myths and prejudices) about treating people with drug problems. Therapists with this outlook will be of no value to you.

You must be able to tell your therapist about your cocaine problem right from the start. There is no value in entering therapy if you don't do this. You need a therapist who will respond supportively to your cocaine problem, who will not judge or condemn you, and who also knows how to help you.

There are several ways to find such an experienced therapist.

- Ask your friends who use or have been in treatment for cocaine or other drug abuse. This includes friends or acquaintances who may have overcome alcohol problems.
- Ask your friends who are in therapy if you can ask their therapist for a referral.
- Call one of the referral services in your city. They usually work anonymously and may have the names of several therapists for you.
- Call any of the emergency drug-abuse or crisis hotlines in your area. Again, you can remain anonymous and get the information you need.
- Call the psychiatric service of a local hospital.
- Call psychotherapy training institutes in your area.
- Call your community mental-health center.

- Call the counseling or psychology departments of local universities.
- Make an anonymous call to the state agency that oversees substance-abuse services in your area.
- Ask your family doctor or your clergyman.
- Contact any of the resources listed in the Where to Get Help section of this book.

How to Choose the Right Therapist. First, find out if he or she is experienced and trained in treating drug problems. Find out specifics—does he work mostly with alcoholics, chronic marijuana smokers, cocaine users, heroin users, all or some of them?

If you're unsure about how to evaluate the answer, ask the therapist in what clinics or training programs he got his training. Don't be timid about asking how long he was there, what kinds of patients he treated. Remember you are not the only one being evaluated. If you need to "shop around," interview three or four therapists until you find the right one.

Ask your potential therapist how he or she feels about drugs and people who use drugs. Ask if he has ever used drugs himself. Watch and listen to the response. Pay attention to his face and tone of voice. Does he sound and look easy? Relaxed, nonjudgmental? Is his manner straightforward and open? Does he seem empathetic to your pain and confident in his ability to deal with your cocaine problem? Is this someone who is in control and who can help you get back in control?

If the answers to all these questions satisfy you, then you've probably found someone who can help you. Trust your instincts. The most important ingredient in therapy is the quality of the relationship. "Chemistry" is important.

Kinds of Therapies and Therapy Tools. Although there are a few different approaches to psychotherapy for cocaine problems, all of them start out with the same initial steps.

The first session will be a consultation, given over to evaluation and assessment, in which the therapist will gather information from you about your medical and psychological history, the specifics of your cocaine-abuse behavior, your living and family situations. From this, he or she will help you work out short- and long-term goals.

It is possible that the therapist may ask you to bring in your spouse or the family members with whom you live. The therapist will be able to help you and them to talk about cocaine or related issues and perhaps make some agreements that will help all of you to know what to expect and to prepare you for the changes you'll all go through.

Your therapist may use any one or combination of therapies.

Individual Therapy. This consists primarily of you and your therapist talking, and mostly of your talking to him or her. The goal is to establish a foundation of trust between you and the therapist so that both of you can explore the problems that led to and sustain your cocaine abuse. Its ultimate goal is to help you alleviate the most damaging symptoms of those problems (in this case cocaine abuse) and to learn to develop better coping skills, a better attitude about yourself and others, and a more pleasing self-image.

Family Therapy. This approach aims to locate and treat any problems that may arise out of your interactions with those in your immediate living situation. Family members are periodically brought into therapy with you so that by exploring your interactions you can develop new ways to communicate and deal with one another.

Group Therapy. Here, therapy usually takes place among six to twelve group members and one or two therapists. All the same factors operate here as in individual therapy, with the added factor that the group structure acts as an artificially created social system and can help its members to encounter and deal with a wider range of issues than individual therapy can. It is also less expensive than individual therapy. It can be especially effective when the group members share the same problem—cocaine abuse.

Behavior Modification. These therapies are based on the idea that outward behaviors are more important than the inner drives, forces, needs, or traits that may underlie them. Destructive behaviors like cocaine abuse are seen as learned, maladaptive responses to past or recent influences in the person's environment, rather than expressions of inner pain or turmoil. The goal in these therapies is to in effect "retrain" the patient by manipulating factors in the environment that precede or follow cocaine use.

Some behaviorists are giving patients a benign liquid that smells like cocaine. After using the pseudococaine but getting no effect, their craving for the drug tapers off. Some therapists just have the cocaine abuser practice saying no to a tray of white powder over and over again until he is desensitized to the cues that made him want the drug so badly. Finally, seeing cocaine or being offered cocaine ceases to be exciting to him.

Aversive therapy is a form of behavior modification. In one version of it, patients are repeatedly shown photographs of the damage caused by cocaine abuse—photographs of damaged nasal membranes or perforated septums, photos of cocaine-damaged lung tissue, pictures of the seizure-battered bodies of cocaine overdose victims, or the scars abusers have gouged in their flesh scratching after coke bugs. Other sorts of behavior modification involve rewarding the patient for successfully resisting cocaine compulsions.

Your therapist may use or suggest you use one of several additional techniques along with your course of therapy. Here are some.

Blackmail. This is used by the Cocaine Clinic in Aspen. Blackmail is effective in preventing the relapses or binges that impede progress in therapy. The patient deposits a signed letter with his therapist. The letter usually contains the most abhorrent self-damaging information the individual can think of. It is often a signed admission of cocaine abuse addressed to one's professional licensing board, one's employer, or a newspaper. One staunch conservative wrote a check to Senator Ted Kennedy's election fund and gave it to his therapist to hold and mail if he used cocaine.

These patients take random urine tests. If they show cocaine use, the letter is mailed. The success rate for abstinence is about 90 percent. When people risk the most important thing they can think of, they tend to stick to their quitting program.

Urine Screenings. These are generally done through a clinic or in conjunction with one. Your therapist may ask you to submit random, frequent urine samples to be tested for cocaine consumption. This is a way to keep things honest and direct without accusations or denials. In the early stages of a serious cocaine problem, and even for a time after therapy begins, this is often a good way to help yourself control the impulse to binge. You won't be tempted to cheat and then hide it from your therapist.

Acupuncture is sometimes used to relieve tension or anxiety, to dispel stress, to help you relax. There is currently research being conducted on the efficacy of acupuncture as a method to reduce addictive cravings.

Hypnosis may help you begin and maintain your abstinence from cocaine.

A very small percentage of problem cocaine users have specific metabolic or physiological sensitivities that cause them to seek and use cocaine not only for its psychological effects, but for the physical boost it gives them. Your therapist may suggest that you be tested for this. If you have one of these conditions, there are several drugs that may help you to stop using cocaine. These are not magic cures; they just help temporarily to alleviate any physically based cocaine cravings. Since their use is still experimental, these drugs are generally prescribed through research programs on cocaine-abuse problems.

In the same way, some people use cocaine to self-medicate an underlying chronic depression. If this turns out to be true for you, your therapist may arrange for you to receive antidepressant medication for a while. This, too, can be helpful.

No matter what type of therapy you enter, there will likely be two principles your therapist will use in order to limit and then eliminate your cocaine problem.

Making Contracts. Contracting in therapy works very similarly to contracting with yourself or a buddy when quitting on your own; it is, however, more structured and the therapist takes a more active part in setting the terms with you. Our contracts with cocaine-abusing patients are written or oral. We find that written ones work best, since we can both refer to them. These contracts spell out very specifically a patient's short-term goals and expectations and include penalties. They also include our expectations. For example, one contract we make with all our patients is that if they come to the office high on cocaine, they will pay for their therapy session, but will also leave *immediately* and lose the session.

The therapeutic contract is a way to anticipate possible problems in a calm and thoughtful way and to come to workable terms and solutions before they happen. When the issues in the contract crop up in treatment, you can avoid engaging in a verbal power struggle—"But you agreed not to . . ." "I didn't say . . ."—by referring to the written contract you've both agreed to and signed.

As with contracts for self-quitters, these are renegotiated every three, six, nine months, and so on, as your needs and goals change. This is also an effective way to look back and see the progress you've made.

Setting Limits. When someone's drug use is out of control, he needs a therapist who can help him hold the line. Your therapist may insist on cocaine-free urines and will resist your efforts to skirt the rules you agree upon. These rules are important because it is a person's diminished ability to set and abide by limits that contributed to drug-abuse behavior in the first place. A good therapist will take an active role in continually setting limits and consistently saying no when it is appropriate. Here's a typical example of how limit setting works.

A patient comes to a session high on cocaine, and the therapist asks him to leave. The patient states that he isn't high—he just drank a lot of coffee. The therapist refers to the contract and gently reminds the patient that they agreed that if he even *appears* high he's required to leave. No matter how the patient tries to engage the therapist, with rational arguments, pleas, anger, accusations, the therapist will escort him to the door and reschedule the next appointment. He makes it clear that he is not angry with the patient, but rather is demonstrating how much he cares. In this way, no matter how out of control a cocaine-abusing patient may feel, he knows he can count on the therapist's consistent but caring setting of limits.

Involving Your Family in Your Problem. It is often beneficial for your family to be included in therapy with you at the very beginning. We believe in utilizing every resource and support system a patient has to help him keep his life intact. A loving family is often the best resource a person can have. By enlisting the cooperation of family members, patients can make tremendous progress.

A patient of ours, Rose, was a Boredom/Stress Reliever. At 28 she was once again unemployed, having lost her job as a receptionist because of lateness. She now spent her time in bed watching TV and using cocaine. Her parents had always paid all the bills (including the tab for cocaine, although they didn't know it at the time). They learned through a call from a hospital emergency room that their daughter was a serious cocaine abuser and had just suffered an overdose. They were referred to Creative Solutions. At first their reaction to Rose's cocaine abuse was outrage, hurt, and confusion, but they followed our suggestions and pulled together as a strong, loving family unit. We met for a series of twelve family sessions and worked out a contract that cut Rose off from any control of her finances. All of Rose's monies would be handled by her parents and would continue to be even after she had gotten a job. Paychecks would be mailed directly to her parent's home and they would give Rose an allowance for carfare and lunch. Rose had a limited time in which to find work (six weeks). Within three months, their financial support would be slowly withdrawn. Rose would stand on her own.

The sessions provided support, direction, encouragement, and advice for Rose's parents. They talked about their fears about what might happen to Rose if they cut her off and about their guilt. When Rose relapsed during the fifth week of treatment we gathered for an emergency family meeting. We decided it was best for Rose to move back home to a structured and supervised atmosphere. We met with

Rose's parents frequently during the first few weeks. They were eager to help Rose get back on the right track but just not sure what they ought to be doing. We began at the beginning. Rose's urine would be randomly collected so we would know for sure whether Rose was cocaine-free. Her bankbooks, jewelry, and any other valuables were locked away. Her parents began to learn how to set limits to deal with their daughter's anger and threats. They learned that Rose's liking them at the moment was not so important. They needed to be firm and clear and protect Rose from herself. Rose remained in this sheltered environment for four months.

It has been eleven months now and Rose has been working steadily for nine months. She has not missed one day of work or come in late. Although she had to give up some of her friends, she says it was worth the trade because she had not used any cocaine since that last "mini-binge" ten months ago. Rose's parents told us that now they understand that saying no when appropriate is the most loving gift they could give their child.

Clinics

If you can't afford to enter private therapy or your health insurance won't cover it, you can enter the outpatient program of a drug-treatment clinic. There are only a few that specialize in cocaine treatment. Most of them are in or near major cities, and they can be difficult to find. The majority of them are publicly funded, but over the past few years a small but growing number of private practitioners have started clinics that deal exclusively with cocaine abuse.

The largest number of clinics are federally funded drug rehabilitation and treatment programs. Most of them are connected with university or teaching hospitals or community service institutions. To locate them, contact university hospitals or teaching hospitals near you. You can also call the department of psychiatry at any medical school near you. Community mental-health centers, information clearinghouses, municipal health departments, and drug or crisis hotlines can also be good sources. You might even contact one of the major TV networks or a local station. Cocaine abuse has been getting a good deal of media coverage lately and they may have a place to refer you to.

Although the number of clinic programs specifically aimed at cocaine abuse have been few until very recently, drug rehabilitation facilities sometimes offer treatment to cocaine abusers in conjunction with their larger programs. If you find the only specialized treatment in your community lies within the confines of a heroin or methadone treatment center, consider it anyway. You won't be the only person there who is not a methadone patient.

What to Expect When You Register at a Clinic. First, you'll need to call and schedule an appointment in advance. On the day you go for your intake evaluation, there may be a long wait. Bring something to occupy you. Also bring documentation (birth certificate, driver's license, union card, credit card). Some clinics may insist on photo I.D.'s. Also bring your health insurance information if you have it. Be prepared.

The first person you see will generally be an intake worker who will register you. This person may be a skilled psychotherapist or a trained ex-addict. You may be asked to fill out questionnaires. This can take anywhere from twenty minutes to a few hours, depending on the clinic. You'll be asked about your race, religion, economic status, your work and family status, your drug problems, and other medical and psychiatric information. If the clinic is connected to a medical school research program, you may be asked to participate in that program. You may be asked to sign a release enabling the clinic to obtain information about you from other clinics, physicians, or psychiatric facilities you may have visited. You'll be given a physical examination.

If you enter a clinic program, you can expect to find a broad range of patients there with you, from down-and-out ex-addicts to prominent citizens. There is also a broad range of services offered under varying conditions. Waiting lists for treatment may be long and no therapy may be available for months, or ever. Clinics vary widely—they are a hit-or-miss proposition and range from excellent to barely adequate. At some, you may be offered counseling or psychotherapy; at others you may be offered basic supportive services like employment referrals and vocational programs. Some clinics may offer you medication with or without psychotherapy. The counselor assigned to you can vary from clinic to clinic and can range from a skilled psychotherapist to an ex-addict counselor or a student who may know less than you do about cocaine and human behavior.

Evaluate a clinic with the same criteria you would use to evaluate a psychotherapist. Find out about the staff experience and training. Look at the general attitude of the staff or the counselor assigned to you. Are they helpful and supportive or cool and remote? Do they seem harried or too busy for you? If you are assigned a therapist or counselor, pay attention to who this person is. Do his values, education, life-style seem similar to yours or what you aspire to? Can you identify with him and make an alliance with him to overcome your problem? Try to discover this person's attitude toward drug use and drug users. Is it nonjudgmental and open? Use your intuition. It's ultimately your relationship with the therapist or counselor that counts. If it feels right, stick with it.

The outpatient routine will vary from clinic to clinic. You may be asked to come to the clinic daily, at least at the beginning, to give a supervised urine sample to be tested for cocaine use and to talk with your counselor and possibly a physician or physician's assistant. You may be asked to come in only once or twice a week, or once every two weeks. This depends on clinic practices and on the nature of your cocaine problem. The clinic program may or may not have a time structure. It can consist of a six-week intensive program to start, followed by a one-year follow-up of counseling and aftercare, or it may be completely open-ended, available to you for as long as you need its services. Much of this depends on whether the program is publicly or privately funded. You'll likely have more options at a privately run facility, although this can be expensive.

Going into the Hospital

These are special inpatient medical settings where people with serious cocaine problems go (or are sent) in order to halt severe abuse or addiction, and to recover enough to embark on a long-term therapy program. Hospital stays for cocaine abuse are necessary when the person requires close medical and psychological supervision for a short period.

Hospitalization may be the only alternative for the most serious class of Cokeaholics. In a hospital, the person is separated from drugs, can't hurt himself or others, is monitored, and can get intense crisis intervention, including therapy, medications, and rehabilitation.

How to Find a Hospital with a Cocaine Treatment Program. There are not many hospitals with programs specially designed to intervene in acute cocaine abuse. There are several, however, and there are substantially more that have good psychiatric care facilities with general drug treatment programs. The best way to locate and evaluate one is to ask your family doctor or psychotherapist. If that's not possible, call university teaching hospitals in your area and inquire there. Effective drug-abuse treatment, especially for cocaine abuse, is a relatively new field and many of the better programs are in teaching or university hospitals that also do research. Another alternative is to try any of the crisis intervention or drug hotlines in your area, or a mental-health center or information clearinghouse. You can also call or write to NIDA (The National Institute for Drug Abuse) in Rockville, Maryland. Check the Where to Get Help list in the back of the book for addresses and phone numbers.

Entering the Hospital. No one ever said going into the hospital for a cocaine problem was a vacation, but cocaine treatment facilities do vary widely from hospital to hospital. Accommodations can run from the barest, most basic amenities, like an army-type cot, to private rooms with silk sheets on the beds and designer chocolates on the night table.

Ultimately, though, the accommodations are unimportant. What is most crucial is that you receive proper treatment for your cocaine problem. For a limited time you must turn control of your treatment, yourself, your day-to-day life over to the experts whom you've sought out and let them help you. After all, you ended up in the hospital because you've already turned control of your life over to cocaine.

The hospital stay for acute cocaine use varies from a few days for emergency treatment to a few weeks or months for intensive rehabilitation. Here is what you can expect.

■ When you first enter, you and your belongings may be searched for cocaine and other drugs.
■ You can expect a long intake interview with one or more psychiatrists and perhaps other staff. These people will try to be helpful and supportive. You may also be given some psychological tests.
■ You'll be given a thorough physical examination and any medical problems like exhaustion, malnutrition, or dehydration will be treated.
■ You may be housed on a locked ward or in a room in a locked wing of the hospital. This may sound threatening, but try not to let it throw you; it is for your own good in the event you're overcome by an irresistible cocaine compulsion. You may eventually be moved to an open, unlocked area.
■ You may be prescribed medication. This may be a tranquilizer, an antidepressant, or medication to help you sleep.
■ As soon as possible you'll be started in rehabilitative treatment. This will usually involve both individual and group therapy, and some family therapy. It may also involve vocational rehabilitation.
■ When you've passed through the most critical phase and are on your way to recovery, you'll be released. You'll probably be released with a carefully constructed discharge plan.

The Discharge Plan. A discharge plan is to help you continue your progress after you leave the hospital. Most treatment for the underlying causes of compulsive cocaine abuse focuses on first bringing the uncontrolled compulsive use under control and then maintaining this while the patient embarks on psychotherapy in the second phase. The discharge plan is the backbone of the second phase.

Here are some elements that may be included in the discharge plan.

■ Relocation. You may be advised to move from where you live if your spouse is a cocaine user and refuses to stop, or if you live with roommates who use drugs. It may mean ending a relationship with a cocaine-using/dealing lover.

■ Employment. Returning to your old job or finding a new one.

■ Family support. A set of guidelines and agreements between you and your family detailing how they can support your progress and how you can accept their support.

■ Psychotherapy. This is crucial for you to continue in order to avoid a relapse and to discover the underlying problems that led you into chronic cocaine abuse to begin with. You may continue therapy outside with the same therapist you began with in the hospital, or you may be referred to a new one.

How to
Help Someone
Else

Don't be a detective or a policeman. No matter how strangely a loved one, child, spouse, friend, or lover, may be acting, it's not a good idea to surmise or deduce that he or she is using cocaine unless they tell you they are directly. If you think someone close to you is developing a problem with cocaine, *ask him or her about it*. Be straight. Don't play doctor or therapist; don't try to make creative diagnoses. When they are ready they'll tell you the truth.

If someone close to you uses cocaine and may be developing a health problem with it, he *may* begin complaining of headaches or insomnia. He may manifest constant and chronic nasal congestion over a long period of time. He can become irritable or depressed in conjunction with some of these other signs.

When cocaine use becomes even more extreme, you may see other symptoms: very noticeable weight loss and chronic lack of energy, loss of normal motivation, suspiciousness and paranoia, neglect of personal hygiene. He may vacillate between an inability to sleep at all to sleeping round the clock for days.

Remember that you cannot solve the problem for him.

251

Only he can solve it for himself when he is ready to. You can support him, empathize, and even offer suggestions, but *he* has to take the steps. You may be able to help him take those steps. Talk to him about it. Be loving, be gentle, show your concern; *don't* give lectures and *don't* give orders or directions. *Don't* tell him what's happening: *ask* him. Don't tell him what to *do;* ask him how he *feels.* Ask him if he thinks he has a cocaine problem. Ask him if he thinks he should do something about it.

You might try to interest him in the quitting principles we've just given you. See if he sees his cocaine use as a problem; see if he feels he has a motivation to stop; see if he knows his reasons for using the drug. Don't threaten, unless you're prepared to carry out your threats. *Actions mean more than words.* Someone with a serious cocaine problem is out of control or nearly so, and if you demonstrate that you too are out of control and too weak to act (threatening to leave him, for instance, and then failing to do it), you may terrify him even more. He may see this as proof that not only can't he stop himself, but no one else can either.

Don't play doctor. If the person admits he has a problem and he wants to try to quit cocaine on his own, very well. If he doesn't think he can, suggest he find professional help— a psychotherapist skilled in treating drug problems. Encourage him to get help. Don't forget to let him know you love him even though he may have a cocaine problem.

Talk about how *you* feel. Be very clear about what you expect and what *you will do* yourself. If you are someone who cares about a cocaine abuser, you will need to set limits for yourself. Limit the time you spend with the cocaine abuser, refuse to lend him money, refuse to make excuses for him. The most effective thing you can do is learn not to be an "enabler" for him. An enabler is someone, usually a spouse, lover, or close relative, who is trying to help or protect someone with a drug problem, but who in doing so is actually *enabling* that person to continue using cocaine. *Enablers don't deliberately do this, and they can change their behavior once it's pointed out to them.* A parent, for example, whose grown son or daughter lives at home without paying rent and spends his money on cocaine instead is enabling that child to continue using cocaine as long as he continues to let him live at home rent-free. This parent might have to start insisting on rent from the child, and if he refuses, ask him to leave. You'd be amazed at how many problem cocaine users will come to terms with their drug use when their enablers learn to say no. Here's a typical example of a question asked of us by an enabler parent.

"My daughter is twenty-seven and lives at home with us. She is unemployed and is using all the money we give her to look for work, buy clothes and food, for cocaine instead. We've tried to reason with her, but she won't talk to us. What can we do?"

Here is the answer we gave.

"Stop giving her money for anything. Do it immediately. Don't give her a dime for carfare, job hunting, anything. If she needs to look for a job, give her subway tokens or bus tickets, and tell her to pack a brown bag lunch. Since she is living under your roof, you can make the rules. If she doesn't like it, tell her she can leave, but be prepared to follow through.

"It may be helpful for all of you to get into short-term family therapy with someone who specializes in drug use. He or she will help you set limits for your daughter and follow through with the rules and support that will begin to alleviate the chaos that descends on families in this situation."

Here is another question, asked of us by a distraught wife.

"My husband says he doesn't have a problem with cocaine, but it's destroying our marriage. He uses it all the time and won't listen to me when I ask him to stop. What can I do?"

Here is our answer.

"'I' is the key word for you in this situation. Don't talk to him about what he's doing; talk to him about how it makes *you* feel. And don't forget that *you* have options and choices. Part of what may be making you feel miserable and helpless is that you believe there is nothing you can do. There may be very little you can get your husband to do at this point, but you can take charge of *your* own life.

"You can tell him that if he doesn't get help, you will leave him, but *mean it*. And do it if he doesn't respond. Move out of the house temporarily if you can. Do whatever you must to protect your peace of mind and ability to function."

Here is another question from a spouse of a cocaine abuser.

"My husband is spending a lot of our money on cocaine. I've asked him to stop and he says he will, but so far it's been six months and he hasn't. Our bank account is dwindling. What can I do?"

"Stop believing him. He can't stop, no matter what he says. You'll probably do better to enlist the help of a therapist or counselor to help you and your husband talk openly about cocaine and try to work toward some sort of agreement. Don't try to handle this problem alone. Find a drug-treatment expert who works with couples."

Here's one last commonly asked question.

"My husband has started sneaking out of the house at night to buy cocaine and has spent over fifteen thousand dollars of our savings on cocaine in the past seven months. He can't go to work, stays in the house in his bathrobe, and uses cocaine all day and all night. I'm frightened for him, but also for myself and the children. What can I do?"

"If you have reason to fear for your physical safety or that of the children, get out of the house immediately and stay with friends, neighbors, or relatives. Enlist the help of a professional. Contact your family physician or your clergyman and get his help in convincing your husband to seek professional help. Don't try to tackle this alone. Your husband needs the help of a professional and you need help and support. *Don't forget about yourself.*"

If someone close to you has a serious cocaine problem and cannot help himself or refuses to go for help, then you may have to wait until he hits rock bottom. Many cocaine abusers will not help themselves until this happens. This can be terrifying to watch, especially if you find there's nothing you can do to prevent it. When your loved one gets to the end of his rope, it's more likely he'll go for help.

If someone close to you is really out of control with cocaine, concentrate on caring for yourself. Protect yourself physically, and protect your financial assets from him if you have to. Take your kids and get out of the house—move if you must. In the long run these individuals will choose to save themselves or they will not. It's up to them. Don't destroy yourself along with them, because they will feel even worse about themselves if they hurt you before they come around to mending their own lives.

If and when they decide to help themselves, you can give them all the love and support they cannot take from you now.

Coping with the Cokeaholic (Before He Goes into Treatment)

There are many crucial developments that take place before the Cokeaholic goes into treatment, and it's useful for those close to him to know what to do and what to expect.

This is not a recommendation for home therapy for the Cokeaholic. These are guidelines for helping the Cokeaholic enter into treatment with a competent professional. Remember: even doctors don't treat their own families.

Rule number one in dealing with a husband, wife, child, parent, or relative is this: love him, but not more than you love *yourself*. Don't let this person destroy you along with himself. If he wants to let you help him or he wants to help himself, fine. If not, concentrate on protecting yourself from his self-destructiveness.

■ If your child is a Cokeaholic, immediately cut off *every* financial resource. This means everything. No one in the family must act as an enabler for him or her.
■ If the family breadwinner is a Cokeaholic, try to cut off his or her access to financial assets. Lock up the bankbooks; take away the checkbooks and credit cards.
■ Don't try to reason with this person; someone in love with cocaine has no other genuine relationships. Forget the long hours of conversation and the wonderful insights, especially if he or she was under the influence of cocaine at the time. Don't wait for the Cokeaholic to say the right words; instead,

look at his behavior. Try to make contracts with him—firm, clear agreements he must keep: no cocaine this week, no sex with this person after he's had cocaine. Do not accept any promises that are not firm agreements. Do not be reticent about insisting that this person stop his cocaine use. Urge him to go for help or into the hospital. Stand your ground.

■ Above all, be prepared to follow through on any agreements you've made with this person. If you say you'll leave unless he stops using cocaine, *then be prepared to leave.*

■ Remember, at some level, the Cokeaholic genuinely *wants to be stopped,* even if he says he does not, or cannot, do it himself.

Look into hospital programs yourself, get the phone numbers you need to call, find out about insurance coverage and fees. Hold the information and be prepared to give it to the Cokeaholic to use, when the moment comes. But understand one thing: the Cokeaholic has to want to help himself. Once the crisis is over and he is in the hospital, and afterward, you can be supportive.

Cocaine Overdose: How to Recognize It and What to Do Until Help Arrives

Any acute health or behavior crisis that occurs under cocaine is usually extreme and very dangerous, either to the user or the people around him. A cocaine emergency is no place for amateur first aid or home remedies, no matter who recommends them.

■ If someone you are with uses cocaine and goes into a seizure, or exhibits signs of heart attack, breathing difficulty, or any other cocaine-induced medical emergency, *call immediately for help.* Don't wait. A few minutes could mean the difference between life and death. Call 911 or your local emergency number; call an ambulance; if the person is conscious, take him directly to a hospital emergency room.

■ If you do take him to an emergency room, be sure to tell the staff there that the person has recently used cocaine. This is crucial, especially if the individual is suffering from an anxiety attack or an episode of paranoia or delusions. Standard emergency treatment for these conditions often involves administering certain tranquilizers, and several of the most common of these can interact with cocaine and cause convulsions or death. If you take responsibility for the life of someone in a cocaine crisis, do it completely: tell the attending physician about the drug use.

Therapy for the Serious Cocaine User

The question both cocaine abusers and their families usually ask after hospitalization is, Can a former Cokeaholic or other serious cocaine abuser ever return to social or recreational use of cocaine?

Many cocaine-treatment experts would answer this with a flat no. Most outpatient treatment programs and posthospitalization discharge plans are based on the principle of complete abstinence from cocaine for the demonstrated problem user. Though this is a controversial issue, this much is true: anyone who has suffered from cocaine-abuse problems will always be at risk to abuse cocaine again. If it happened to you once, the odds are that it will happen again. Although many recovered Cokeaholics report they can use cocaine in a social or recreational fashion, we usually answer this question with one of our own. Why on earth would anyone who knows they are a bad risk willingly put themselves at risk again?

It should be emphasized that anyone who has suffered from paranoid episodes or delusional thinking under the influence of cocaine can expect such psychotic reactions to recur with even the smallest dose of cocaine, even after many months of complete abstinence.

In general terms, psychotherapy for a Cokeaholic follows the same broad contours as that for less severe abusers trying to solve their cocaine problems themselves. The aims are to uncover the underlying issues that made the person abuse cocaine and help him learn how to deal effectively with them without drugs. If, for example, the person is a self-medicator with an underlying depression, the goal is to address the discomfort he is medicating.

Much like self-treatment of mild cocaine overuse, or psychotherapy for moderate cocaine abuse, if you were a serious user your therapy focuses on the goals of structuring time, learning what your feelings really are and how to deal with unpleasant feelings without drugs. You must learn to express feelings instead of keeping them inside or pushing them away with cocaine. Therapy works to help you avoid becoming dependent on cocaine again. The most basic rule in treating drug abuse is that the therapist cannot do this successfully while you are under the influence of the drug. Too much time is structured around helping you stay away from cocaine and not enough on your real problems. As a result, limit-setting and contracting with the therapist about cocaine use are given special attention.

Many Cokeaholics can work up to the point where they can avoid cocaine for weeks or months at a time, but they will relapse or binge periodically. In a successful treatment course, the period of abstinence between cocaine binges will get progressively longer and longer, and the episodes of use will become fewer and fewer. The person learns how to handle his feelings and how to identify the signals for his cocaine craving and cope with them without drugs. He will break his agreements less and less often and will eventually stop needing to make them. The person learns how to manage his inner states without drugs and how to negotiate his way around the potential points where he may relapse. He learns to eliminate his access, to stay away from people and places where drugs are used, and not to handle drugs. He learns that if he finds himself in a stressful situation—unemployed, bored, or feeling badly about himself—that he may be prone to relapse. He will discover how to take care of his situation as soon as possible. He learns how to avoid or break the associations with his cocaine cues. He learns that any ideas he may have about suddenly being able to use cocaine regularly without getting into trouble will get him into trouble and that he will do well not to give in to them.

In short, he learns how to cope, to take care of himself—without cocaine.

As we've seen, cocaine problems can range from minimally disruptive habits that are relatively easy to break, through a wide field of abuses and dependencies that are highly expressive of an individual's inner turmoil and emotional discomfort, to full-blown addictions that chaotically destroy everything in their path.

Ultimately, though, cocaine is only a substance, a powder, the chemical distillation of the leaves of a plant. It has potent chemical action, but nothing more. No mood-altering drug, including cocaine, can overcome a human being who has decided to resist it, who is committed to maintaining control of his life. Most of the stories in this book bear this out in one way or another. We hope what you have just read has helped you solve the mystery of how you can go about finding a way to live your life and satisfy your needs and desires without the influence of cocaine.

A person will always be more powerful than a drug if he chooses to be and then learns how to succeed at it. If you have a cocaine problem, don't be afraid. No matter how immense, hopeless, or out of control it may seem, it can be solved. *You* can solve it, alone or with the right kind of help.

Cocaine Abuse Self-Test

$\mathbf{W}$e have designed this test to help you determine what your potential is for becoming a cocaine abuser and to help you rate your involvement with cocaine. For each statement below, circle the number that best describes how suitable that statement is for you. Circle the numbers as follows:

1 if the statement *never* applies to you
2 if it *rarely* applies
3 if it *sometimes* applies
4 if it *usually* applies
5 if it *always* applies.

Then add up your score and read the scoring section at the end of this test to find out if your cocaine use is about to become a problem.

I believe that my work or study performance is better after using cocaine.	1 2 3 4 5
Taking cocaine makes me feel more comfortable with other people.	1 2 3 4 5
In a social setting	1 2 3 4 5
In an intimate, one-to-one setting	1 2 3 4 5
I like myself better when I'm high on cocaine.	1 2 3 4 5
I am able to feel more like a take-charge person after taking cocaine.	1 2 3 4 5
If I'm feeling disappointed or depressed, I feel that using cocaine will help me.	1 2 3 4 5

Cocaine Abuse Self-Test

Cocaine helps me

	Feel less nervous	1 2 3 4 5
	Be less inhibited	1 2 3 4 5
	Feel less guilty	1 2 3 4 5
	Forget about my troubles	1 2 3 4 5

I worry about money after using cocaine.   1 2 3 4 5

I have trouble stopping using cocaine.   1 2 3 4 5

I think about using cocaine and look forward to having
it—at times.   1 2 3 4 5

I have had arguments with my spouse or other family
members because of cocaine.   1 2 3 4 5

I feel people are saying negative things about me after I
use cocaine.   1 2 3 4 5

I notice a "crash" (down, depressed, dysphoric effect)
after using cocaine, when it begins to wear off.   1 2 3 4 5

The only problem I've ever had with cocaine is the cost
and/or availability of it.   1 2 3 4 5

I buy my own cocaine.   1 2 3 4 5

I will use cocaine only when it is offered to me.   1 2 3 4 5

I have gotten bad effects from cocaine.   1 2 3 4 5

If offered to me, I would use cocaine again now.   1 2 3 4 5

Sex is not as satisfactory or exciting without cocaine.   1 2 3 4 5

I feel I am better accepted if I bring cocaine to certain
settings.

	Among my co-workers	1 2 3 4 5
	On a date with a new person	1 2 3 4 5
	With friends at a get-together	1 2 3 4 5

When I take cocaine, I am able to express my true feelings
(anger, love, etc.).   1 2 3 4 5

There are times after taking cocaine that I wish I hadn't
taken it.   1 2 3 4 5

Taking cocaine is exciting.   1 2 3 4 5

I like the feelings I get from cocaine.   1 2 3 4 5

Cocaine makes me feel uneasy in my skin.   1 2 3 4 5

As soon as I take some cocaine, I want more.   1 2 3 4 5

I would use cocaine again if available to me.   1 2 3 4 5

I usually associate cocaine with

Sex	1 2 3 4 5
Work	1 2 3 4 5
Feeling bad	1 2 3 4 5
Fatigue	1 2 3 4 5

Now Add Your Score

37–90   You are a user with a low potential to abuse, if all your life circumstances stay the same.

91–125   You may be a social cocaine user, but you have many strong positive feelings about cocaine. It means something to you, and you may feel it actually improves your emotional well-being or basic talents. Watch out for increases in your cocaine use if your access to it increases, the stress in your life rises, or you are faced with strong psychological discomfort over a sustained period.

126–155   Although your level of cocaine use may still be under control, the drug is a hazard for you. You exhibit some of the basic qualities for frequent or overindulgent use. Cocaine has high value for you, and your use is showing negative effects in other parts of your life. These may not be obvious to you now, but they could get out of hand. Watch out for patterns of abusive or dependent cocaine behavior.

156–185   You have a strong potential to develop a cocaine-abuse problem. The drug has as much value to you as other significant things and relationships in your life. You count on it to solve social and emotional difficulties that you should use your coping skills to deal with. You may also have a tendency to develop marked anxiety or paranoid reactions to the drug. On balance, cocaine is not a good bet for you. Try to stop. If you insist on using it, try to watch your frequency and dose very carefully. Be on the lookout for any patterns that develop in your cocaine use. Be alert to changes in your access or life stress that may push your cocaine use out of control. Consult the "Where to Get Help" pages that follow.

Where to Get Help

The number of organizations springing up to meet the demand for assistance with cocaine problems is increasing exponentially. Some of the organizations are good, some are not. (The 800-COCAINE organization has had more than two thousand requests within four months from various groups wishing to be named as resources on their 800 hotline referral list.) The following names were compiled through physicians and groups with whom we are personally acquainted or who have been referred to us by colleagues. When we have not had the benefit of direct recommendations, we have sought suggestions from other professional organizations. Though this list is by no means comprehensive, it does represent a list of trusted professionals.

Alabama
Claudio Toro, M.D., Medical Director
Hillcrest Hospital
6869 Fifth Avenue, South
Birmingham, AL 35212
205-833-9000

Michael Kehoe, M.D., Medical Director
University of Southern Alabama
Medical Center
2451 Fillingin Street
Mobile, AL 36617
205-471-7477

Arizona
Robert Mayer, M.D.
Phoenix Camelback Hospital

5055 North 34th Street
Phoenix, AZ 85018
602-941-7509

Dennis C. Westin, M.D., Medical Director
Palo Verde Hospital
801 South Prudence Road
Tucson, AZ 85710
602-298-3363

Arkansas
Donald Butts, M.D., Medical Director
Charter Vista Hospital
P.O. Box 1906
Fayetteville, AR 72702
501-521-5731

Karen Keller, Program Director
RESTORE
Riverview Medical Center
1310 Cantrell Road
Little Rock, AR 72201
501-376-1200

California
David B. Bergman, M.D., Medical
Director
Southwood Mental Health Center
950 Third Avenue
Chula Vista, CA 92011
619-426-6310

Ms. Ann Munoz, Director,
Renewal Unit
Dominguez Valley Hospital
3100 Susana Road
Compton, CA 90221
213-639-2664

John P. Feighner, M.D., Medical
Director
San Luis Rey Hospital
1015 Devonshire Drive
Encinitas, CA 92024
619-753-1234

Richard A. Rawson, Ph.D.
Director
Cocaine Abuse Treatment Services
827 Foothill Boulevard
LaCanada, CA 91011
213-790-4044

Mr. David Leblanc
Doctor's Hospital of Lakewood
Clark Avenue Division
5300 N. Clark Avenue
Lakewood, CA 90712
213-866-9711

Dixon Young, M.D., Director,
Renewal Unit, 3rd Floor
Century City Hospital
2070 Century Park East
Los Angeles, CA 90067
213-277-4248

Ms. Mary McNally, Director,
Renewal Unit
Renewal Hospital of Ojai
1306 A Maricopa Highway
Ojai, CA 93023
805-646-5567

Ms. Vel Gilbert, Director, Renewal
Unit
Ontario Community Hospital
550 N. Monterey
Ontario, CA 91764
714-984-2201

Ms. C. J. Hawkins, Director
Renewal Unit
Doctor's Hospital of Pinole
2151 Appian Way
Pinole, CA 94564
415-724-5000

Ms. Pat Gallagher, Director,
Renewal Unit
Alisal Community Hospital
333 N. Sanborn Road, Box 2159
Salinas, CA 93902
408-424-0381

David Smith, M.D., Director,
Haight-Ashbury Free Clinic
409 Clayton Street
San Francisco, CA 94117
415-626-6763

Colorado
Robert P. Snead, M.D., Medical
Director
Boulder Psychiatric Institute
3000 Pearl Street
Boulder, CO 80301
303-441-0526

Thomas Crowley, M.D., Professor
of Psychiatry
University of Colorado School of
Medicine
1827 Gaylord
Denver, CO 80206
303-388-5894

William W. McCaw, M.D.,
Medical Director
Mount Airy Psychiatric Center
4455 East 12th Avenue
Denver, CO 80220
303-322-1803

Connecticut
Roger Meyer, M.D.
University of Connecticut School
of Medicine
University of Connecticut Health
Center
Farmington, CT 06032
203-674-3423

Herbert Kleber, M.D., Director,
Substance Abuse Unit
Connecticut Mental Health Center
34 Park Avenue
New Haven, CT 06510
203-789-7282

Lane Ameen, M.D., Medical
Director
Elmcrest Psychiatric Institute
25 Marlborough Street
Portland, CT 06480
203-342-0480

Delaware
Cor DeHart, M.D., Medical
Director
Rockford Center
1605 North Broom Street
Wilmington, DE 19806
302-652-3892

District of Columbia
Mark Hertzman, M.D., Chief
Resident, Director,
Substance Abuse Unit
George Washington University
Hospital
901 23rd Street NW
Washington, DC 20037
202-676-3355

Howard Hoffman, M.D., Medical
Director
Psychiatric Institute of Washington
4460 MacArthur Boulevard NW

Washington, DC 20037
202-467-4600

Florida
Moke Williams, M.D.,
Coral Ridge Psychiatric Hospital
4545 North Federal Highway
Fort Lauderdale, FL 33308
305-566-7102

Jesse J. Kaye, M.D., Medical
Director
Lake Hospital of the Palm Beaches
1710 Fourth Avenue North
Lake Worth, FL 33460
305-588-7341

Theodore J. Machler, M.D.,
Medical Director
Medfield Center
12891 Seminole Boulevard
Largo, FL 33540
813-581-8757

David G. Pinosky, M.D., Medical
Director
Highland Park General Hospital
1660 Northwest 7th Court
Miami, FL 33136
305-326-7008

Steve Targum, M.D.
Sarasota Palms Hospital
1650 South Osprey Avenue
Sarasota, FL 33579
813-366-6070

Georgia
Ronald Bloodworth, M.D.
Psychiatric Institute of Atlanta
811 Juniper Street, N.E.
Atlanta, GA 30308
404-881-5800

Mr. Al Stines, Director, Substance
Abuse Unit
Charter Lake Hospital
P.O. Box 7067
Macon, GA 31209
912-474-6200

Mark Gould, M.D., Medical
Director
Brawner Psychiatric Institute
3180 Atlanta Street, S.E.
Smyrna, GA 30080
404-436-0081

Idaho
Ms. Gail Ater, Director,
The Walker Center
P.O. Box 541
Gooding, ID 83330
208-934-8461

Mr. Eugene Cwalinski, Director,
Substance Abuse Unit
Mercy Medical Center Care Unit
1512 12th Avenue Road
Nampa, ID 83651
208-466-4531

Illinois
Sidney Schnoll, M.D., Ph.D.,
Director, Chemical Dependency
Unit
Northwestern Memorial Hospital
320 East Huron
Chicago, IL 60611
312-649-8713

Charles R. Schuster, Ph.D.
University of Chicago Department
of Psychiatry
5841 South Maryland
Chicago, IL 60637
312-962-6360

Indiana
Alvin Hvidston, Director,
Chemical Dependency Unit
St. Vincent's Stress Center
8401 Harcourt Road
Indianapolis, IN 46260
317-875-4710

Iowa
Barbara Martens, Business
Coordinator
Sedlacek Treatment Center
c/o Mercy Hospital
701 Tenth Street, S.E.

Cedar Rapids, IA 52403
319-398-6226

Kansas
Robert Conroy, M.D.
C. F. Menninger Memorial
Hospital
3616 West Seventh Street
P.O. Box 829
Topeka, KS 66601
913-273-7500

Kentucky
Mr. Ray Wilson
Our Lady of Peace Hospital
2020 Newburg Road
Louisville, KY 40232
502-451-3330

Louisiana
Stanley Roskind, M.D., Medical
Director
Jo Ellen Smith Psychiatric Hospital
4601 Patterson Road
New Orleans, LA 70114
504-363-7676

Gene Usdin, M.D., Professor of
Psychiatry
Louisiana State University
1403 Delachaise Street
New Orleans, LA 70115
504-891-7000

Maine
Stanley J. Evans, M.D., P.A.,
Director
Mercy Hospital Alcohol Institute
Portland, ME 04111
207-774-1566

Maryland
Bruce Taylor, M.D., Director of
Admissions
Taylor Manor Hospital
College Avenue
Ellicott City, MD 21043
301-465-3322

266

John E. Meeks, M.D., Medical Director
Psychiatric Institute of Montgomery County
14901 Broschart Road
Rockville, MD 20850
301-251-4500

Massachusetts
Steve Mirin, M.D., Director, Drug Dependence Treatment
McLean Hospital
115 Mill Street
Belmont, MA 02178
617-855-2151

Bernard Gray, Ph.D., Executive Director
Norman Zinberg, M.D.
Comprehensive Mental Health Services
1643 Beacon Street
Waban, MA 02168
617-969-8870

Michigan
Raymond E. Buck, M.D., Medical Director
Psychiatric Center of Michigan
35031-23 Mile Road
New Baltimore, MI 48047
313-725-5777

Mr. Robert Kercorian, Director, Substance Abuse
Harold E. Fox Center
900 Woodward
Pontiac, MI 48053
313-858-3177

Mr. Steven Hnat
Substance Abuse Unit
Henry Ford Hospital
6773 West Maple Road
West Bloomfield, MI 48033
313-661-6100

Minnesota
Daniel Anderson, M.D.
Hazelden

15425 Pleasant Valley Road
Center City, MN 55012
612-257-4010

Joseph Westermayer, M.D.
Department of Psychiatry
University of Minnesota Hospital
Box 393 Mayl
420 Delaware Street, S.E.
Minneapolis, MN 55414
612-373-7952

Mississippi
Mr. Bill Sellers, Administrator
Delta Medical Center
P.O. Box 5247
Greenville, MS 38704
601-334-2200

Mr. John Reedy, Administrator
Riverside Hospital
P.O. Box 4297
Jackson, MS 39216
1-800-962-2180

Missouri
Samuel Guze, M.D.,
Department of Psychiatry
Washington University School of Medicine
4940 Audubon
St. Louis, MO 63110
314-454-3875

William Clary, M.D., Medical Director
Ozark Psychiatric Clinic
1900 South National, Suite 1800
Springfield, MO 65804
417-881-3124

Montana
Mr. David Cunningham, Executive Director
Rim Rock Foundation
P.O. Box 30374
Billings, MT 59107
406-248-3175

267

Mr. Robert Barren, Director,
Alcohol & Drug Program
St. James Hospital East
25 Continental Drive
Butte, MT 59701
406-723-4341

Nebraska
Mr. Jim Mays, Director, Alcohol
Treatment Center
Immanuel Medical Center
6901 North 72nd
Omaha, NE 68122
402-572-2016

Nevada
Mr. Mark Augenstien
Care Unit Hospital
1401 Lake Mead Avenue
North Las Vegas, NV 89030
702-642-6905

William Thornton, M.D., Medical
Director
Truckee Meadows Hospital
1240 East Ninth Street
Reno, NV 89512
702-323-0478

New Hampshire
Ms. Barbara Noyer, Director of
Personnel
Hampstead Hospital
East Road
Hampstead, NH 03841
603-329-5311

New Jersey
Peter Mueller, M.D.
Princeton Hospital
905 Herrintown Road
Princeton, NJ 08540
609-924-4061

Russel Ferstandig, M.D.
179 S. Maple Avenue
Ridgewood, NJ 07450
201-445-9777

William Vilensky, M.D.
Suite 106, Kennedy Professional
Mall
40 Laurel Road
Stratford, NJ 08084
609-346-7025

Jane Jones, M.D.
Psychiatric Associates of New
Jersey
19 Prospect Street
Summit, NJ 07901
201-522-7000

New Mexico
John McCormack, M.D.
Vista Sandia Hospital
501 Richfield Avenue, N.E.
Albuquerque, NM 87113
505-898-1661

Joel Hochman, M.D.
St. Vincent's Hospital
664 Camino Del Monte Sol
Santa Fe, NM 87501
505-982-2529

New York
Robert Bertoni
Bry Lin Hospital
1263 Delaware Avenue
Buffalo, NY 14209
716-886-8200

Irl Extein, M.D.
Falkirk Psychiatric Hospital
P.O. Box 194
Central Valley, NY 10917
914-928-2256

Nannette Stone and Marlene
Fromme
Creative Solutions
55 West 90th Street
New York, NY 10024
212-496-0618

Arnold Washton, Ph.D.
The Regent Hospital
425 East 61st Street
New York, NY 10021
212-935-3400

North Carolina
Jack W. Bonner III, M.D., Medical
Director
Highland Hospital
49 Zillicoa Street
P.O. Box 1101
Asheville, NC 28802
704-254-3201

Dennis Christianson, M.D.,
Medical Director
Appalachian Hall
P.O. Box 5534
Caledonia Road
Asheville, NC 28813
704-253-3681

Everett Ellinwood, Jr., M.D.
Duke University Medical Center
Box 3870
Durham, NC 27710
919-684-5225

North Dakota
Will Wells, M.D., Clinical Director
Hartview Foundation
1406 N.W. 2nd Street
Mandan, ND 58554
701-663-2321

Ohio
Bill Moore
Emerson A. North Hospital
5642 Hamilton Avenue
Cincinnati, OH 45224
513-541-0135

William Webber, M.D.
Woodruff Hospital
1950 East 89th Street
Cleveland, OH 44106
216-795-3700

Oklahoma
Mr. Bill Steele, Director, Chemical
Dependency Unit
Presbyterian Hospital
707 N.W. 6th Street
Oklahoma City, OK 73102
405-232-0777

Oregon
Daniel Bloch, M.D., Medical
Director

Cedar Hills Psychiatric Hospital
10300 S.W. Eastridge Street
Portland, OR 97225
503-292-9101

Pennsylvania
Ken Sandler, M.D.
The Fairmont Institute
561 Fairthorne Street
Philadelphia, PA 19128
215-487-4102

Jerry A. Romoff, Administrator
Western Psychiatric Institute and
Clinic
3811 O'Hara Street
Pittsburgh, PA 15261
412-624-2000

Rhode Island
Andrew Slaby, M.D., Professor of
Psychiatry
Brown University Division of
Biology & Medicine
Rhode Island Hospital
Providence, RI 02902
401-277-5488

South Carolina
Douglas F. Crane, M.D., Medical
Director
Fenwick Hall
P.O. Box 688
Maybank Highway & River Road
Johns Island, SC 29455
803-559-2461

Christopher Caston, M.D.
711 N. Church
Suite 110
Spartanburg, SC 29303
803-585-0328

South Dakota
Mr. Charles Brewer, Coordinator
of Patient Care
River Park, Inc.
P.O. Box 1216
Pierre, SD 57501
605-224-6177

Tennessee
Robert Booner, M.D., Medical Director
Peninsula Psychiatric Hospital
Route #2, Box 233
Louisville, TN 37777
615-573-7913

Susan Reimer, Administrator
Park View Hospital
Parthenon Pavilion
2401 Murphy Avenue
Nashville, TN 37203
615-327-2237

Texas
Lawrence Arnold, M.D., Medical Director
Brookhaven Psychiatric Pavilion
Seven Medical Parkway
Dallas, TX 75234
214-247-1000

Frederick Goggans, M.D.
Psychiatric Institute of Fort Worth
815 Eighth Avenue
Fort Worth, TX 76104
817-335-4040

Utah
Donnis Reece,Ph.D., Program Administrator
St. Benedict's ACT Center
1255 East 3900 South
Salt Lake City, UT 84117
801-263-1300

Vermont
Robert Landeen, M.D.
Brattleboro Retreat
75 Linden Street
Brattleboro, VT 05301
800-451-4203

Mr. Norman Reuss
Champlain Drug Services
45 Clarke Street

Burlington, VT 05401
802-863-3456

Virginia
Director, Substance Abuse Unit
Serenity Lodge
2097 South Military Highway
Chesapeake, VA 23320
804-543-6888

C. Gibson Dunn, M.D., Medical Director
Springwood Psychiatric Institute
Route 4, Box 50
Leesburg, VA 22075
703-777-0800

Joseph Garten, M.D.
Psychiatric Institute of Richmond, Inc.
3001 Fifth Avenue
Richmond, VA 23222
804-329-4392

Washington
Elliot Oppenheim, M.D.
8430 Main Street
Edmonds, WA 98020
206-774-5113

Kay E. Seim, Administrator
Kirkland Care Unit Hospital
10200 N.E. 132nd Street
Kirkland, WA 98033
206-821-1122

West Virginia
Edwin L. Johnson, Administrator
Highland Hospital
300 56th Street
Charleston, WV 25304
304-925-4756

Wisconsin
Jerry Reichert, Administrator
St. Croixdale Hospital
445 Court Street North
Prescott, WI 54021
715-262-3286

Craig Larsen, M.D., Medical
Director
Milwaukee Psychiatric Hospital
Dewey Center
1220 Dewey Avenue
Wauwatosa, WI 53213
414-258-4094

Wyoming
Durward Burnett, M.D. Substance
Abuse Unit
Wyoming State Hospital
P.O. Box 177
Evanston, WY 82930
307-789-3464

Bibliography

Anderson, K. "Fighting Cocaine's Grip: Millions of Users, Billions of Dollars." *Time*, April 11, 1983, 22–33.

Ashley, R. *Cocaine: Its History and Effects.* New York: St. Martin's Press, 1975.

Brecher, J. "Drugs on the Job." *Newsweek*, August 22, 1983, 52–60.

Byck, R., ed. *Cocaine Papers: Sigmund Freud.* New York: Stonehill, 1974.

Center for Disease Control. "National Surveillance of Cocaine Use and Related Health Consequences." *Morbidity and Mortality Weekly Report*, May 28, 1982, 265–76. Washington, D.C.: U.S. Department of Health and Human Services.

Deneau, G. W., T. Yangita, and M. H. Seevers. "Self-administration of Psychoactive Substance by the Monkey: A Measure of Psychological Dependence." *Psychopharmacologia* 16 (1969): 30–48.

Ellinwood, E. H., Jr., and M. M. Kilbey, eds. *Cocaine and Other Stimulants.* New York: Plenum, 1977.

Goodman, L. S., and A. Gilman, eds. *The Pharmacological Basis of Therapeutics.* 4th ed. New York: Macmillan, 1970.

Mule, S. J., and M. Saunders, eds. *Proceedings of the Symposium on Cocaine.* Sponsored by the New York State Division of Substance Abuse Services, New York, New York, May 3–4, 1982.

National Institute on Drug Abuse, Division of Research, Rockville, Md. National Household Survey of Drug Use 1983.

Petersen, R. C., and R. C. Stillman, eds. *Cocaine 1977.* National Institute on Drug Abuse Research Monograph no. 13 (ADM) 77-471. Washington, D.C.: Government Printing Office, 1977.

Phillips, J. L., and R. Wynne. *Cocaine: The Mystique and Reality.* New York: Avon Books, 1980.

Spotts, J. V., and F. C. Shontz. *Cocaine Users.* New York: Free Press, 1980.

Van Dyke, C., and R. Byck. "Cocaine." *Scientific American* 246 (1982): 128–46.

Washton, A. M. "Adverse Effects of Cocaine Abuse on Health and Functioning." In *Problems of Drug Dependence, 1983*, edited by L. S. Harris. National Institute on Drug Abuse Research monograph. Washington, D.C.: Government Printing Office. In press.

———. "The Cocaine Epidemic." Testimony before the U.S. House of Representatives Select Committee on Narcotic Abuse and Control, June 6, 1983.

Wetli, C. V., and R. F. Wright. "Death Caused by Recreational Cocaine Use." *Journal of the American Medical Association* 241 (1979): 2519–22.

Index

Index

Index

Index

Romances, cocaine, 22–23
Routine Users, 76–93

Seizures, 192, 193
Selling of cocaine, 7–18
Set and setting, 33–34
Sex, 20–21
  reasons for using cocaine and,
    201–2
Shooting cocaine, 32–33
Sleep cycles, 210
Smoking freebase, 31–32
Snorting (sniffing), 29–30
  danger of, 191
Social gatherings, 202–3
Social Sniffers, 49–75, 196
Speedball, 193
Stimulant effects, 26
Strengths, quitting cocaine and
  finding your, 208
Stress, 44
  learning new ways to deal with,
    221–22
  use of cocaine to relieve, 123–44,
    204–5
Structuring your time, quitting
  cocaine and, 208, 222–24
Substitute habits, 219–20
Symbolic use of cocaine, 42–43

Telephone-referral helpline, 4–5,
  263
Therapy, 257–58. *See also*
  Psychotherapy
  in clinics, 245–47
  in hospitals, 247–50
  organizations involved in, 263

Time, quitting cocaine and
  structuring your, 208, 222–24
Tocra, 7
Treatment for cocaine abuse, 4. *See
  also* Therapy
Tyrosine, 210

Ugly reminders, quitting cocaine
  and, 227–28
Urine screenings, 242
Use of cocaine, defined, 37–38
Use-recovery-relapse cycle, 43–44
Users of cocaine
  Boredom/Stress Relievers, 123–
    44
  Cokeaholics, 49, 145–86
  number and characteristics of,
    3–4, 13–15
  Performance Users, 94–122
  recreational, 37–38
  Routine Users, 76–93
  Social Sniffers, 49–75
  types of, 49
  women, 21–22

Vin Mariani, 9

Women, 21–22
  pregnant or nursing, 194
Work, 18–19, 203–4
  as motivation for quitting
    cocaine, 199

Youth culture, 14